PARAMETER SETTING

STUDIES IN THEORETICAL PSYCHOLINGUISTICS

1987

PARAMETER SETTING

Edited by

THOMAS ROEPER and EDWIN WILLIAMS
Dept. of Linguistics, University of Massachusetts, Amherst, U.S.A.

D. REIDEL PUBLISHING COMPANY

A MEMBER OF THE KLUWER ACADEMIC PUBLISHERS GROUP

DORDRECHT / BOSTON / LANCASTER / TOKYO

Library of Congress Cataloging-in-Publication Data

Parameter setting.

(Studies in theoretical psycholinguistics)
Papers from a conference held at the University of Massachusetts in
May 1985.
Bibliography: p.
Includes index.
1. Language acquisition—Congresses. 2. Grammar, Comparative
and general—Congresses. I. Roeper, Thomas. II. Williams, Edwin.
III. Series.
P118.P29   1987   401'.9   86–31665
ISBN 90–277–2315–X
ISBN 90–277–2316–8 (pbk.)

Published by D. Reidel Publishing Company
P.O. Box 17, 3300 AA Dordrecht, Holland

Sold and distributed in the U.S.A. and Canada
by Kluwer Academic Publishers,
101 Philip Drive, Norwell, MA 02061, U.S.A.

In all other countries, sold and distributed
by Kluwer Academic Publishers Group,
P.O. Box 322, 3300 AH Dordrecht, Holland

Printed in The Netherlands

TABLE OF CONTENTS

v

INTRODUCTION

In May 1985 the University of Massachusetts held the first conference on the parameter setting model of grammar and acquisition. The conference was conceived in the belief that there is a new possibility of tightly connecting grammatical studies and language acquisition studies, and that this new possibility has grown out of the new generation of ideas about the relation of Universal Grammar to the grammar of particular languages. The papers in this volume are all concerned in one way or another with the 'parametric' model of grammar, and with its role in explaining the acquisition of language.

Before summarizing the accompanying papers, I would like to sketch the intellectual background of these new ideas.

It has long been the acknowledged goal of grammatical theorists to explicate the relation between the experience of the child and the knowledge of the adult. Somehow, the child selects a unique grammar (by assumption) compatible with a random partially unreliable sample of some language. In the earliest work in generative grammar, starting with Chomsky's Aspects, and extending to such works as Jackendoff's Lexicalist Syntax (1977), the model of this account was the formal evaluation metric, accompanied by a general rule writing system. The model of acquisition was the following: the child composed a grammar by writing rules in the rule writing system, under the constraint that the rules must be compatible with the data, and that the grammar must be the one most highly valued by the evaluation metric. In principle, such a a strategy could give a unique grammar for any set of data, thus turning the question into a 'formal' (but empirical) problem.

The parameterized model of grammar grew out of the failure, on the part of grammarians, to make any progress in understanding grammar selection with this 'evaluation metric'. The only general component of the evaluation metric that ever received any real scrutiny was 'short-ness' of grammars, and this failed in such pervasive ways that it became tedious to mention it.

Furthermore, but more or less independently, there was dissatis-faction on the part of psychologists with this 'formal' account of

Thomas Roeper and Edwin Williams (eds.), Parameter Setting, vii—xix.
© *1987 by D. Reidel Publishing Company.*

acquisition — it was not at all clear how rule generation and evaluation related to actual acquisition. The evaluation model led to no clear predictions testable in the realm of actual acquisition.

The parameterized model has no rule writing system. Rather, the rules of grammar (or the 'principles', as it is now fashionable to call universal rules) are specified as a part of the innate. The rules, however, are slightly 'under-specified' — that is, certain 'parameters' are left unspecified, to be filled in by the child according to the language he is exposed to. So, instead of selecting a rule from a space of infinitely many rules of some rule writing system, the child simply sets the value of an open parameter in some rule already given in Universal Grammar, and thereby derives a language particular rule. It certainly sounds easier.

The history of the notion of "universal but parameterized rule" probably begins with Bach (1965), a paper that suggests that certain rules, such as *Wh*-movement, are given as part of Universal Grammar, for languages to use, or not (an 'existence' parameter). Chomsky (1965) explicitly mentions the possibility of 'substantive universals', that is, the specification in UG of fixed (unlearned) rules of grammar, but there is no mention there of the possibility that these rules might be 'parameterized'. In Williams (1976, 1977, 1977a, 1981) a parameterized theory of the base component is given, with head-position and presence vs. absence of the specifier and complement left open as parameters for each phrase, and this scheme was compared to Jackendoff's (1977) 'evaluation metric' theory. I personally regard Jackendoff's work there as the most excellent work in a failing paradigm, and its failure despite its virtues is what convinced me that a more substantive approach to grammar selection was needed. Until then, it was always conceivable that we still needed to find the right notation for the rule writing system, or the right evaluation metric.

The parameterized model at least appears to make easier the acquisition of language — rather than searching an infinite range of grammars, the child is seeking answers to a few simple questions ("is the base head final"; "is *Wh*-movement present?", etc.). Of course, the parameter setting model is still approachable, at least in principle, by purely 'grammatical' means — the theorist picks the parameters so as to give a map of attested linguistic variation. No doubt most of the work on parameters in the near future will have this character. But there is the exciting posibility, pursued in the present set of papers, that this map can be directly interpreted as the structure of the language acquisition device, including UG. To connect grammatical studies to acquisition studies in a fruitful way, there, of course, must be some idea of what the parameters and rules are, but perhaps more importantly, there must be some general idea of what a parameter can be. Only some general (but contentful) idea of parameter could generate research at the juncture of grammatical studies and acquisition studies.

At present, there is one research-generating idea at that juncture — that idea is the "no-negative-evidence" hypothesis, which says that the data of the "language acquisition device" (idealized child) consists of positive instances of sentences from the target language only. It may well be that the hypothesis is a complicated half-truth, as much a part of the idealization of the problem as a part of the answer to the problem. At the present, however, when we have no idea where the truth lies, this hypothesis serves the very useful function of directing research on the acquisition of grammar, and also serves as a pro-tem means of evaluating the consequences of proposals about the nature of grammar for the study of acquisition.

So, when the parameters postulated do not give a straightforward course of acquisition consistent with the "no-negative-evidence" hypothesis, then special comment is called for, but otherwise not. In this sense, it serves as a criterion of successful theorizing.

For example, the obvious initial 'setting' for the null subject parameter, whatever that parameter actually is, is the setting that would forbid null subjects; a child then encountering a single sentence without a subject would then reset the parameter. Suppose on the other hand that the setting giving null subjects were the initial setting; how would a child know to reset the parameter for non pro-drop languages? The presence of subjects in sentences alone would not suffice — subjects occur in both languages. The child would have to notice that the subject was never omitted, and this would require the survey of a good amount of data, not a single sentence.

Hyams (1983) and Hyams (present volume) suggest that the initial setting IS the one giving null subjects, contrary to the reasoning just given, but, in the face of the "no-negative-evidence" hypothesis, goes on to tie the parameter to features of the language not obviously connected with pro-drop, but for which a course of acquisition consistent with the "no-negative-evidence" exists.

The role of the "no-negative-evidence" hypothesis goes back at least to Gold (1967) where he showed that no general infinite class of languages could be learned from positive instances only. The cases where positive instances failed were cases in which there were an infinite number of languages 'nested' by the subset relation; positive evidence alone could not distinguish among the infinite number of languages that contained the entire input sample. These cases are not as pathological as one might think, given the cases discussed in Wexler and Manzini (this volume), where some of the humanly accessible languages are nested by the subset relation. Gold's work showed that the space of human languages would have to have some very special properties if they were to be learned only from positive instances of sentences of the language.

The first application of the "no-negative-evidence" hypothesis to a parameterized model of grammar was in Williams (1976), where a parameterized account of the phrase structure component was given consistent with a "Principle of Minimum Falsifiability", equivalent to the "no-negative-evidence" dictum. Berwick (1985) supplies a formalization of the principle in terms of sets and subsets (the 'subset principle'), and this formalization is taken up in the paper by Wexler and Manzini in the present volume. The subset principle says that when the two settings of a parameter give two different languages L1 and L2, L1 a subset of L2, then the default (or initial, or unmarked) setting should be the the the one giving the smaller language L1. The reason is, simple data (one sentence from L2 not in L1) will suffice to trigger the resetting of the parameter to L2, but no such simple data would serve to trigger the resetting to L1 if L2 were taken as the initial setting. In fact, negative data would be needed in that case. It is clear that the subset principle is in the spirit of the "no-negative-evidence" dictum, and in fact can be considered a concrete formalization of it.

Before turning to the papers, I would like to raise two points about the adequacy of the parameter setting model of grammar in a theory of acquisition.

First, there must be some further work on some implicit assumptions that make the parameter setting model a successful predictor of acquisition stages. One assumption is that the evidence needed to set a parameter is 'simple'. The other is that the setting of one parameter is independent of the setting of another parameter. These assumptions could be false, and in fact probably are — the setting of the bounding node of subjacency is probably contingent on the presence of *Wh-*

movement in the language, so these two are not independent (they are intrinsically dependent — one might imagine also 'formal' UG-specified dependencies as well). The question is, how complicated are such contingencies — in the worst case, one can imagine the parameters were so paralyzingly interconnected that they all had to be set "at one time" and the evidence was the union of all the evidence relevant for any of them. Under this circumstance, the language learner is hardly better of than he was with the evaluation metric. There certainly has been some very interesting work on this topic — I would cite particularly Culicover and Wexler's (1980) work on the acquisition of transformations, and the work of Dresher on phonology. The parameter setting model holds out the hope of a much more fine-grained understanding of how grammar selection relates to the primary data, as each parameter can be scrutinized to determine its dependence on other parameters, and to determine what would constitute a 'fair sample' of the language for setting that parameter.

The second point I would like to raise in connection with the parameter setting model in acquisition studies has to do with a neglect of those aspects of language that do not lend themselves to parameterization. The neglect is understandable; it is simply the result of the success of the parameter setting model. However, the extent of linguistic structure for which the parameter setting model is inappropriate may be wider than is recognized. It will be unanimously conceded, for example, that the rote learning of words is not a matter of parameter setting. But there are in fact broad-scale structural aspects of grammar that may not reduce to parameter setting. For example, nearly every language has some kind of nominal or verbal paradigm, which is essentially an n-dimensional matrix of forms, mapped in a systematic (but not necessarily bi-unique) way onto a set of morphological distinctions. The number of dimensions of this matrix, the size of each dimension, and the mapping of the matrix onto the set of distinctions, are all subject to great variation from language to language, and the idea of 'setting parameters' seem to be of no help here.

Another domain apparently beyond parameter setting would be the identification of affixes. When does the learner abstract from word to morpheme? A clue to this may be the cases in which the abstraction is incomplete — for example, the suffix -y in English forms such as pretty, petty, happy, etc. The -y here is arguably not a separate affix, but it nevertheless signals that the word of which it is a part is an adjective, as words ending in -*y* are very often adjectival. Native speakers sense this connection, even if reluctant to acknowledge -*y* as an affix in these cases. Perhaps this is an instance in which the acquisition device has detected a statistical regularity but has failed to identify an affix. This statistical regularity is grasped by a kind of low-level induction device looking for correlations of word-shape and other word-properties, such as gender, number, category, etc., this device being a part of the word-structure learning faculty.

There is probably room for low level 'concept formation' as well — languages seem to have language particular categories; in English, for example, -*ly* adverbs seem to have unique properties, properties not shared by the other adverbs in English. For example, only they occur freely in all the AUX positions. Hence, they must be identified as a subcategory of English adverb, but the particular subdivision that English evidences may not be repeated in any other language, and hence is not plausibly 'parametric'.

It would be quite surprising if parameter setting exhausted the possibilities — knowledge of language involves a number of different types of knowledge, and acquisition will procede most efficiently if the means of learning each type is tailored to that type.

In the papers that follow, two (plus the responses to them) are presentations of parameterized models of parts of grammar. These are the papers by Wexler and Manzini and by Hyams. In both these cases, the setting of the parameters discussed (pro-drop in the case of Hyams, and binding domains in the case of Wexler and Manzini) is consistent with the "no-negative-evidence" dictum. Furthermore, acquisition evidence is supplied to validate the stages of acquisition predicted by the predicted initial settings of the parameters.

Hyams paper presents one of the most 'orthodox' and also one of the best known accounts based on the subset hypothesis. Previous accounts (e.g. Rizzi, 1982) have suggested that the unmarked grammar of subjects would have them obligatorily present always; a language with optional subjects must be arrived at. This set-up is what the subset hypothesis (which is a formalization of the "no-negative-evidence" hypothesis) would lead you to expect, since a pro-drop language has all of the sentences of its non-pro-dropping twin, and it has in addition all of the sentences with subjects dropped — so every non-pro-drop language is a subset of some pro-drop language.

But how does one square this with the fact that children speaking

English go through an initial stage with dropped subjects? The clear conclusion is that pro-drop is the initial hypothesis. But then how does one advance to the non-pro-drop hypothesis, giving a language which is a superset of the language of the current grammar? In fact, Hyams points out that in fact neither language is a subset or superset of the other. This is because pro-drop languages do not have overt expletives, only non-pro-drop languages do — so each language contains sentences that the other does not (pro-drop Ls contain sentences with no subjects; non-pro-drop Ls contain languages with expletive subjects). Given this, the course of acquisition could go either way, depending on which is the initial hypothesis — in either there would be simple triggering evidence. Hyams presents evidence on the implication of the structure of the AUX in pro-drop to argue that the pro-drop hypothesis is initial, which is of course consistent with the known course of acquisition of non-pro-drop languages.

Hyams proposal, if correct, calls into question the literal applicability of the subset principle, since the languages that are to be distinguished through learning are not in the subset relation, and yet the "no-negative-evidence" hypothesis, of which the subset principle is an intended formalization, seems equally applicable here as in other cases.

Lebeaux in responding to Hyams' paper is not so much concerned with her particular application of the subset principle, as he is with one of her assumptions about the sequence of grammars that the child passes through, particularly the assumption that each of these is a possible adult grammar. Lebeaux suggests that in fact the grammars grow in complexity, in an intuitive sense of that term. So, for example, he suggests that the reason that children commence with pro-drop, and later pass on to non-pro-drop, is that initially they have no mechanism of case assignment other than 'structural', where structural case is case that is associated with configurations, rather than with case-assigning lexical items; structural case assignment is by assumption optional. Later, the child acquires the ability to assign case lexically, where lexical case assignment is obligatory. The later grammar is clearly 'more complex' than the former.

The attractive feature of Lebeaux's conception is that it gives order to the parameters — less complex grammars will precede more complex grammars, in some intuitive sense of that term (though Lebeaux suggests that some sort of evaluation measure (!) might be involved). From the standpoint of the standard conception of parameter setting, the choice of ordering of parameters is at best consistent with only the "no-negative-evidence" hypothesis, at worst arbitrarily stipulated. Lebeaux's suggestions raise the question, is there a general theory of parameters beyond the subset principle, and if so, is it 'consistent' with the subset principle (does it give orderings of hypotheses (or, parameter settings) consistent with it.)

Wexler and Manzini, in their paper, apply the subset principle to the binding theory. The default value of the domain parameter of each binding theory element is set in a way consistent with the subset principle — it is small for anaphors, and large for pronouns. This model denies that there is any general binding domain for a language, only item-particular domains. This is forced by the author's assumption that parameters are associated with lexical items (as in Borer, 1985), not grammars as a whole — so the domain parameter could be set differently for each item subject to the binding theory, and they give some evidence that this is so.

In his reply, Safir suggests that the hypothesis that parameters are lexical leads to an 'atomization' of the theory, in that language particular features of structure that cannot be associated with particular words cannot be learned. It is presently an open question whether such features exist. Safir concedes on the basis of Wexler and Manzini's discussion of binding theory in Icelandic that there might not be any super-lexical generalization of binding domains.

Safir challenges the assumption made by Wexler and Manzini that the subset relations that govern parameter setting are learned, on the grounds that the computations involved are too complicated to attribute to the child. In fact though, it seems to me that whatever the facts of this matter might be, it has no bearing on the empirical content of the theory as a theory of learning, for apparently the calculations and the learning do not interact in any way (though one might challenge this simplifying assumption).

In the remainder of the papers in this volume (and the responses to them) the main goal is not to present particular parameters, but to scrutinize the parameterized model itself from the point of view of methodology, and from the point of view of the general problem of language learning; the general point of these papers is that the parameterized model can account for only part of the complete story of language acquisition, and in fact that the setting of parameters itself might be contingent on development that is not 'parametric' in nature.

In their paper, Nishigauchi and Roeper emphasize one important point about the deductive parameterized model: that that model, by itself, does not make acquisition predictions — it must be supplemented with principles of acquisition that relate linguistic data to the parameter-setting devices. First, there must be some prior structure assigned to a string before it can serve as the grounds for setting some parameter, and this prior structure must involve something other than parameter setting (surely the identification of words in the string is not the result of parameter setting). Seconds, there must be some relation between a particular piece of data and the change in grammar which it triggers, and this relationship is governed by principles of acquisition that are logically independent of, but supplemental to, the actual setting of parameters. On this last point, Nishigauchi and Roeper propose that reference serves to bootstrap the system in a number of cases. For example, the English complementer 'for' and expletives 'it' and the 'there' can be regarded as purely 'empty' grammatical objects; however, Nishigauchi and Roeper argue, it is no accident that these are homophonous with non-'empty' items — the purposive Prep 'for' and the referential pronouns 'there' and 'it' — it is via their referential analogues that the system grasps these items in the first place, only later assigning them their 'empty' grammatical functions.

Nishigauchi and Roeper propose other acquisition principles as well, among them a 'modularity' principle similar in spirit to that which appears in Wexler and Manzini's contribution.

In their paper, Borer and Wexler suggest that certain substantive principles and operations of grammar emerge spontaneously through maturation in the first several years of the child's life, rather than through any kind of learning, including parameter setting. They defend the intellectual coherence of this view, and give several instances of acquisition which they feel supports the idea. The alternative to the 'maturation' hypothesis is the 'continuity' hypothesis, according to which the principles and operations available to the child remain constant through the course of acquisition.

This 'maturation' hypothesis they feel is favored empirically over the 'continuity hypothesis' by cases in which a child maintains for a period of time either a non-optimal grammar or a grammar clearly falsified by simple data.

Borer and Wexler judge that the 'continuity' hypothesis is 'simplest' in some sense, and suggest that it is therefore a priori to be preferred. It might be worthwhile to consider it an 'idealization' whose harmfulness to deeper understanding cannot be assayed at present, but which serves as a specific context within which to reason about acquisition and conduct research. It is of course proper to question idealizations, but the refutation of an idealizing assumption does not help unless the specific context it provides is replaced. The question then is, does the 'maturation' hypothesis provided a sufficiently specific context for research. Wexler and Borer seek to show that it does, by providing a number of cases in which the maturation of a particular principle can be invoked to explain a particular fact of acquisition. They do not, however, provide any general idea of what matures when. They may in fact not believe this possible, but this means that the continuity hypothesis still serves as the context of research, while debate procedes on particular cases.

Weinberg's reply to their paper attempts to show that the idealization to the continuity hypothesis is harmless enough for the cases Borer and Wexler present, by offering alternative accounts of the cases they feel point to maturation as the only reasonable case. She draws an important distinction between two types of case they consider, cases where the child maintains a false hypothesis in the face of simple falsifying evidence because the needed principle or operation is not available at the time, and cases where a child alters a grammatical description on the emergence of a new principle, despite the lack of falsifying evidence for the old description. She rightly notes that the later type of case is a bit more puzzling than the first — why should the child reanalyze?

Solan's paper presents again a parametric model, but in addition Solan discusses the difficulties in connecting parametric models to acquisition data; in addition, he provides an interesting instance of a case in which acquisition results can bear on a question of grammar proper.

Solan proposes that certain deficits in the child's early use of pronouns reflects not a mis-set parameter, but rather a confusion on the part of the child as to what principles apply to what lexical items; in particular, which items principles A and B of the binding theory apply to — the child, according to Solan, initially has all elements (pronouns and anaphors) subject to A, and not B. The alternative is an account in which the child has correctly classified the elements as pronominal or anaphoric, but has still to set the parameters of the domains for principles A and B. Solan gives evidence that the correct account is the first one. Actually, in any view, the child must learn this classification; the question is, does this learning interact with the BT in any way; Solan suggests not. The broadest question raised here is, what is the nature of the pre-parametric learning that must take place — clearly, some limited amount of the language must be learned before the questions about how to set parameters can be raised. The child must learn what the objects are that the parameters are about, and the crux of the problem is, how 'global' is this learning — can it, for example, be made contingent on the setting of some parameters.

Finer presents a parametric account of the data Solan discusses which avoids this question entirely. Finer's account is 'conservative' in the sense that it accounts for the data in the only known terms, namely, the parametric model, and is perhaps slightly to be preferred on these grounds, but both authors treat the argument as entirely an empirical matter.

Solan points also to certain features of the acquisition data which suggests, in a way that data from adult language cannot, that the binding theory of the kind proposed by Freidin (to appear) (and incidentally by Huang, 1982, as well) is preferred to the 'standard' binding theory as in Chomsky (1981). Again, Finer points out an alternative account of the data consistent with the standard theory. Here as well the authors succeed in posing the question as an entirely empirical matter, and it is encouraging to see grammatical studies and acquisition studies so finely wed.

In the two final papers, Phinney and White examine the role of the parameter setting model in the acquisition of a second language by adults. The general question is, what is the role of the parameters set for the native language (L1) in the acquisition of the second language (L2) — does the language learner assume the settings of his native language, and reset them where appropriate, or does he assume the settings of UG (where UG specifies unmarked default settings), and procede as in the acquisition of L1?

Where L1 has an unmarked value for some parameter, and L2 has a marked value, Phinney and White are in agreement that learning will proceed as in acquisition of L2, positive data in L2 providing the trigger for the marked setting. For this case, it is difficult to know if the learner is using UG default settings, or the settings of L1, since these are the same.

Where L1 is marked, and L2 is unmarked, the authors disagree on the course of acquisition, and the difference seems to boil down to a difference on the question whether it is UG or the settings of L1 that the learner starts from. White suggests that the learning unmarked settings for L2 is very difficult, requiring negative evidence, as the "logic or markedness" would suggest. She cites data in the acquisition of Spanish subject drop (L2) by English speakers (L1) to support this. Her assumption is that the learner is resetting L1 settings. Phinney on the other hand assumes that L1 default settings are available to the L2 learner, and consequently, learning unmarked settings will be quite easy, requiring no evidence at all. Interestingly, Phinney cites data from English speakers learning Spanish as well.

The papers in this volume are remarkably coherent in their view of the nature of the parameterized model, and in its potential role in acquisition studies. Surely, a good deal is still to be gained from studying the most elementary questions about what the parameters are, what the initial settings are, and to what extent the observed course of acquisition confirms these findings. I believe though that every one of these paper at least hints at much more difficult questions, ones that may be realistically confronted in the near future: questions about the complexity of primary data needed to set parameters, about the independence of the parameters with respect to the data, and about the 'locality' (over the primary data) of decisions made in the process of acquisition. It is only because the parameterized model is capable of such concrete predictions about acquisition that such question can be posed at all — it is difficult to imagine, for example, what the analogous questions might be for the 'evaluation metric' model. When serious research begins on these questions, the study of language acquisition will enter a new realm.

REFERENCES

Bach, E.: 1965, 'On some recurrent types of transformations', in C. W. Kreidler (ed.), *Sixteenth Annual Roundtable Meeting on Linguistics and Language Studies*, Georgetown University Monograph Series on Language and Linguistics, 18. Washington D.C.
Berwick, R.: 1985, *The Acquisition of Syntactic Knowledge*, MIT Press.
Borer, H.: 1984, *Parametric Syntax*, Foris Publications, Dordrecht.
Chomksy, N.: 1965, *Aspects of the Theory of Syntax*, MIT Press.

Chomsky, N.: 1981, *Lectures on Government and Binding*, Foris Publications, Dordrecht.
Culicover, P. and K. Wexler: 1980, *Formal Principles of Language Acquisition*, MIT Press.
Freidin, R.: to appear, 'Fundamental issues in the theory of binding', in B. Lust (ed.), *Acquisition Studies in Anaphora: Defining the Constraints*, D. Reidel, Dordrecht.
Gold, E.: 1967, 'Language identification in the limit', *Information and Control 10*, 447—474.
Huang, J.: 1982, *Logical Relations in Chinese and the Theory of Grammar*, MIT dissertation.
Hyams, N.: 1983, *The Acquisition of Parameterized Grammars*, CUNY dissertation.
Jackendoff: 1977, *Lexicalist Syntax*, MIT Press.
Rizzi, L.: 1982, *Issues in Italian Syntax*, Foris Publications, Dordrecht.
Williams, E.: 1976, 'The natural philosophy of languange acquisition', ms. UMASS.
Williams, E.: 1977, 'Markedness and phrase structure', Glow Presentation (appears as Williams, 1981).
Williams, E.: 1977a, *Presentation, International Conference on Child Language*, Tokyo.
Williams, E.: 1981, 'Language acquisition, markedness, and phrase structure', in S. Tavakolian (ed.), *Language Acquisition and Linguistic Theory*, MIT Press.

EDWIN WILLIAMS

NINA HYAMS

THE THEORY OF PARAMETERS AND
SYNTACTIC DEVELOPMENT

1. INTRODUCTION

Within recent theories of Generative Grammar, UG has taken the form of a parameterized system. The parameters of UG express the limited range of variation which is permitted with respect to a set of core principles. For example, the X-Bar schemata given in (1) specifies that the categorial rules must conform to an 'endocentric requirement'; that is, each phrase must contain a lexical head of its own feature specification. However, languages may vary as to the linear position of the head with respect to its complements (represented by . . .) (Stowell, 1981).

$$(1) \qquad X^n \rightarrow \ldots X^{n-1} \ldots$$

Similarly, it has been proposed that the principle of Subjacency is subject to parametric variation (Rizzi, 1982). We may think of the core rule as specifying that a moved element may not cross two 'bounding nodes'. What counts as a bounding node may vary (within limits) from language to language, being chosen from among the set S, S-bar, NP, and so on. Rizzi has argued that this is one respect in which Italian and English differ. The bounding nodes in English are NP and S, while in Italian they are NP and S-bar. Within a parameterized theory of UG, language acquisition (or more narrowly, grammatical development) is viewed as a process in which the child 'fixes' the set of parameters for the particular language he is to acquire.

The purpose of this paper is to provide an elaboration of the relationship between the parameters of UG and actual grammatical development. We will be assuming as a working hypothesis (and in fact, we take as the null hypothesis) that grammatical development is a 'continuous' process; that is, we assume that the intermediate grammars constructed by the child in the course of acquisition (though perhaps not fully specified) are constrained by the principles of UG. This continuous model of grammatical development can be schematized as in (2).

1

Thomas Roeper and Edwin Williams (eds.), Parameter Setting, 1—22.
© 1987 by D. Reidel Publishing Company.

(2) $G_0, G_1, G_2, \ldots, \ldots, G_s$

         G_0 = UG; G_s = the adult grammar

Continuity is, of course, not a necessary assumption. It is certainly a logical possibility that the intermediate grammars are constructed according to principles which are fundamentally different from those which characterize the adult system. If this is the case, then language acquisition is a kind of 'metaphoric' process (Gleitman, 1981) and the model we are suggesting may be inappropriate. At the present, however, there is little evidence to suggest that the early grammars do contain 'unlinguistic' rules. In face, an adequate description of even the earliest multiword utterances require rules which are not qualitatively different from adult grammatical rules (cf. Hyams, 1983; Levy, 1983; Pinker, 1984).[1]

Given the continuous model of development schematized in (2) and a system of parameters outlined previously, there are certain predictions which follow concerning the actual course of acquisition, i.e. the set of intermediate grammars. The most obvious prediction is that the values chosen by the intermediate grammars along particular parameters will not fall outside the permitted range. For example, an intermediate grammar will not have PP as a bounding node for Subjacency, assuming this is not a 'possible' bounding node. A second, perhaps less obvious, prediction is that an early grammar of a language L may differ from the adult grammar of L with respect to the value chosen along a particular parameter (provided both are within the permitted range). In this instance we expect that the child's language and the adult language will differ in certain systematic ways, these differences being derived from the parametric variation between the two grammars. That the child grammar and the adult grammar could differ in this way is made plausible by the following considerations. First, as noted by White (1980), the child does not have teleological knowledge of the adult grammar, and hence the latter is not really the 'target' from the child's perspective. Rather, the child is attempting to construct a grammar for a certain range of data. It is important to note, however, that the data base for the child grammar and the data base of the adult grammar are not necessarily the same insofar as the child 'selectively attends' to data (Newport et al., 1977). In fact, it may be useful to distinguish, as White suggests, between 'input data' (the data available to the child in the linguistic environment) and 'intake data' (the linguistic data to which the child actually attends). Different data bases will obviously result in grammars which differ in certain respects. Finally, we expect that the child grammar will differ from the adult grammar in the instance in which a particular parameter comes fixed at an 'initial', setting (i.e. the value assumed in advance of experience with a particular language) which happens not to be the correct setting for the adult grammar. In this paper we will present an instance of this last case and the particular parameter which we discuss is the so-called 'pro-drop' (or 'null subject') parameter (Chomsky, 1980, 1981; Taraldsen, 1980; Jaeggli, 1982; Borer, 1981; Safir, 1982; Rizzi, 1982). The pro-drop parameter is intended to explain (among other things) the property exhibited by languages like Italian and Spanish of allowing phonologically-null subjects in tensed sentences. Examples are given in (3) and (4).

(3)   Vado al cinema stasera   (Italian)
(4)   Voy al cine esta noche   (Spanish)
        '(I) go to the movies tonight'

Specifically, we will argue that the early grammar of English (and all other languages) is a pro-drop grammar, this reprsenting the 'initial' setting along the pro-drop parameter. The particular formulation of the parameter which we propose explains various well-known properties of early language, notably the optionality of lexical subjects and the absence of modals and auxiliaries.

In Section 2 we outline the particular version of the pro-drop parameter which we assume, which we refer to as the AG/PRO parameter. We will focus on the adult grammars of Italian (and Spanish) and English and thereby provide the theoretical framework within which to view the acquisition data. In Section 3 we discuss the effects of the parameter during actual grammatical development. Included in this section is an account of the kind of 'triggering' data which could induce a resetting of the pro-drop parameter in the English speaking child, and hence account for the transition to the adult system.

2. THE AG/PRO PARAMETER

As a point of departure, we assume the Extended Projection Principle (Chomsky, 1981), i.e. the requirement that all sentences have subjects.

This is expressed by the base rule in (5), which is universal (abstracting away the order of constituents).

(5)   S → NP INFL VP

As is well-known, however, languages exhibit variation with respect to whether the subject need be phonologically realized (cf. examples (3)—(4)). That is to say that in pro-drop languages a lexical subject is entirely optional though the subject, even when phonologically null, has a definite pronominal reference. Rizzi (1982) has proposed that this variation can be explained by assuming that in languages like Italian and Spanish, INFL may be specified as [+pronominal]. A [+pronominal] INFL licenses an empty category in subject position.[2] Following in the spirit of Rizzi's proposal, we propose that the difference between pro-drop and non-pro-drop languages is that in the former the AG (= agreement) features contained in INFL (cf. (6) below) constitute a particular kind of pronominal, namely, the element PRO.[3] Thus, on our analysis languages may vary as to whether AG is or is not PRO. Where AG is PRO it licenses an empty category in subject position, as in Italian and Spanish;[4] where AG is not PRO a null subject is impossible, as in English. We henceforth refer to this parameter as the AG/PRO parameter. The expansion of INFL which we assume is as in (6).

(6)   INFL → (AG) AUX

AG is the set of features for person, number and gender associated with the subject (= PRO in pro-drop languages). The AG features are present in tensed clauses and absent in gerunds and infinitivals. We further assume (in the spirit of the Standard Theory) that the tense specification of the sentence is contained inside AUX, as are various auxiliary elements, for example, the English modals. As we will observe later, however, there is language particular variation with respect to whether AUX may contain lexical material, and this variation is derivable from the AG/PRO parameter.

Within the theory of grammar we are assuming (the Government-Binding Theory, Chomsky, 1981), the defining characteristic of PRO is that it may only appear in ungoverned positions (cf. Note 3.). The definition of government which we adopt, following Aoun and Sportiche (1983), is given in (7).

(7) α governs β in the structure $[\ldots \alpha \ldots \beta \ldots \alpha \ldots]$ where
                                                                          γ

  (i) $\alpha = X^0$
  (ii) where ϕ is a maximal projection, ϕ dominates β iff ϕ dominates α.

Zagona (1982) has observed that in addition to the null subject phenomenon, there is a second property which distinguishes pro-drop from non-pro-drop languages, and this concerns the behavior the auxiliary systems in these two language types. There is considerable evidence that in English the modals and, in certain instances, the auxiliaries *have* and *be* constitute a separate consituent from the VP; that is, they appear under AUX. Typical syntactic diagnostics for the AUX analysis include tag-formation, negative placement, VP deletion and Subject-AUX inversion, each of which is illustrated in (8).

(8) a.   Peter hasn't eaten, has he?
    b.   John will not finish this paper.
    c.   Mary isn't coming tonight, but Sue is.
    d.   Will Robert find his sunglasses?

Moreover, the English modals distinguish themselves from main verbs by their complete lack of verbal morphology. In Italian (and Spanish) in contrast, the auxiliaries and 'modals' (e.g. *potere* (can), *dovere* (must)) exhibit all the syntactic and morphological behavior of verbs. There is no evidence to suggest that in these languages auxiliary elements appear under the separate AUX constituent. There is no process of tag-formation as such. Negative markers cannot intercede between an auxiliary and main verb, nor can pronominal object clitics. The negative marker and the clitic must precede both the auxiliary and main verb, as exemplified below.

(9) a.   *Mario ha non mangiato
         (cf. Mario non ha mangiato)
         'Mario has not eaten'

    b.   *Mario ha lo mangiato
         'Mario has it eaten'
         (cf. Mario lo ha mangiato)

Auxiliaries cannot be stranded under VP deletion.

(10)   *Maria non è arrivata ancora, ma Gianni è
       'Maria hasn't (= isn't) arrived yet, but Gianni has (= is)'

Finally, auxiliaries and modals cannot be inverted with the subject in tensed clauses.

(11) a. *Ha Gianni mangiato
        'Has Gianni eaten'

   b. *E Gianni arrivato
      'Is Gianni arrived'

   c. *Puo Gianni aiutarci
      'Can Gianni help us'

With respect to their morphology, the Italian modals (and auxiliaries) exhibit the full range of inflection for person, number and tense, in marked contrast to the English modals. Zagona has related the null-subject phenomenon to the differences in the auxiliary systems of Spanish and English by proposing that in Spanish and other pro-drop languages, the head of INFL is 'nominal' (following Rizzi's analysis) and thus licenses a null element in subject position, while in English the head of INFL is 'verbal', thereby licensing a null element inside the VP. On her analysis, then, languages vary according to whether INFL is 'nominal' or 'verbal' in nature. We would like to propose, in contrast, that the impossibility of generating (or raising) auxiliaries into AUX follows from the fact that a lexical element in AUX would govern AG.[5] Where AG is PRO (in pro-drop languages), the resulting configuration is in violation of the principle that 'PRO must be ungoverned' (cf. Chomsky, 1981, for discussion). This contrast between English and Italian is schematized in (12).

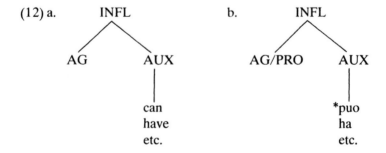

(12) a.   INFL   b.   INFL
          AG   AUX   AG/PRO   AUX
                   | |
                  can   *puo
                  have   ha
                  etc.   etc.

Returning to the data in (11), we assume, following Safir and Pesetsky (1981) that Subject-AUX inverted structures are generated by the rule 'Move INFL', an instantiation of 'Move α', which adjoins INFL to the left of S. We further assume, as seems optimal, that 'Move INFL' applies freely, its output being constrained solely by an independently needed PF condition blocking free occurrences of 'bound morphemes', as in (13).

(13) $*X + \text{Af(fix)} + Y$ where $X, Y = \emptyset$

Thus, in English, 'Move INFL' will yield a well-formed output iff AUX is lexically specified, since in that instance the AG features (and tense features) may affix onto the adjacent auxiliary element, as in (14).

(14)

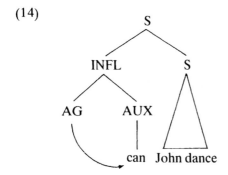

In Italian (and Spanish) in constrast, 'Move INFL' will not yield a grammatical output since no lexical element can appear in AUX (given the condition on PRO). Hence, there will be no adjacent stem onto which the AG and tense features can affix. In short, inversion in tensed sentences in Italian and Spanish is blocked by the principle that PRO be ungoverned, not by any condition on the application of 'Move INFL'.

Note that this analysis makes the following prediction. 'Move INFL' should yield a grammatical output in Italian just in case INFL does not contain AG, since in this instance there is nothing to block the occurrence of lexical auxiliaries in AUX. As noted earlier, AG is present in tensed sentences, but not in gerunds and infinitivals. Hence, our analysis predicts that inversion will be possible in these constructions. The following data (from Rizzi, 1982) confirm this prediction.

(15) a. Avendo Maria accettato di aiutarci, potremo risolvere il problema

'Having Maria accepted to help us, we can resolve the problem'

  b. Essendo Gianni disposto ad aiutarci, potremo risolvere il problema

'Being Gianni willing to help us, we can resolve the problem'

  c. Gianni sostiene non essere lui in grado di dare un contributo

'Gianni maintains not to be he able to make a contribution'

  d. Dovendo tuo fratello tornare a casa, non possiamo allontanarci molto

'Having (= musting) your brother to return home, we can't go very far'

  e. Ritengo dover tuo fratello tornare a casa

'I believe to have (= must) your brother to return home'[6]

To sum up, in English the modals are generated in AUX, while *have* and *be* may raise into AUX from their base-generated position in the VP (Emonds, 1976). In Italian (and Spanish), on the other hand, the modals *potere* (can) and *dovere* (must) are main verbs — specifically, raising verbs (cf. Rizzi, 1976; Burzio, 1981), while the auxiliaries *avere* (have) and *essere* (be) form a verbal complex with the main verb inside the VP. We may assume that relevant structures to be as follows.

(16) a. $[_s \text{Gianni}_i [_{INFL}] [_{VP} \text{puo} [_s [e_i] \text{ andare via}]]]$
'John can go away'

  b. $[_s \text{Gianni} [_{INFL}] [_{VP} [_V \text{è andato}] \text{ via}]]$
'Gianni has gone away'

In Italian, however, the modals and auxiliaries may raise into INFL (and hence undergo inversion) just in case AG is absent. Thus, certain striking differences in the auxiliary systems of pro-drop and non-pro-drop languages follow as effect of the AG/PRO parameter. In the following section we will examine the effects of the AG/PRO parameter in actual grammatical development.

3. THE GRAMMAR OF EARLY ENGLISH

The early stages in the acquisition of English are marked by the prevalent use of what we might pretheoretically refer to as 'subjectless sentences'. The following (non-imperative) sentences (taken from Bloom, Lightbown, and Hood, 1975) are representative of the general phenomenon.

(17)   Read bear book
         Want go get it
         Ride truck
         Bring Jeffrey book
         Want look a man
         See under there

Sentences of this sort have been remarked upon by Bloom (1970), Brown, Cazden, and Bellugi (1973), Braine (1973), McNeill (1966), Menyuk (1969), and Gruber (1967) among others. The most important fact to note about these sentences is that they co-exist with sentences containing overt subjects. This is illustrated by the 'minimal pairs' in (18) (sentences taken from the same transcript) (Bloom *et al.*, 1975) and the 'replacement sequences' (Braine, 1973) given in (19); that is, a subjectless sentence immediately followed by an expanded version of the sentence with a subject.

(18)   Throw it away   Mommy throw it away
         Want go get it   I want take this off
         Go in there   Foot goes over there
         Change pants   Papa change pants
         Take a nap   Mama take a nap

(19)   Fall . . . Stick fall
         Go nursery . . . Lucy go nursery
         Push Stevie . . . Betty push Stevie
         Crawl downstairs . . . Tommy crawl downstairs
         Build house . . . Cathy build house

The data illustrated in (18) and (19) clearly show that the absence of subjects is not due to a performance limitation on sentence length since the child is able to produce the longer sentence. (Note in this regard that many of the sentences during this period reach four, five and six words.) Neither is it the case that the absence of a lexical subject correlates with in any straightforward way with syntactic complexity.

Lexical subjects may be absent in simple utterances as they may in more complex sentences, illustrated below (from Bloom *et al.*, 1975).

(20)   Want Kathryn ə put in ə tank
        Kathryn want build another house
        Want look a man
        I want kiss it

Thus, it does not appear to be the case that 'missing' subjects are due to an increased 'cognitive load' associated with greated syntactic complexity. Finally, the systematicity of the phenomenon precludes an analysis of these sentences as simple performance errors.

While 'missing' subjects are pervasive, sentences with missing objects are strikingly rare. An account in terms of processing or cognitive limitations does not predict such an asymmetry. Note, moreover, that the 'missing' subject is not semantically restricted, i.e. it is not uniformly an *agent of action*, for example.[7] Nor is it restricted as to grammatical person. The null subject may refer to the child himself or to some other person or object. This is best illustrated by the 'replacement sequences' in (19).

Subjectless sentences in early language share two important properties with adult pro-drop languages. First, as has been illustrated, the lexical subjects are entirely optional. Second, as first noted by Bloom (1970), the 'missing' subject has a definite pronominal reference which can be inferred from context, as illustrated by the following dialogue.

(21)   (Eric has just eaten)
        Mother: You ate the apple all up.
                There's no more apple.
        (Eric starts to cry and hits the toys)
        Eric: Want more apple.

In (21) it is clearly Eric who wants some more apple and not some unspecified individual.

The optionality of lexical subjects and the definite reference associated with the missing element constitute prima facie evidence for a pro-drop analysis of subjectless sentences in child language. There is, however, a stronger prediction which follows from the particular pro-drop analysis proposed in this paper. Recall that given that AG/PRO parameter, a pro-drop language cannot contain lexical elements in AUX since AG (= PRO) would be governed in violation of the condition on PRO. It is well-known that children acquiring English systematically omit modals and auxiliaries (Brown and Fraser, 1964; Bellugi, 1967; Brown, 1973). On the basis of the data we examined (from Bloom, 1970; Bloom *et al.*, 1975, and Bellugi, 1967) the English auxiliary *be* and the modals are systematically absent during the period of subjectless sentences.[8] The modals and *be* elements emerge shortly after the point at which the child begins using lexical subjects consistently; that is, following the point at which the early grammar shifts away from a pro-drop grammar towards the adult grammar of English.[9] In (22) and (23) we have indicated the ages and stages which correspond to the two grammar types for the children studied in Bloom (1970) and Bloom *et al.* (1975). The ages and stages given in (22) is the period characterized by a grammar in which AG is PRO (henceforth referred to as G_1; that is, the period in which subjectless sentences are prevalent and modals entirely lacking. Those given in (23) represent the point of shift, or the resetting of the AG/PRO parameter. (We return to this shortly.) At this point, the children being using lexical subjects consistently and the auxiliaries emerge shortly thereafter.

(22) G_1 (AG = PRO)

Eric I → Eriv V (20;2—25;1)
Gia II → Gia V (20;2—25;2)
Kathryn I → Kathryn III (21;0—24;2)

(23) G_2 (AG ≠ PRO)

Eric VI (26;3)
Gia VI (27;1)
Kathryn (26;4)[10]

Although the AG/PRO analysis directly predicts the impossibility of lexical material in AUX during the period of subjectless sentences, it does not explain why the auxiliaries are entirely lacking. In principle, there is a second option available to the child, namely, he could analyze the modals and *be* as main verbs, as they are in Italian and Spanish, for example (cf. (16)). What then excludes this alternative analysis? Let us begin with the modals, reserving discussion of *be* until Section 3.2. Note that in order for the child to (mis)analyze the modals as main verbs he must be able to identify them as verbs. In English, one of the essential properties which distinguishes modals from verbs is the lack of morphological marking on the former. Thus, if the child is sensitive to the relationship which exists between particular inflectional forms and particular grammatical classes, it is unlikely that he will (mis)analyze modals as main verbs. There is evidence from both naturalistic and experimental studies that children do in fact have knowledge of form-class relationships at a very early age. Maratsos (1982) points out that early language is generally lacking in form-class errors; that is, children do not attach verb inflection to members of other grammatical categories. He notes, for example, that although children use terms like *away, off, bye-bye* to denote actions, they do not produce errors such as the following.

(24)   Gia awaying   (unattested)
        Car outing   (unattested)

In addition, there is cross-linguistic experimental evidence that very young children use the information provided by inflection in comprehending sentences whether or not they use these inflections productively in their own speech (Slobin, 1982). Thus, the acquisition data from production and comprehension supports the hypothesis that children are sensitive to inflectional morphology and that this information is used by the child in determining category membership. To the extent that this is so English speaking children will not analyze modals as verbs. Thus the two analyses for the English auxiliaries which are in principle available to the child are in fact excluded. The absence of inflection on the modals blocks a main verb analysis, while the presence of AG/PRO in INFL blocks the modals from appearing under AUX. In effect, the early grammar 'filters out' input data which are unanalyzable.[11] It is expected, however, that once AG is no longer pronominal, the modals will emerge since at that point a possible analysis presents itself, namely, the AUX analysis. As noted earlier, this is the case. The modals emerge only after the AG/PRO parameter has been reset, as evidenced by the fact that the child is using lexical subjects consistently.

The analysis we are suggesting makes two further predictions. First, it follows from this account that once the auxiliaries emerge they will appear simultaneously in declarative and interrogative (i.e. inverted) structures. Recall that what blocks AUX inversion (i.e. 'Move INFL') in pro-drop languages is the impossibility of lexical material in AUX; the rule is otherwise free to apply. As noted by Bellugi (1967) the auxiliaries are introduced in declarative, negative and interrogative sentences at the same point in development. Bellugi (1967) identifies this stage as Stage C. Some examples follow (from Bellugi, 1967 — Stage C).

(25)   He won't come
        I can't see it
        The sun is not too bright
        Could I use this one?
        Will you help me?
        Did you make a great big hole in there?

The second prediction concerns the relative acquisition of the English modals and the modals in a pro-drop language, for example, Italian. Recall that in Italian the modals receive the full range of verbal inflection. We thus expect that the Italian modals, *potere* (can) and *dovere* (must), will be acquired earlier than the English modals since the former can be identified and analyzed as main verbs. That is to say that the Italian child needn't await the availability of the AUX node for these elements. This second prediction is also confirmed by the acquisition data. The Italian modals are acquired significantly earlier than the English modals and in fact they are acquired at roughly the same point at which English speaking children acquire the semi-auxiliaries *have to* and *going to* (Hyams, 1983). In the section that follows we discuss this comparative evidence for the analysis presented in this paper.

3.1. *Some Comparative Evidence*

On the above analysis the late appearance of modals is explained by strictly grammatical factors — the impossibility of lexical material in AUX and the morphological differences which exist between verbs and modals. A priori, there is a plausible alternative explanation, namely that the modals are late acquired because of their semantic or conceptual complexity. There are, however, two immediate problems with a semantic/conceptual account. First, as Bellugi (1967) and others have noted, the English semi-auxiliaries *hafta* and *gonna* are acquired significantly earlier than the 'real' modals. They appear during the period which we have characterized as G_1. Bellugi places the acquisition of the semi-auxiliaries during her Stage B — 3 to 8 months prior to Stage C[12] (which marks the emergence of the modals). Examples are given below (from Bellugi, 1967; Bloom *et al.*, 1975).

(26) a. I gonna cut some more
    b. I going give it to somebody
    c. I hafta eat my ice cream

Note that the semi-auxiliaries *hafta* and *gonna* are semantically equivalent to the modals *must* and *will*. Thus, a semantic account cannot explain the real-time lag which exists between the acquisition of modals and semi-auxiliaries in English. Moreover, as noted above, Italian speaking children acquire the modals *potere* (can) and *dovere* (must) significantly earlier than their English cohorts; the Italian modals appear at roughly the same point as the the English semi-auxiliaries, that is, during Bellugi's Stage B. Some examples follow (from Hyams, 1983).

(27)   Io deo lavorare co cacciavite [deo = devo]
        'I must work with (the) screwdriver'

        Non posso più chiamare nonnina
        'I cannot call Grandma anymore'

Again, an account along semantic/conceptual lines would fail to explain the lag between the emergence of the English and Italian modals.

Given the analysis proposed in this paper the prior appearence of the English semi-auxiliaries and the Italian modals relative to the English modals receives a straightforward explanation. Both the Italian modals and the English semi-auxiliaries bear verbal inflection and hence may be analyzed by the child as verbs. While the English semi-auxiliaries are not inflected as heavily as the Italian modals, they are nevertheless morphologically distinguishable from the English modals which bear no inflection whatsoever. The semi-auxiliary *have to* has three forms — *hafta, hasta* and *hadta*. Similarly, the semi-auxiliary *going to* bears the progressive suffix-*ing*, one of the first verbal inflections to be acquired by English speaking children (Brown, 1973). Young children use both the contracted and non-contracted form of *going to* (cf. (26a,b)). It is thus expected that these verbal elements will appear prior to the modals. In particular, they may emerge prior to the shift away from G_1 since they are analyzable as main verbs.[13]

3.2. *The English Auxiliary Be*

The analysis of semi-auxiliaries proposed in this section raises an immediate question with respect to the emergence of the auxiliary *be* in

English. Unlike the modals, *be* is inflected (although the inflection is highly irregular). It should thus be possible for the child to analyze this element as a verb. This prediction is only partially true, however. Brown (1973) notes a curious asymmetry in the child's use of this verb. While *be* is systematically absent in progressive and predicative constructions, as in (28), it is never ommitted in sentences like those in (29). The sentences in (28) and (29) co-occur in the acquisition data during the period characterized by G_1.

(28)   You so big
        Adam home
        No the sun shining
        He eating ice cream

(29)   Here it is
        There it is

As Brown notes, children fail to omit *be* in precisely those cases in which it is impossible to contract *be* in the adult language (cf. *Here it's, *There it's).[14] Summing up Brown's results, the 'uncontractible *be*' emerges significantly earlier in development than the 'contractible *be*', the latter appearing at the same point as the modals. On our analysis, the appearance of *be* in (29) is expected. By hypothesis, the inflection on *be* enables the child to identify it as a main verb. The alternative analysis, in which *be* is in AUX is excluded by AG/PRO. Strictly speaking then, it is the non-occurrence of *be* in examples like (28) which needs to be explained. We believe that the absence of *be* in these cases is directly related to its contractibility in the adult language, (i.e. the input data). Note that in those contexts in which *be* may undergo contraction, namely, in progressive and predicative constructions, (cf. It's raining, He's happy) the status of *be* as a main verb is less than obvious. Assuming that for the child, as for the adult, there is a strict locality condition on contraction, (i.e. *be* must in AUX (Emonds, 1976), a main verb analysis is impossible in these cases. At the same time, the presence of AG in INFL excludes an AUX analysis. Thus, the 'contractible' *be*, like the modals, is filtered out of the input data. It emerges alongside the modals at the point at which it may appear in AUX, that is, following the restructuring of G_1. As with the modals, *be* appears simultaneously in declarative, negative and interrogative structures (Bellugi, 1967). In the section that follows we discuss the restructuring of G_1.

3.3. *The Resetting Of The AG/PRO Parameter*

It is obvious that if an early grammar differs from the adult 'target' grammar, there must be mechanisms which insure a restructuring in the proper direction; that is, the early grammar must be 'delearnable' in the sense of Klein (1982). One kind of mechanism is the availability of 'triggering' data, that is, data which are inconsistent with a current grammar and which serve to force a resetting of a parameter. In this section we will consider the kinds of triggering data which might induce a resetting of the AG/PRO parameter in the development of English.[15]

There are at least two potential triggers, the expletive pronouns *it* and *there*, and what we refer to as "infelicitous referential pronouns". We discuss each of these in turn. Pro-drop languages like Italian and Spanish lack expletive pronouns. It seems reasonable to assume that the absence of expletive pronouns is related to the fact that in pro-drop languages the use of pronouns is reserved for purposes of contrast, emphasis, or to introduce a change of discourse topic.[16] Given that expletives cannot be used contrastively, emphatically, etc. (since they are semantically empty), we do not expect them to occur in languages in which pronouns have a pragmatic, as opposed to strictly grammatical function. It is thus possible that once the English speaking child learns the English expletives the latter trigger a restructuring according to (roughly) the following line of deduction. *It* and *there* are not being used for pragmatic purposes since they do not contribute to the meaning of the sentence. Thus they must be present for strictly grammatical reasons, namely, a null subject is impossible. If a null subject is impossible, AG is not PRO. This hypothesis is supported by the acquisition data. Expletives are absent prior to the point of restructuring and then appear in the data at the time which we have identified as the point of restructuring (cf. (23)). The sentences in (30) occur during the period referred to as G_1. These are sentences which would require expletives in the adult language (from Bloom *et al.*, 1975).

(30) Outside cold   ('It's cold outside')
      That's cold   (referring to the weather)
      No morning   ('It's not morning')
      Is toys in there   ('There are toys in there')
      No more cookies   ('There are no more cookies').

The following sentences, which occur at the point of restructuring, contain the first occurrences of expletives.

(31)   No, it's not raining
        It's not cold outside
        There's no more
        There's no money

Given the logic of a parameterized theory of grammar, we expect that restructuring will be triggered by relatively simple data which are readily available to the child. Ideally, we would like a theory in which the class of 'triggering data' is restricted in a principled fashion. A very strong claim (certainly too strong) is that all restructuring is induced by the acquisition of particular lexical items and their associated properties. For this reason the hypothesis that lexical expletives trigger a restructuring is attractive. There is, however, another set of potential triggering data for the particular parameter under discussion. This is the use of referential pronouns, e.g. *he, she*, etc. in what we might call 'pragmatically infelicitous' circumstances. At some point in development the English speaking children must learn that in English contrast and emphasis are indicated by stress. He will, however, hear unstressed referential pronouns, and hence will know that they are not present for pragmatic purposes. Thus, again, according to the same line of deduction used in the case of expletives, the AG/PRO parameter will be reset. On this account as well, the emergence of lexical expletives at the point of restructuring is predicted since a null subject is no longer licensed anywhere. Expletives would not, however, constitute the triggering data in this instance. In short, there are various lexical pronouns in English which do not serve any pragmatic function, either because they are semantically empty or because they are unstressed. Their presence in the sentence is necessitated by strictly grammatical factors, namely, that the grammar of English does not license phonologically-null subjects. Thus, in principle either class of elements (or both) could trigger a resetting of the AG/PRO parameter.[17]

4. CONCLUDING REMARKS

The analysis proposed in this paper attempts to provide a principled account of various (apparently unrelated) acquisition phenomena by approaching the acquisition data from within an independently motivated theory of grammar. At the same time, such an approach broadens the empirical coverage of the theory of grammar, in particular, the theory of parameters.

It is worth noting at this point that the acquisition analysis proposed in this paper, in which pro-drop constitutes the initial hypothesis of the child, is not what has standardly been assumed based on the analysis of adult pro-drop and non-pro-drop languages. White (1983) and others have proposed that the initial value along the pro-drop parameter must be [-pro-drop] given that in this case the child acquiring a pro-drop language would have positive evidence that his hypothesis is wrong, i.e. he would hear sentences in which the subject is absent. If, on the other hand, the English speaking child were to begin with a pro-drop grammar, he would never have disconfirming evidence since lexical subjects are possible in pro-drop languages. Although the logic of this approach is entirely correct, it (implicitly) assumes that what the child must learn in this instance is the surface behavior of the particular language he is acquiring. If, on the other hand, the child is really learning an abstract property of INFL (whether it is pronominal or not) then there are various kinds of disconfirming evidence for the English speaking child, as outlined earlier.[18]

Given the logic of a parameterized theory of grammar, the 'fixing' of a particular parameter should have complex consequences throughout the grammar of a particular language. Such a system goes a long way towards explaining how it is possible for a child to arrive at an adult grammar in a relatively short period of time. There is, however, a further consequence of such a model for actual acquisition. The richer the deductive structure associated with a particular parameter, the greater the range of potential 'triggering' data which will be available to the child for the 'fixing' of the particular parameter. In a theory of acquisition which does not assume an ordered (or orderly) presentation of data, this result seems optimal.

NOTES

[1] Pinker (1984) also argues for a continuous model of development. He refers to this as the 'continuity hypothesis.' In general, claims concerning continuity do not require that *all* principles of UG be available at the initial state. It is possible that certain principle are maturationally determined to emerge at later points in development. For discussion of this issue, see Borer and Wexler (this volume).

[2] More specifically, Rizzi proposes that a pronominal INFL functions like a clitic which 'properly governs' an [e] in subject position. The reader is refered to Rizzi (1982) for further discussion. For discussion of the notion 'proper government', see Chomsky, 1981; Rizzi, 1982.

[3] PRO is the element typically found in subject position of tenseless clauses, as follows.

    (i)   I want [PRO to go]
    (ii)   [PRO to leave] would be a mistake
    (iii)   [PRO drinking turtle blood] is disgusting

Jaeggli (1982) has proposed that PRO may also appear in a second 'transparent' position, COMP, as the output of PRO-movement in topicalized structures. See also Chomsky (1981) for a PRO-movement analysis of purposive infinitivals.

[4] Following Chomsky (1982) we assume that the null element occupying subject position is *pro*. On our analysis, the condition on *pro* is that is be governed by AG/PRO. For the definition of government see (7) in the text.

[5] On our analysis the head of INFL is determined according to the following 'Head Assignment Principle':

    (i)   Where AUX is lexically specified AUX heads INFL: otherwise AG heads.

[6] Rizzi (1982) notes that inversion in these cases is not only possibile but in fact obligatory. He proposes that the obligatoriness can be accounted for by assuming that Italian has a marked rule of nominative Case assignment as follows:

    (i)   Assign Nominative Case to NP in the context of AUX _____

If the rule fails to apply the structure is ruled out by the Case Filter. Henceforth we assume Rizzi's account of the obligatoriness of inversion in thes instances. Our analysis focuses on the fact that inversion is possible in these cases but not with tensed auxiliaries.

    Rizzi notes that these inverted sentences are of a rather formal style, the gerunds being less formal than the infinitives.

[7] This suggests that an adequate characterization of the null-subject phenomenon in early language cannot be stated in terms of semantic roles without a significant loss of generality. Indeed, facts such as these provide empirical evidence against the semantically-based child grammars proposed by Bowerman (1973) and Schlesinger (1971). For further discussion of this issue, see Hyams (1984).

[8] Participial forms (e.g. eaten, gone, etc.) are absent from the data through Stage V (Brown, 1973) suggesting that young children simply do not know the present perfect tense. We will therefore not discuss the English auxiliary *have*.

[9] The resetting of the parameter is discussed in Section 3.3.

[10] Bloom (1970) and Bloom *et al.* (1975) do not report the data for Kathryn beyond Time III (age 24;2). Thus, the point of shift for this child is a projection based on the fact that her language at Time III exhibited many of the properties which usually precede the shift (found in Gia V and Eric V).

[11] This is reminiscent of Roeper's 'input filter'. See Roeper (1978) for discussion.

[12] The amount of time between Stages B and C varies considerably from child to child. As noted in the text, the children studied by Bellugi ranged from a 3 to 8 month interval between the two stages.

[13] Two other 'modallike' elements which occur during Bellugi's Stage B are *can't* and *don't*. Following Bellugi, we assume that these elements are not in fact analyzed as negated modals by the child. Rather, they are simple negative markers analogous to *no*

and *not* which are also used by the child at this stage. See Bellugi (1967) and Hyams (1983) for further discussion.

[14] In his study of the acquisition of 'the 14 grammatical morphemes' Brown (1973) distinguishes the 'contractible *be*', the element which can be contracted in the adult language, from the 'uncontractible *be*' which cannot be contracted. In terms of the order of emergence of these forms in child language, the uncontractible form ranks 6.50 while the contractible form is the last of the 14 morphemes to appear.

[15] We assume, following Baker (1979), that the triggers are 'positive' data, that is, data in the environment which cannot be generated or are somehow incompatible with the child's current grammar.

[16] Chomsky (1981) suggests that the use of pronouns is governed by an Avoid Pronoun Principle which states (roughly) "Avoid pronouns where a null pronominal is possible".

[17] K. Wexler and L. White (p.c.) have independently suggested a third possible trigger — modals and *be* in sentence initial position in yes/no questions. Wexler and White note the results of Newport, Gleitman and Gleitman (1977) who found that sentence initial auxiliaries are particularly salient to the child in that the frequency of yes/no questions in the input data seem to be one of the few environmental factors which has a direct effect on language development in young children. It is thus possible, as suggested by Wexler and White, that when the child begins to attend to sentence initial auxiliaries, he is forced to an analysis in which these elements appear in AUX, and hence AG is not PRO.

[18] The Subset Principle (Berwick, 1982) is directly related to the issue of the availability of disconfirming evidence. Jacubowitz (1984), following Berwick, has argued that the child initially chooses the parameter value which generates the 'smaller' language, i.e. if the language generated by value x along parameter P is a subset of the language generated by value y along parameter P, the child will choose value x. An interesting question which is raised by the Subset Principle is what happens in the case in which a value x along parameter P generates a 'smaller' language with respect to a range of data A, but a larger language with respect to a range of data B. For example, in the version of the pro-drop parameter presented in this paper, English is a subset of Italian relative to the null-subject phenomenon, but Italian is a subset of English relative to the auxiliary system (e.g. we find inversion in tensed sentences in English but not Italian). If our analysis is correct, it suggests that the Subset Principle must be relativized to particular data. See Wexler and Manzini (this volume) for extensive discussion of the role of the Subset Principle in acquisition.

REFERENCES

Aoun, J. and D. Sportiche: 1983, 'On the formal theory of government', *The Linguistic Review* **2**, 211—236.

Baker, C. L.: 1979, 'Syntactic theory and the projection problem', *Linguistic Inquiry* **10**, 533—582.

Bellugi, U.: 1967, *The Acquisition of Negation*, unpublished Harvard University doctoral dissertation.

Berwick, R.: 1982, *Locality Principles and the Acquisition of Syntactic Knowledge*, MIT doctoral dissertation.

Bloom, L.: 1970, *Language Development: Form and Function in Emerging Grammars*, MIT Press, Cambridge, Massachusetts.

Bloom, L., P. Lightbown, and L. Hood: 1975, *Structure and Variation in Child Language*, Monograph of the Society for Research in Child Development, Vol. 40, No. 2.

Borer, H.: 1981, *Parametric Variation in Clitic Constructions*, MIT doctoral dissertation [revised version published as *Parametric Syntax*, Foris Publications, Dordrecht, 1984].

Borer, H. and K. Wexler: 1984, 'The maturation of syntax' (this volume).

Bowerman, M.: 1973, *Early Syntactic Development*, Cambridge University Press, Cambridge.

Braine, M.: 1973, 'Three suggestions regarding grammatical analyses of children's language", in C. Ferguson and D. Slobin (eds.), *Studies in Child Language Development*, Holt, Rinehart and Winston, New York.

Brown, R.: 1973, *A First Language: The Early Stages*, Harvard University Press, Cambridge, Massachusetts.

Brown, R., C. Cazden, and U. Bellugi: 1973, 'The child's grammar from I to III', in C. Ferguson and D. Slobin (eds.), *Studies in Child Language Development*, Holt, Rinehart & Winston, New York.

Brown, R. and C. Fraser: 1964, 'The acquisition of syntax', in U. Bellugi and R. Brown (eds.), *The Acquisition of Language*, Monographs for the Society of Research in Child Development, 29.

Burzio, L.: 1981, *Intransitive Verbs and Italian Auxiliaries*, MIT doctoral disseration [to be published by D. Reidel, Dordrecht].

Chomsky, N.: 1980, 'On binding', *Linguistic Inquiry* 11, 1—46.

Chomsky, N.: 1981, *Lectures on Government and Binding: The Pisa Lectures*, Foris Publications, Dordrecht.

Chomsky, N.: 1982, *Some Concepts and Consequences of the Theory of Government and Binding*, Linguistic Inquiry Monograph, MIT Press, Cambridge, Massachusetts.

Emonds, J.: 1976, *A Transformational Approach to English Syntax*, Academic Press, New York.

Gleitman, L.: 1981, 'Maturational determinants of language growth', *Cognition* 10, 103—114.

Gruber, J.: 1967, 'Topicalization in child language', *Foundations of Language* 3, 37—65.

Hyams, N.: 1983, *The Acquisition of Parameterized Grammars*, CUNY doctoral dissertation. [published as *Language Acquisition and the Theory of Parameters*, D. Reidel, Dordrecht, 1986].

Hyams, N.: 1984, 'Semantically-based child grammars: Some empirical inadequacies', Proceedings of the Stanford Child Language Conference.

Jacubowitz, C.: 1984, 'On markedness and binding principles', in the Proceedings of NELS 14.

Jaeggli, O.: 1982, *Topics in Romance Syntax*, Foris Publications, Dordrecht.

Klein, S.: 1982, *Syntactic Theory and the Developing Grammar: Reestablishing the Relationship between Linguistic Theory and Data from Language Acquisition*, unpublished UCLA doctoral dissertation.

Levy, Y.: 1983, 'It's frogs all the way down', *Cognition* 15, 75—93.

Maratsos, M.: 1982, 'The child's construction of grammatical categories', in E. Wanner and L. Gleitman (eds.), *Language Acquisition: The State of the Art*, Cambridge University Press, Cambridge.

McNeill, D.: 1966, 'Developmental psycholinguistics', in F. Smith and G. Miller (eds.), *The Genesis of Language: A Psycholinguistic Approach*, MIT Press, Cambridge, Massachusetts.

Menyuk, P.: 1969, *Sentences Children Use*, MIT Press, Cambridge, Massachusetts.

Newport, E., L. Gleitman, and H. Gleitman: 1977, 'Mother, please, I'd rather do it myself; Some effects and non-effects of maternal speech style', in C. Snow and C. Ferguson (eds.), *Talking to Children; Language Input and Acquisition*, Cambridge University Press, Cambridge.

Pinker, S.: 1984, *Language Learnability and Language Learning*, Harvard University Press, Cambridge, Massachusetts.

Rizzi, L.: 1976, 'La montée du sujet, le *si* impersonnel et une régle de restructuration dans la syntaxe italienne', in *Recherches Linguistiques* **4**, Paris-Vincennes.

Rizzi, L.: 1982, *Issues in Italian Syntax*, Foris Publications, Dordrecht.

Roeper, T.: 1978, 'Linguistic universals and the acquisition of gerunds', in H. Goodluck and L. Solan (eds.), *Papers in the Structure and Development of Child Language*, University of Massachusetts Occasional Papers in Linguistics, vol. 4.

Safir, K.: 1982, *Syntactic Chains and the Definiteness Effect*, MIT doctoral dissertation [published by Cambridge University Press, Cambridge, 1985].

Safir, K. and D. Pesetsky: 1981, 'Inflection, inversion and subject clitics', in V. Burke and J. Pustejovsky (eds.), *Proceeding of NELS* **11**.

Schlesinger, I. M.: 1971, 'Production of utterances and language acquisition', in D. I. Slobin (ed.), *The Ontogenesis of Grammar*, Academic Press, New York.

Slobin, D.: 1982, 'Universal and particular in the acquisition of language', in E. Wanner and L. Gleitman (eds.), *Language Acquisition: The State of the Art*, Cambridge University Press, Cambridge.

Stowell, T.: 1981, *Origins of Phrase Structure*, MIT doctoral dissertation [to be published by MIT Press].

Taraldsen, T.: 1980, 'On the NIC, vacuous application and the *that*-t filter' [Distributed by Indiana University Linguistics Club].

Wexler, K. and R. Manzini: 1984, 'Parameters and learnability in binding theory' [this volume].

White, L.: 1980, *Grammatical Theory and Language Acquisition*, McGill University doctoral dissertation [Distributed by Indiana University Linguistic Club].

White, L.: 1983, 'The pro-drop parameter and L2 acquisition', McGill University manuscript.

Zagona, K.: 1982, *Government and Proper Government of Verbal Projections*, University of Washington/Seattle doctoral dissertation.

DAVID LEBEAUX

COMMENTS ON HYAMS

INTRODUCTION

Assuming, as usual, a theory of language acquisition in which the grammars of each stage pass into the next,

(1) $G_0 \overset{f_0}{\frown} G_1 \overset{f_1}{\frown} G_2, \ldots, G_n$

We may inquire into the functions f_0, f_1, $\ldots$, f_n which relate the successive grammars; we may also inquire into the nature and structure of the intermediate grammars, G_i. An instance of *parameter setting* constitutes a particular sort of restricted f_i, namely one in which the flanking grammars, G_i and G_{i+1}, are roughly equivalent in complexity, and both are possible end points. Hyams' paper develops, in some detail, a particular instance of the parameter setting approach — namely, by analyzing the early optional lack of subjects as following from a setting of the pro-drop parameter. From this she attempts to predict the properties of both the input and output grammars (G_i and G_{i+1}) at a particular point in time in the acquisition of English, as a consequence, so to speak, of the conversion of English as Italian to English as English.

In Hyams' approach, as in all others, a particular sort of answer is being given to questions such as the following: Is language acquisition continuous? What is the nature of the difference between adjacent grammars? Are all the G_i possible terminal grammars? Is there some sense in which G_i is simpler than G_{i+1}, either in terms of markedness, or some other criterion? Can it be shown, for some G_i, that the acquisition device *must* pass through a simpler grammar G_j, in order for G_i to be reached? It is these questions which form the conceptual backing for any particular research in language acquisition; it is to these that I will be referring, even if implicity, in the following discussion.

23

Thomas Roeper and Edwin Williams (eds.), Parameter Setting, 23–39.
© 1987 by D. Reidel Publishing Company.

1. A PARAMETER SETTING ACCOUNT

The hypothesis that early English passes from a positive setting of the pro-drop parameter to a negative setting allows, as Hyams notes, a number of properties of the initial grammar to be explained. The propensity of children to drop subjects but not objects (in (1)), i.e. a subject/object asymmetry in this regard, mimics or models a similar possibility in adult Italian.

> (2) a. Kathryn see ball; see ball
>   b. (I) read bear book
>   c. Want look a man
>   d. Ride truck; Gia ride bike

In addition, early grammars in English, but not Italian, apparently drop modal constituents, and in general AUX. This difference is traced to the difference in the analysis of these constituents in English and Italian. In English, this class of verbs is assumed to be of a special sort, namely auxiliary verbs, which do not undergo agreement morphologically (at least for modals), are fronted for questions, and so on. No such special class exists in Italian, and the semantically identical class is simply analyzed as raising verbs (Rizzi, 1982). Assuming that (i) the child *is* able to analyze the initial instances of these elements as auxiliaries, and (ii) the possibility of a true auxiliary verb in the language is ruled out in this early stage by the prop-drop parameter (namely, according to Hyams, because AGR = PRO, and PRO would be governed by AUX if generated alongside it), the fact that these elements are filtered out in the early grammar of English would be explained. So the pro-drop hypothesis would explain the lack of these verbs in English, as well as the optional dropping of the subject.

There is an element to this analysis which is counterintuitive — namely, the child must be assumed to be sophisticated enough to analyze the elements under discussion as auxiliaries in English rather than main verbs (since if they were analyzed as main verbs they would not be filtered out), but not to be able to use this knowledge to determine that AGR $\neq$ PRO, though that further conclusion would be automatic under the assumptions that Hyams advocates. (Since if AGR did equal PRO, there would have to be a governed PRO, it being governed by AUX: an impossibility.) In the terminology of Roeper

(1978), while the analysis of these elements as auxiliaries *could* be a trigger to the lack of pro-drop in English, they are apparently not so used, and the child waits instead until a different property of non pro-drop languages is detected: namely, the existence of expletive elements in English. Thus an apparent conclusion of great sophistication, namely, the differentiation of the class of auxiliary verbs from main verbs in English and Italian for the same semantic class, is paired, by hypothesis, with the lack of a simple deductive step. Yet it is difficult to see how the analysis could be changed to avoid this counter-intuitiveness.

2. MARKEDNESS

The 'Italianizing' of early English brings with it a number of explanatory benefits, in the manner discussed above. Nonetheless, problematic features arise. One has to do with the nature of the trigger for the reanalysis of English as not a pro-drop language, and the early filtering out of auxiliaries. A more central consideration for the theory of language acquisition as a whole would involve the notion of markedness. Under the simplest interpretation of the term, an interpretation which, I would argue, should be strenuously held on to, a marked option corresponds exactly to a property of the acquisition device: namely, a grammatical option which is considered secondarily in comparison to the paired unmarked choice. That is, the marked option is some feature or property which requires more information to be set in its direction. This is, of course, the traditional view. There is, however, a possible more inclusive view, that the unmarked option is the one which is adopted first by the child, whether this is a property of the grammar *per se*, or of the entire computational device. Rizzi (1985) notes the possibility of such an interpretation in order to allow for Hyams' observations to be compatible with his conclusion that pro-drop is the grammatically marked, not the unmarked, option. In such a case one might reserve the notion of markedness to apply to the grammar G (Eng), and attribute the delay in acquisition to the externalized language L (Eng), assuming that Rizzi is correct in his attribution of the relative markedness of the two options. But then that leaves open the question of *why* the externalized language and the grammar should differ in their markedness.

There is another way of considering this which brings the point home more firmly. According to Hyams, the child starts out with an Italian grammar in this respect; and then moves to English (3). However, since the notion of parameter which she adopts is cut off from the idea of development (and perhaps intentionally so), one might equally well imagine that the child could in general start off with an English-type grammar involving obligatory subjects, and only later move to Italian: that is, the setting could be as in (4) rather than (3).

(3)   Italian   → English
        (pro-drop)   (not)

(4)   English → Italian
        (not)   (pro-drop)

Since it is relatively clear that the latter not only does not happen but *could* not happen (it would involve, for example, the Italian child allowing initially inversion of the auxiliary), it appears that there is a problem, perhaps a fairly significant one, with Hyams account.

As noted above, the problem seems to reside in the relatively 'external' notion of parameter which Hyams adopts. Because of this, the setting of a parameter initially in a given direction is a matter of choice, though encoded in UG: the situation is basically symmetrical. However, there are a number of instances — and the early dropping of subjects is one of them — in which it appears that the situation is basically asymmetrical: that is, that a particular ordering $G_i \rightarrow G_{i+1}$ is much more likely than the reverse $G_{i+1} \rightarrow G_i$. Assuming the most usual notion of parameter-setting, this ordering must be assumed to be simply stipulated, as an individual, isolated property of UG, and does not follow from any more general feature of the system. Indeed, in earlier work (Chomsky, 1965), a particular ordering might be assumed to follow from a more general feature — namely, the application of the evaluation metric to the data — but in more recent work that conception has not generally found favor. Nonetheless, I would argue that the insight lying behind the evaluation metric, that there is a *necessary* ordering of G_i and G_j for some related G, is a correct one, where 'necessary' means something more than a simple stipulated markedness property of UG. What would appear to be lacking in current theory is a notion of development which would induce just such an ordering.

Ideally, this would go beyond the relatively unconnected notion of parameter-setting as commonly understood, so that a particular ordering of grammars in development could be found as necessary. With respect to the ordering in acquisition being discussed here, this would mean that the early optional dropping of subjects would be necessary before the final end state could be reached: i.e., that (3) but not (4) is a possible course of development. It is toward such a reconceptualization, and a retrieval of the importance of the proper role of development that I will try to draw a focus.

3. GUILFOYLE'S ANALYSIS, AND SUBJECT-DROP RECONSIDERED

Suppose that we assume that the special property of the early grammar is not that AGR = PRO, but rather in the case-marking and government of the subject position. We may follow in this a line of thought suggested by Guilfoyle. Guilfoyle (1984) suggests that it is tense which marks subjects for case, and the lack of subjects in early grammar is related to the lack of TNS in these constructions. When TNS then appears, she suggests, the subject may be properly case-marked, and so uniformly appear.

This sort of approach seems promising, but the particular claim that early sentences lack tense in the syntax would presumably require some rule 'writing in' tense at the level of LF, since it is certain that children correctly differentiate semantic tense at the point of development that we are talking about. Let us assume rather that the case-marking element, whether AGR or TNS or some other property of INFL, is present in the early S's, and that the difference is located instead in the position of the element in the tree: that in early grammars it is already adjoined to the verb at the point at which case-marking takes place, giving rise to the situation in (5) and (6). See also Berwick (1985) for a similar view.

(5)   Adult grammar (English):
   (a) Case-marking (by AGR or TNS)
   (b) Affix-hopping (Adjoins case-marking element to verb or its neighbor)

(6)   Child's grammar:
    (a)   Case-marking element is already adjoined.

Assuming that strict *c*-command is necessary for the case-marking of
the subject, the case-marking element is able to case-mark and govern
the subject in the adult grammar, but not the child's, since it is already
adjoined.

With respect to pro-drop, this corresponds to the account found in
Chomsky (1981) or Huang (1984), where the relevant difference is in
the position of 'Rule R', affix-hopping, in the grammar. In the
Chomsky-Rizzi account in LGB, English differs from Italian in that
Rule R applies in the syntax in Italian, i.e. in the course of the
derivation from DS to SS, while it applies at PF in English. Since INFL
would govern the subject position at *s*-structure in English, the possibility of the ungoverned null element, PRO, would be excluded in
English but not Italian. The child's grammar differs from the adult
grammar in the application of Rule R: the child analyzes INFL as
present and adjoined directly to the verb, as it appears in the surface
form, and not adjoined there by affix hopping. As such, it does not
govern and case-mark the subject, and lexical subjects are discarded.
The difference between the child's and adult's structure for English can
be seen in (7) and (8) below. This analysis of the difference removes it
from an understanding in which the subject drop in early speech is
traced to a difference in categorial status of AGR, and places it in the
structural analysis of the constructions.

(7)

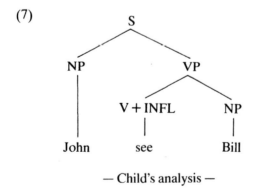

— Child's analysis —

(8)

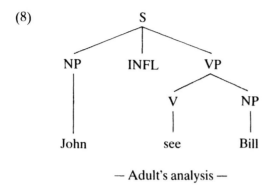

— Adult's analysis —

The analysis of the early verb as containing TNS or INFL, and this having later to be teased out, accords well with a more general process in acquisition: namely, that an element which is initially taken as an unanalyzed whole is later broken into subcomponents. Thus, in the context of morphology, is often noted that children begin with a plural form which is correctly used (e.g. feet), later productively overgenerate a form involving the plural marker (feets, foots), and then finally return to the correct use of the form. This pattern of acquisition can be explained by assuming that the child starts out with a semantically correct, but morphologically unanalyzed form (e.g. feet, dogs) — this form is marked for plural semantically, but the plural morpheme has not yet been discovered — and that later the plural morpheme -s is analyzed out morphologically and then productively used (Lebeaux, 1983; Pinker, 1984). With respect to the verbal complex, the situation is presumably the same; the child begins with a verb which includes INFL: semantically and syntactically V + INFL but with no morphological analysis. At a later stage, the structure at surface (or s-) structure is morphologically analyzed $((\ )_V INFL)_V$. At a still later stage, INFL is analyzed as hopping onto the verb via affix-hopping. It is this final stage which is crucial for the syntax, but it is dependant on the morphological analysis being antecedently done. At the earliest stage, INFL is analyzed with the verb, hence does not govern and case-mark the subject position.

This analysis has as a by product a rather startling consequence. Namely, that early subjects are only apparent, and must instead be analyzed as either topics (in the case of full NP subjects), or possibly as subject clitics (in the case of pronouns). This is because a full lexical subject would not be marked for case, and so would violate the case filter. The only 'real' subjects, in the sense of elements filling the (NP, S) position, would be null, since only these would not need to be marked for case.

In fact, just such a conclusion was suggested in early work by Jeff Gruber, where early sentences were analyzed as having generally topic-comment structure (Gruber, 1967). There is a less radical possibility as well, involving a change in the means by which case is gotten on to the subject noun phrase, so that this doesn't require government by INFL. Assume that case-marking may be done in at least two ways, under government by a lexical head (what is usually called *structural case*, Chomsky, 1981), or truly phrase-structurally. (We may ignore lexical and inherent case, for present purposes.) Refining the latter notion, let us assume that an element is phrase-structurally case-marked by virtue of its relation to its immediately dominating element. The TOP position, then, would be phrase-structurally case-marked by virtue of its position (NP, S´) (adopting *Aspects* notation); the subject position of noun phrases, which I will assume is also phrase-structually case-marked, by virtue of its position (NP, NP). Phrase-structural case-marking, then, differs from structural case-marking in two ways: (i) structural case-marking is done by a c-commanding, lexical head, X^0, a sister of the case-marked element, while phrase-structural case marking is by virtue of the relation of an element to its mother node (just as grammatical relations are defined in *Aspects*), (ii) phrase-structural case-marking, but not structural, is optional, no head *must* assign it.

With respect to acquisition, this formulation of case-marking would allow the child to case-mark the subject in structures like (7) above, even in the absence of a c-commanding INFL. More generally, simple NP VP structures with an already adjoined INFL would be acceptable because the subject could be phrase-structurally case-marked, given that the child assumes the (NP, S) position to be a position of phrase-structural case. The case marking possibilities in sentences even with an adjoined INFL would thus be extended to subject position, by using the same mechanism which marks the subject of noun phrases. The phenomenon of subject drop, in such a system, would thus be accommodated to the 'subject drop' which occurs in noun phrases in the adult system, and thus not properly speaking to be included under pro-drop at all.

4. EMPIRICAL CONSIDERATIONS

I have presented above two sorts of theories to account for the phenomenon of subject drop in early speech. In one, Hyams' account, the phenomenon of subject drop is identified with pro-drop, an area of parametric difference between English and certain Romance languages such as Italian and Spanish. In the other, my account, subject drop is traceable to a difference in the way that case is assigned to the subject position in the adult's grammar and the child's, which is due in turn to the child's analysis of INFL as initially being adjoined to V, and thus incapable of assigning case. These theories differ both empirically and conceptually. The empirical difference, as expected, will ultimately be resolved by discovering in a refined way the nature of the case system that the child uses, and how this fits in with the adult system. One place at which to probe the system is in the handling of expletives.

4.1. *Expletives and Case*

In Hyams' account, expletives play a crucial role: they act as a trigger for the re-analysis of the system and the rejection of pro-drop by the child. This is because the presence of an expletive in subject position, a semantically unnecessary element, argues for its obligatory syntactic presence in a non pro-drop language like English, and thus, from the point of view of the child, constitutes evidence that the target language is not pro-drop. The logic of the exclusion of expletive elements is thus the same as that used for the Avoid Pronoun principle: lexical material, including expletives, should be avoided if possible if unnecessary. Since expletives are present in adult speech they act as a trigger for the rejection of the pro-drop hypothesis, but prior to that they are excluded by a version of the Avoid Pronoun principle.

The situation with the adjoined INFL account is somewhat different. The exclusion of expletive elements in early speech is traced, not to the presence of pro-drop, but rather to a property of the case-assignment system.

Consider the contrast between (9a) and (b), a contrast which has never been satisfactorily explained — and rarely noted — in theoretical work.

(9) a.   it being obvious that John is well-intentioned
    b.   *its obviousness that John is well-intentioned

That is, gerunds allow expletive subjects while simple derived nominals do not. Similarly, expletives in topic position are disallowed.

(10)   *It, it is obvious that John is well-intentioned.

It might initially be thought that functional reasons account for the ungrammaticality of (10), but the contrast in (9) shows that such an explanation would be insufficient. In fact, the generalization that covers both (9b) and (10) is the following (adopting the definition of phrase-structurally case-marking above):

(11)   Expletive elements are disallowed in phrase-structurally case-marked positions.

The principle (11) distinguishes (9a) from (b), since the latter position is phrase-structurally case-marked, while the former is case-marked by the gerund marker -*ing*. Further, the topic position (NP, S″) is phrase-structurally case-marked, while the subject position, in the adult grammar, is not, thus accounting for the ungrammaticality of (10). Principle (11) therefore holds for the adult grammar. It extends automatically to the child grammars as well, given the analysis above. Apparent subjects in child grammars are actually either: (i) topics, or (ii) real subjects, but phrase-structurally case-marked. In either case, the relevant position would be one of phrase-structural case-marking. Hence, by (11) expletive elements are excluded.

There is one clear advantage to (11) over an explanation involving the Avoid Pronoun principle. The latter principle, unlike the former, is a functional principle, and not expected to be unduly strong or universal. However, the contrast in (9) shows that functional considerations are insufficient, and that, in fact, the exclusion is strong. Indeed, using the Avoid Pronoun principle to exclude expletives has an internal difficulty in Hyams' account even apart from this. This is because the presence of expletives in adult speech has a key role in her logical-deductive system: it allows for the child to deduce that the language is not pro-drop. However, if the presence of expletives is just vaguely excluded by a functional principle such as Avoid Pronoun, the presence of such expletives can hardly be sufficient grounds for the child to determine the pro-drop parameter one way or the other. The latter is strict in a way that the former is not.

4.2. *Object-particle Constructions*

A second group of constructions differentiating the accounts are object-particle constructions. The relation of acquisition data to linguistic theory is again subtle and indirect.

Miller and Ervin (1971) note the plethora of sentences such as the following in early speech:

(12)   White sweater on.
        Blue sweater on.
        Mommy sweater on.
        Susan coat on.
        This dress off.
        Put that on.

They make the following comment:

The particle complement was usually a N^m or noun phrase of model language, but V^m was not uncommon: 'White sweater off', said while taking her sweater off; 'white sweater on', a request directed to her mother to put her white sweater on her; 'salt on', pretending to salt food; 'scarf off', said while taking her scarf off. The model language provides analogues in which the noun is the object: 'I took my sweater off'; 'put my white sweater on!' 'I put the salt on'; 'I took my scarf off'. There are also analogues in which the noun is the subject, but these seem less likely to have been the model for the child: 'my seater is off'; 'my white sweater should be on'; 'the salt is on'; 'my scarf is off'. The fact that there were no sentences like 'Susan off' or 'Mommy on', that is, transitive two-word verb sentences of the model analogue with the verb and object deleted, strengthens the view that the N^m usually represents the object of action.

With respect to the issues under discussion, these sentences play a rather crucial role. Note that Miller and Ervin exclude the view that these sentences in general involve a null copula auxiliary ("my sweater is off") or a deleted or null main verb. This, however, leaves two problems: what is the structure of these constructions? And how is the subject case-marked?

There are basically four possibilities for the contemplated structure of these constructions:

(13) a. Subject-predicate constructions with a missing copula: "White sweater (is) on"
     b. Subject-verb-particle constructions with missing verb or verb complex: "White sweater (is being put) on"

(13) c. Subject-particle constructions with the subject understood as object of action: "White sweater on" (i.e. the surface structure as is)

   d. Subject-verb-object-particle constructions with missing subject and verb: "(You put) white sweater on"

By *missing* in the above account I mean either deleted or simply null lexically, but with the appropriate non-terminals: e.g. for (13b),

$$((\text{white sweater})_{NP} ((\quad)_V (\text{on})_P)_{VP})_S$$

As noted above, Miller and Ervin exclude the first two in the quoted passage for a context in which a white sweater is being put on: the first because it does not match the pragmatic context correctly, the second because the phenomenon of deleted verbs is in general not common at this stage in development. This leaves as alternatives (c) and (d). There are, I believe, some reasons to adopt the simplest, (c).

The first comes from recent work by Richie Kayne (1984), and constitutes a plausibility argument for the possibility of the posited structure. Kayne suggests, roughly, that the object of a verb in a verb-object-particle construction is related to the particle in some sort of semantic unit. Assuming that this is so, bare structures like (13c) would be viable as a sort of primitive predication structure (though not one of the usual sort), without having to supply, e.g., an auxiliary verb. A second, more direct argument for the structure in (13c) would involve the general lack of verb deletion (or verb interpretation) structures at the point of development at which such examples as in (12) are common. The lack of such structures in general would argue that the surface structures in (12) should not be analyzed in this way. While more extensive data is needed, Miller and Ervin's comments, and the lack in general of such constructions suggest that (13c) is the correct choice.

Given this structure, then, the question of case again becomes paramount. How does the subject get case in structures like (14)?

(14)

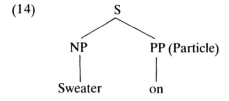

Unlike the null verb hypothesis (13d), there is no way for the NP to receive lexical case as an object (of a null verb). Further, unlike the majority of early sentences, there is no plausible analysis in terms of a null auxiliary. Nor is there a place for INFL in this structure, since, as already noted, *sweater* bears the relation of object (in a V-Obj-Part structure) to its particle, not a subject. The only alternative left is that the sentence is analyzed as is, and that phrase-structural case, not structural case, is assigned to the subject in (14), and in general to elements in the position (NP, S). This, then, argues for a general case-assignment rule of this type in early speech.

4.3. *Case*

So far, discussion of the subject position has been restricted to the assignment of abstract case, Case, to that position. A more direct way of examining early grammars would be by reference to morphological case. Suppose that, as suggested above, INFL actually is adjoined to V in early grammars. Then there is no 'normal' way to get nominative case onto the subject. Rather, one of two things must happen: (i) the apparent subject must not be in subject position, but in a different position, e.g. topic or clitic, to which case is assigned, or (ii) the apparent subject *is* an actual subject, and there is some other way than simple structural case assignment of getting case onto that element. It was suggested above that the way of getting case onto that position was by phrase-structural case assignment to the (NP, S) position.

These two proposals together would have the following effect, no matter which of the two were correct:

(16)   The subject is case-marked in a different fashion in child grammars, but not adult grammars.

This is because the object would presumably be case-marked, as in adult grammars, by the *c*-commanding verb, while the subject, unlike the subject in the adult grammar, would not be case-marked by a *c*-commanding AGR or TNS. At a more detailed level of analysis, the proposal (16) requires the mechanism of phrase-structural case-marking. Is there any evidence in child speech?

In fact, there appears to be some. Suppose, first, that the child is marking the subject position phrase-structurally. It was suggested above that phrase-structural case-marking was done by reference to the dominating mother node, rather than by a sister lexical node. For subject position of NPs, it would be the (NP, NP) configuration which allows such marking in the adult grammar. To get such marking on the sentence subject, it is necessary only to assume that the child initially adopts an 'overgeneralization' of phrase-structural case-marking, allowing positions of the form (NP, $X^2_{(-v)}$) to be phrase-structurally case-marked. Such 'overgeneralization' (actually, underdifferentiation) is common in early acquisition in other areas. Then the (NP, NP) position would be phrase-structurally case-marked, but so would, by the same rule, the (NP, S) position.

According to Anne Vainikka, there is evidence from child language of extensive genitive marking (as well as accusative) of the sentence subject position. While she gives no full statistical data, Vainikka notes extensive use of constructions such as the following, at a stage in Maria Roeper's speed, and that of other children.

(17)   My did it
        My going now
        My touching Mommy
        ⋮

The possibility of such case-marking apparently differs with the semantics of the verb, and other such criteria. But the use of such genitive case-marking would seem *prima facie* extremely peculiar to expect. There can be no question of confusion, for example, between different cases associated with the verb's argument complex, since genitive is not a case associated with any member of that. But it is precisely the characterization of phrase-structural case marking, cutting across NP and S, which would predict this result.

The account above gives some reason to believe that the child adopts phrase-structural case-marking of subjects. But there is no reason not to believe that the other account, in which the apparent subjects are actually analyzed as topics, does not hold over a range of data as well. Gruber (1967) and Guilfoyle (1984) adopt just such a structure as (18).

(18)

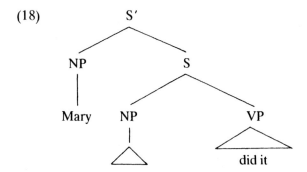

Gruber argues that at one stage of development topic-comment structures are paramount. He gathers data from question inversion, case-
marking of subject pronouns, and distributional analysis of dislocated
subjects (e.g. it broken, wheels; car, it broken). This is not the place to
give a full precis of his position. I will simply note that if he is right that
topic-comment structure characterizes a significant stage or body of
data in child speech, the necessity for such a stage is explained by the
hypothesis here: the adjoined INFL requires that the subject receive
Case in some other way, and placing it as a topic would be just such a
way.

5. SOME FINAL CONSIDERATIONS

At the present point in acquisition research, where many of the basic
issues have not yet been resolved, each proposal consists of both a
concrete analysis, and a more general articulation of a point of view,
where the orientation determines what sort of answer is given to the
group of questions with which I began this paper. Here I have tried to
indicate, along with the points of concrete analysis, a sort of analysis of
Hyams' paper which notes where these broader issues may enter. One
issue, and a quite integral one, has to do with the nature of parameter
setting in acquisition.

This term may be taken in either its broader or narrower sense. In
considering the course of development as a series of single steps
$G_i \rightarrow G_{i+1}$ (for each module), where a function f_i relates the
grammars, these 'broader' and 'narrower' senses translate into different

possible values for the f_i. Parameter setting in its narrowest sense would refer to a change between grammars $G_i \rightarrow G_{i+1}$ in which (1) G_i and G_{i+1} are not inherently ordered by general principles of the grammar, and (ii) both G_i and G_{i+1} are possible terrminal points of development. It is this notion of parameter setting which underlies Hyams' account of pro-drop as an account of language development.

A broader notion of parameter setting could also be invoked. By doing so, we may be able to achieve a rather rich goal: to give some content to the notion of 'development' in the development of a grammar. Informally, this means that there is some change in the complexity or richness of the grammar over time; formally we may divide this into three characteristics: that with respect to G_i, G_{i+1}, G_{i+1} is essentially ordered after G_i where *essentially ordered* means: (i) G_i is less complex than G_{i+1} along some metric, (ii) to get to G_{i+1} it is necessary to pass through G_i, and (iii) possibly, that G_i is not a general final state.

The third attribute would be a possible but not a necessary characteristic of a developmental system. The second attribute, as well as the first, introduce an *asymmetry* into the system; the second attribute, that in order to get to a particular grammar a less mature grammar must first be passed through, would characterize, for example, a system such as that oulined above, where both the posited stage in which INFL is adjoined to the verb and the concommitant stage of phrase-structural case-marking would by necessity precede the corresponding stages in the finaly grammar.

Whether development in the sense of (i)–(iii) above really takes place, and the position that it has in language acquisition, is a serious open question. I have suggested that the position that the researcher takes with respect to these questions is generally implicit, but that it forms the conceptual backbone of the work. Aside from simple empirical differences, the conception of language development offered by Hyams and that offered here differ precisely in this conceptual core. It is to this conceptual issue for language acquisition, as much as to the specific empirical formulations, that I wish to draw attention.

ACKNOWLEDGEMENT

* I would like to thank Anne Vainikka and Tom Roeper for discussion of the issues raised herein.

REFERENCES

Berwick, R.: 1985, *The Acquisition of Syntactic Knowledge*, MIT Press, Cambridge, MA.

Chomsky, N.: 1981, *Lectures on Government and Binding*, Foris Publications, Dordrecht.

Chomsky, N.: 1965, *Aspects of the Theory of Syntax*, MIT Press, Cambridge, MA.

Guilfoyle, E.: 1984, 'The acquisition of tense and the emergence of lexical subjects', unpublished paper, McGill University.

Gruber, J.: 1967. 'Topicalization in child language', *Foundations of Language* **3**.

Huang, J.: 1984, 'On the typology of zero anaphora', *Language Research* **20**, 2.

Hyams, N.: 1987, conference paper, T. Roeper and E. Williams (eds.), *Parameter Setting*, D. Reidel, Dordrecht.

Hyams, N.: 1983, *The Emergence of Parameterized Grammars*, PhD. thesis, CUNY.

Kayne, R.: 1984, 'The Principle of Verb-Particle Constructions', unpublishd manuscript, Paris VIII.

Lebeaux, D.: 1982, 'The acquisition of affixation', unpublished paper, Harvard Univ.

Miller, W. and S. Ervin: 1971, 'The development of grammar in child language', in Bar-Adon and W. Leopold (eds.), *Child Language*, Prentice-Hall, NJ.

Pinker, S.: 1984, *Language Learnability and Language Development*, Harvard Univ. Press.

Roeper, T.: 1978, 'Linguistic universals and the acquisition of gerunds', in H. Goodluck and L. Solan (eds.), *Papers in the Structure of Child Language*.

Rizzi, L.: 1982, *Issues in Italian Syntax*, Foris Publications, Dordrecht.

Rizzi, L.: 1986, 'Null objects in Italian and the theory of pro', *Linguistic Inquiry* **17**, 3.

KENNETH WEXLER AND M. RITA MANZINI

PARAMETERS AND LEARNABILITY
IN BINDING THEORY*

1. INTRODUCTION

1.1. *The Modular Approach*

Modern theory has provided evidence that universal grammar contains principles of a general, but specifically linguistic, form that apply in all natural languages. A goal of this paper is to extend the notion of principle theory to language acquisition. In such a theory each choice that the child makes in his or her growing language is determined by a principle of language or by a principle of learning or by the interaction of these two kinds of principles. The language principles and the learning principles are obviously related (they interact). However, it seems to be a promising approach to see if the two kinds of principles can be separated to some degree. That is, we attempt a modular approach to language acquisition theory. Some aspects of language and its acquisition seem better stated not in linguistic theory, but outside it, in, say, a learning module.

The general idea is that there are aspects of, say, markedness theory that are not part of linguistic theory, but are part of the learning theory. It may be possible to remove certain substantive assumptions about markedness, which are motivated primarily by learning conditions, from linguistic theory. The markedness hierarchies would instead be calculated from principles of the learning module.

An especially impressive demonstration of modularity would exist if the learning module predicted different markedness hierarchies on the same parameter depending upon the cases, for a substantive assumption of markedness within linguistic theory would not do this. We will suggest such a case.

One of the major insights of modern work in language acquisition and linguistic theory is the extent to which the question of how language is acquired is intertwined with the question of how linguistic theory should characterize variation in languages. In this paper the mechanisms underlying variation will be seen to have natural inter-

41

Thomas Roeper and Edwin Williams (eds.), Parameter Setting, 41–76.
© 1987 *by D. Reidel Publishing Company.*

pretations with regard to acquisition mechanisms. Once again, the solutions to problems of acquisition will be seen to have a highly specific linguistic content and to depend at the same time upon specialized learning principles. In our view not only does this view appear to be correct, but it is highly desirable, as it leads to a highly deductive theory.

1.2. *Binding Theory*

The theory that we develop of the learning of values of parameters is meant to be a general theory, which will apply in principle to all parameters. To illustrate and motivate the theory, we will apply it in this paper to a particular case, the learning of the values of parameters associated with binding theory (Chomsky, 1981). In this regard, it will be necessary first to develop a theory of the parameters associated with binding theory. It is important to realize, however, that the two theories are independent of each other. In particular, the learning theory, the theory of parameter setting that we develop, could be correct even if the binding theory and its associated parametric theory are incorrect. Nevertheless, the fact that a number of principles developed in the parameter setting theory do seem to have empirically motivated in-stantiations in binding theory does offer support for the parameter setting theory. In other words, the parameter setting theory makes certain predictions about properties of parametric systems, and binding theory appears to conform to these properties, which are not *a priori* necessary.

Later in this paper we will develop the statement of some aspects of binding theory, and associated parameters, in some detail. For now, however, we will state a few well-known properties in a non-formal manner, so that we can use these properties to illustrate the parameter setting principles. Anaphors and pronominals enter into binding theory. Under binding theory, in English, an anaphor, like *herself*, must be bound locally (binding principle A), and a pronoun, like *her*, must be free locally (binding principle B). For an element X to be 'bound' means for X to be c-commanded by a co-indexed element; and 'free' means not bound. As for the definition of 'local', we will consider only the simplest cases where 'local' can be taken to mean "in the same sentence as".

What must be learned with respect to binding theory? Presumably, very little. As Chomsky (1980) points out, a child has to learn that *herself* is an anaphor. Presumably every other fact about the distribution, possible antecedents, etc., of *herself* will then follow from binding theory. Likewise the child has to learn that *her* is a pronoun but other facts about the distribution of *her* and its antecedents will follow. Thus a very little amount of learning will entail a large amount of growth of knowledge in the child.

It is becoming increasingly clear, however, that the properties of binding are not completely universal. For example, in languages like Japanese there appears to be an anaphor that must be bound, but doesn't have to be locally bound; rather, the binder (co-indexed *c*-commanding NP) can be arbitrarily distant in the sentence from the anaphor. If there is variation of this sort (and other sorts), then something must be learned besides whether a nonreferential item is a pronoun or anaphor. This variation and its relation to acquisition (parameter setting) will be explored in some detail in Section 2.

1.3. *The Subset Principle*

How are the values of parameters learned from experience? Following the general consensus in the field (Wexler and Hamburger, 1973; Baker, 1979), we assume that only 'positive data' is available to the learner. That is, the learner is not corrected for ungrammatical sentences; in general s/he receives no direct information about ungrammaticality. The lack of negative data leads to the following well-known learnability dilemma. If the child ever overgeneralizes, that is, picks the value of a parameter which gives too large a language, then there is no way (given only positive data) to correct the overgeneralization, since all new (positive) data will be generated by the (overgeneral) grammar. To be precise, this problem arises in the case where the overgeneral language is a superset of the correct language. For, otherwise, there will be data which indicates to the learner that the language s/he has selected is wrong.

To overcome this problem, it is often suggested that some kind of markedness theory will allow values of parameters to be learned; and in fact, the logic is more general, applying not only to the parameter setting case, but to any model of language variation and acquisition where subsets and supersets arise. In particular, it is suggested that the markedness hierarchy can be constructed in accordance with the

'Subset Principle'. The term 'Subset Principle', together with the appropriate logic, was first used by Berwick (in press), and our formulation is closely related to his.

The idea is the following. Suppose one value of a parameter yields a language $L(i)$ and another value of the parameter yields a language $L(j)$. Suppose further that $L(i)$ is a smaller language than $L(j)$, that is, that $L(i)$ is contained in $L(j)$. $L(i)$ is a strict subset of $L(j)$. Then the learning strategy specified by the Subset Principle is that the learner select the value which yields $L(i)$ first. If this is the correct choice, there will never be evidence that it isn't, and the learner will stay with the value. If this is the wrong choice, then there will be positive evidence (sentences from $L(j)$ which are not in $L(i)$) which the learner will eventually hear; this evidence must exist, because $L(i)$ is a strict subset of $L(j)$. The Subset Principle specifies that when positive evidence which shows that $L(i)$ is the wrong language is encountered, the learner will switch to the parameter value which yields language. In short, the Subset Principle is a method for specifying a markedness hierarchy when alternative values yield languages which are in a subset relation.

To fix notation, let us formalize the Subset Principle in the following way. Let i and j be values of a linguistic parameter p. $L(p(i))$ is the language — we take a language to be a set of sentences — which is attained by letting p have the value i. Likewise for j. Then we can state the Subset Principle. Suppose $L(p(i)) \subseteq L(p(j))$. Then i is less marked then j. In acquisition terms, if i is a less marked value than j, then i is tried by the learner before j, and only positive evidence that i is wrong moves the learner to j. In the simplest case the positive evidence can be just one sentence S. $S \in L(p(j)) - L(p(i))$; that is, one sentence S which is in $L(p(j))$ but not in $L(p(i))$.

Suppose that there was no Subset Principle. Furthermore, suppose the learner assumes first that j is the correct value. S/he will then always be correct on any sentence that is encountered. Even if i is the correct value, there will be no positive evidence which will guide the learner to select i.

To consider the anaphor example that we mentioned earlier, suppose that the difference between *herself* in English and *zibun* in Japanese is that *herself* must be bound locally whereas *zibun* can be bound 'anywhere' (that is, the binder can appear in any position in the sentence which commands *zibun*). It is clear that (everything else being equal), if an anaphor is taken to be necessarily locally bound, then a smaller language will result than if it is taken to be bound anywhere. That is, let i be the value of the parameter that says that an anaphor must be bound within its sentence. Let j be the value which says that the item can be bound anywhere. Then $L(p(i) \subseteq L(p(j))$. For example, let w be an anaphor. Condider the sentence, "*John* thinks that Mary likes w." In this sentence, w is non-locally bound. Therefore, the sentence is in $L(p(j))$, but not in $L(p(i))$. Now consider the sentence, "*John* shaved w." In this second sentence, w is locally bound. So the sentence is in $L(p(i))$. But it is also in $L(p(j))$. So indeed $L(p(i)) \subseteq L(p(j))$.

In summary, suppose that i and j as given (locally bound vs. non-locally bound anaphors) are values for the 'anaphor parameter' and languages choose one of them. Then we can let the Subset Principle decide which is unmarked. Its choice will be i (locally bound). If this choice is wrong, positive evidence will be available which will allow the learner to choose j (bound anywhere).

In order for the Subset Principle to determine a strictly ordered learning hierarchy — this is what we will mean when we say that the Subset Principle as we define it here applies — it is necessary that two values of a parameter in fact yield languages which are in a subset relation to each other (i.e., one is a subset of the other). This requirement we call the 'Subset Condition'. It is necessary for the Subset Condition to hold in order for the Subset Principle to apply.

It is a consequence of the modular theory of parameter setting or learning that markedness hierarchies can be calculated by the Subset Principle in interaction with principles of Universal Grammar, making it unnecessary to state the hierarchies as substantive universals within linguistic theory. In fact, the interaction can yield different hierarchies even of the same linguistic parameter. An example which we will treat in detail concerns the differences between anaphors and pronouns. Since anaphors are governed by Principle A, which says that they are bound, the generated language will be smaller when the anaphor is bound locally than when it is bound anywhere. We have already seen an example of this case. A pronoun, however, is governed by Principle B. Suppose that parametric variation which is possible for anaphors is also possible for pronouns, so that in some languages pronouns must be free 'everywhere', instead of 'locally'. A calculation similar to the one we gave for anaphors will show that when pronouns must be free locally the language is a superset of the language generated when pronouns must be free everywhere. (For example, where *w* is a pronoun, "*John* thinks that Mary likes *w*" is in the former language but not in the latter one.) Therefore, for pronouns, the local domain of binding is marked with respect to the entire sentence ('everywhere') domain of binding. But we have already seen that for anaphors precisely the opposite is the case, that is, the local domain of binding is unmarked with respect to the entire sentence ('anywhere') domain of binding. Therefore, a substantive universal listing the markedness hierarchy cannot be stated, at least independently of whether the hierarchy refers to a pronoun or an anaphor. But the different hierarchies are exactly what would be expected from the interaction of the Subset Principle and the Binding Theory. To the extent that empirical evidence corroborates the different hierarchies, this provides evidence for the relevance of the Subset Principle.

1.4. *The Many-Parameter Problem: The Independence Principle*

A special problem arises when we take into account the fact that there is more than one parameter in a language. The problem, and the term "many-parameter problem", were introduced in a talk by Bob Matthews in 1982 at Western Ontario (R. Matthews, personal communication). So just setting one parameter does not allow the 'language' to be calculated. How should the other values be set when the languages are calculated? What we have to assume is that, for every parameter *p* the languages must be nested (form subsets of each other), for all values of all other parameters. This is what we will refer to as the 'generalized' Subset Condition.

It turns out, however, that the (generalized) Subset Condition is not sufficient to insure that the Subset Principle can apply. We also have to insure that the particular subset relation of the languages formed by two values (say *i* and *j*) of a parameter are not affected by the setting of the other parameters. If *i* produces a subset of *j* for some setting of the other parameters, then it will produce the same subset for all other values of a parameter. This property is called *Independence*. The Subset Condition and Independence are necessary and sufficient for the Subset Principle to apply in all cases.

The idea of these conditions is that one can set the parameters independently of each other. If there are chains of derivational implications between parameters, it may be that there really is only one parameter. It seems to us that Independence is really what linguists have implicitly had in mind when they talk about parameter setting in a manner akin to the Subset Principle. However, as far as we know, nobody has explicitly realized what it is necessary to assume in order to deal with the more than single parameter case. What is intriguing is that it appears that parameters that are stated in a natural linguistic way seem to satisfy, in many cases, the Subset Condition and Independence which, *a priori*, it would be quite easy to violate. In later sections we will give a detailed study of parameters and demonstrate how the Subset Condition and Independence hold. It is an important question for future study how generally true these conditions are.

1.5. *The Lexical Parameterization Hypothesis*

A further property that will emerge is that all anaphors in one language do not appear to obey exactly the same laws. To the extent that this is true it suggests that different lexical items can be associated with different values of lexical items; hence, as argued first by Borer (1984), that parameterization is essentially lexical. In a sense this should not be too surprising because it has long been recognized by linguistic theory that the lexicon states much or most of the idiosyncracies in a language. The basic view of grammar is not changed. Simply something more has to be said about a non-referential lexical item than whether it is an anaphor or a pronominal. As long as this statement of properties can be associated with an adequate learning theory, we will not have lost anything.

It does seem worth noting, however, that there are conceptual differences: the idea of parameter used here and the standard notion. Usually a parameter is taken to be associated with a whole language or grammar — an example is Rizzi's discussion of the Subjacency Parameter (See Chomsky, 1980, 1981). The problem for the child is how to use limited data to set a value for the parameter. But the parameter, once set, has extensive consequences for variation throughout the language. The kinds of parameters we are discussing, however, are set by the child for a particular lexical item. On the one hand the consequences of setting a lexical parameter would not be as broad as in the case of a language-wide parameter. On the other hand, the learnability problems might be considerably less severe.

It is important finally to make clear the status of lexical parameterization with respect to the parameter setting (learning) theory that we develop. The principles of learning (Subset Principle, Subset Condition, Independence and other aspects of the construction of the markedness hierarchy and acquisition theory) are necessary for any kind of parameter setting theory of the kind discussed here, whether parameters are selected for a grammar as a whole or for lexical items. In other words, two aspects of theory, the learning theory and the necessity for the association of parameters with lexical items, are independent.

2. PARAMETERS

As we saw above, binding theory, as introduced in Chomsky (1981), consists essentially of two principles, a binding principle A stating roughly that an anaphor must be bound locally, or, to be more precise, in the domain referred to as governing category, and a binding Principle B stating that in the same domain a pronominal must be free, i.e., nonbound, as in (1) (for an extension of the binding principles see Manzini, 1983; see Chomsky, in press, and Manzini, forthcoming, for a state of the art discussion):

(1) A.   An anaphor is bound in its governing category
    B.   A pronominal is free in its governing category

In (1) the term 'bound' means 'c-commanded and coindexed,' as in the definition of binding in (2); and correspondingly the term 'free' means 'not both bound and coindexed':

(2) α binds β iff
       α and β are coindexed and α c-commands β

Furthermore, the notion of governing category for an element is defined essentially as in (3), as the minimal category which contains the element under consideration and has a subject:

(3) γ is a governing category for α iff
       γ is the minimal category which contains α and has a subject

Consider, for example, English and in particular the English reflexive *himself* or the personal pronoun *he*. Obviously *himself* is an anaphor, in that it cannot have any reference independently of an antecedent in the sentence; *he* is a pronominal, in that it can depend for its reference on an antecedent in the sentence or in the discourse, or refer deictically. It is easy to see that the theory in (1)—(3) correctly accounts for the distribution of *he* and *himself*, as well as for the distribution of their antecedents.

Consider first *himself*, as in (4), where italics is used as an alternate notation for coindexing:

(4) a.   *John* criticized *himself*
    b.   *John* heard criticisms of *himself*
    c.   **John* heard [my criticisms of *himself*]
    d.   **John* heard [me criticize *himself*]
    e.   **John* forced me [to criticize *himself*]
    f.   **John* knew that [I criticized *himself*]

It is easy to see that the theory in (1)—(3) correctly accounts for both the well-formedness of the examples in (a)—(b) and the ill-formedness of the examples in (c)—(f). Consider first (a)—(b). In (a)—(b) the minimal category which contains *himself* and a subject, namely *John*, is the matrix sentence. Hence by the definition of governing category in (3) the matrix sentence is the governing category for *himself*; and by binding principle A *himself* must be bound in the matrix sentence. But in (a)—(b) *himself* is indeed bound in the matrix sentence, by *John* again; hence both (a) and (b) are correctly predicted to be well-formed.

Consider on the other hand (4c)—(4f). In (c) the minimal category which contains *himself* and a subject, namely the genitive *my*, is the embedded nominal, as bracketed; in (d)—(f) the minimal category which contains *himself* and a subject, namely the accusative subject *me* in (d), an empty subject PRO in (e) and the nominative *I* in (f), is the embedded clause, again as bracketed. Hence by the definition of governing category in (3) the governing category for *himself* is the embedded nominal in (c) and the embedded clause in (d)—(f); and by binding principle A *himself* must be bound in the embedded nominal in (c) and in the embedded clause in (d)—(f). But in (c) *himself* is bound, by *John*, outside the embedded nominal, and in (d)—(f) *himself* is bound, by *John* again, outside the embedded clause. Hence binding principle A is violated, and all of (c)—(f) are correctly predicted to be ill-formed.

Consider, then, *he*, as in (5):

(5) a. **John* criticized *him*
    b.   *John* heard [me criticize *him*]
    c.   *John* forced me [to criticize *him*]
    d.   *John* knew that [I criticized *him*]

According to the definition of governing category in (3), the matrix sentence is the governing category for *he* in (a) and the embedded clause the governing cagetory for *he* in (b)—(d). For, in (a) the matrix sentence is the minimal category which contains *he* and a subject, namely *John*; in (b)—(d) the minimal category which contains *he* and a subject — *me* in (b), an empty subject PRO in (c), and *I* in (d) — is the embedded clause. Hence by binding principle B, in (a) *he* must be free, i.e., not bound, in the matrix sentence; in (b)—(d) *he* must be free, i.e., not bound, in the embedded clause. But in (b)—(d) *John* does bind *he* outside the embedded clause; hence the theory in (1)—(3) correctly predicts (b)—(d) to be well-formed. On the other hand, in (a) *he* is bound by *John* in the matrix sentence; hence binding principle B is violated, and (a) is correctly predicted to be ill-formed.

Thus the theory of binding in (1)—(3) correctly accounts for English *himself* and *he*, and indeed for a significant number of pronominals and anaphors across languages.

Consider, however, Icelandic, and in particular the Icelandic reflexive *sig* as described, for example, in Johnson (1984). As its English counterpart *himself*, Icelandic *sig* obviously is an anaphor, in that it cannot have any reference independently of an antecedent in the sentence. But Icelandic *sig*, contrary to English *himself*, cannot be correctly accounted for by the binding theory in (1)—(3).

Consider indeed the examples in (6), where *sig* is roughly translated as REFL, for 'reflexive':

(6) a. **Jón* segir að [Maria elskar   *sig*]
         Jon says that Maria loves   REFL

    b.   *Jón* segir að [Maria elski   *sig*]
         Jon says that Maria loves (subjunctive) REFL

    c.   *Jón* skipaði Haraldi að [raka   *sig*]
         Jon ordered Harald to shave REFL

    d.   *Jón* heyrdu [lysingu *Maria*   af sér]
         Jon heard   Maria's description of REFL

All of (6a)—(6d) are predicted by the theory in (1)—(3) to be ill-formed. For, according to the definition of governing category in (3), the governing category for *sig* is the embedded sentence in (6a)—(6c) and the embedded nominal in (6d), since the embedded sentence in (6a)—(6c) and the embedded nominal in (6d) obviously are the minimal category which contains *sig* and a subject. By binding principle A, then, *sig* must be bound in the embedded sentence in (6a)—(6c) and in the embedded nominal in (6d); and since in (6a)—(6c) and (6d) *sig* is bound, by *Jón*, outside the embedded sentence and the embedded nominal respectively, all of (6a)—(6d) are ultimately predicted to be ill-formed. But while (6a) is actually ill-formed, (6b)—(6d) are not; hence the theory in (1)—(3) correctly accounts for (6a), but obviously makes the incorrect predictions for (6b)—(6d).

The fact that the theory in (1)—(3) cannot account for Icelandic *sig*, however, does not mean that the distribution of *sig* and its antecedents is completely free. On the contrary, one can easily show that *sig* must in general be bound, as it is in (6); hence at least the part of binding theory which states that an anaphor must be bound applied to *sig* as well. Furthermore, the contrast between examples of the type of (6a) and examples of the type of (6b)—(6d) suggests that *sig* not only must be bound, but must also be bound within a domain of some sort. Hence one can in fact assume that binding principle A, as stating that an anaphor is bound in its governing category, applies in its entirety to *sig* as to its English counterpart *himself*; except that the notion of governing category, defined as in (3) for English *himself*, must be defined in some different way for Icelandic *sig*.

Let us then assume, following Johnson (1983, 1984), that in the case of *sig* the definition of governing category in (7), rather than the definition of governing category in (3), applies:

(7) γ is a governing category for α iff
       γ is the minimal category which contains α and has an indicative TNS

It is not difficult to see that the definition of governing category in (7) taken together with binding principle A actually accounts for all of the data in (6).

Consider first (6a). In (6a) the embedded sentence has an indicative Tense; hence the minimal category which contains *sig* and an indicative Tense obviously is the embedded sentence. Consider on the other hand (6b)—(6d). Contrary to (6a), the embedded sentence in (6b) only has a subjunctive Tense; the embedded sentence in (6c) has no Tense at all; and the embedded nominal in (6d) obviously does not have an INFL, let alone a Tense. Hence in (6b)—(6d) the minimal category which contains *sig* and an indicative Tense is the matrix sentence. According then to the definition of governing category, in (6a) the governing category for *sig* is the embedded sentence; in (6b)—(6d) the governing category for *sig* is the matrix sentence. Hence by binding principle A, in (6a) *sig* must be bound in the embedded sentence; in (6b)—(6d) *sig* must be bound in the matrix sentence. But in (6a) *sig* is bound by *Jón* outside the embedded sentence; hence, correctly, the theory predicts that (6a) is ill-formed. In (6b)—(6d), on the other hand, *sig* is in fact bound by *Jón* within the matrix sentence; hence, correctly again, the theory predicts that (6b)—(6d) are well-formed.

Thus, summing up, while the theory of binding in (1)—(3) correctly accounts for English, as in (4)—(5), Icelandic, as in (6), is correctly accounted for by a revision of the theory with (7) substituted for (3). On the one hand, then, the definition of binding in (2) and the binding principles in (1) invariably hold; on the other hand, different definitions of governing category hold in different cases, (3) holding for English, as in (4)—(5), and (7) for Icelandic, as in (6).

If so, one is led in turn to the conclusion that while the theory of binding as a whole is a subtheory of Universal Grammar, indeed as in Chomsky (1981), one of the notions which crucially enter into it, the notion of governing category, is a parameter of the theory, much in the sense of Chomsky again. In particular, the two definitions of governing category in (3) and (7) represent two values of the parameter; the value represented by the definition in (3) is associated with English, as exemplified in (4)—(5); the value represented by the definition in (7) is associated with Icelandic, as exemplified in (6).

To be more precise, the definitions of governing category in (3) and (7) do not just differ one from another; they also obviously have an identical common core. By collapsing then (3) and (7) one can obtain the definition of governing category in (8), where the parameter is now seen to be internal to the definition of governing category itself:

(8) γ is a governing category for α iff
        γ is the minimal category which contains α and
        either has a subject
        or has an indicative Tense

In (8) obviously the two values of the parameter correspond to the two terms of the disjunction; the value corresponding to the first term of the disjunction is the value associated with English, as in (4)–(5), while the value associated with the second term of the disjunction is the value associated with Icelandic, as in (6).

But while the parametrized definition of governing category in (8) accounts not only for English *himself* and *he*, but also for Icelandic *sig* and for an increased number of other pronominals and anaphors across languages, it only partially accounts for the total observed range of variation. A discussion of what a complete such account requires would inevitably exceed the limits of this paper; following Manzini and Wexler (1984), then, here we will simply assume that a number of new values must be introduced, and that in particular, once introduced the new values of the parameter, the definition of governing category in (9) is obtained (alternative accounts can be found notably in Yang, 1984, and Koster, 1984):

(9) γ is a governing category for α iff
        γ is the minimal category which contains α and
        a. has a subject, or
        b. has an INFL, or
        c. has a TNS, or
        d. has an indicative TNS, or
        e. has a root TNS

Evidently the definition of governing category now includes a five-valued parameter, with the five values of the parameter corresponding to the five members, (a), (b), (c), (d), and (e) of the disjunction in (9). A value (a) of the parameter in (9) obviously identifies with the first value of the parameter in (8) or the value associated with English, as in the examples in (4)–(5); value (d) in (9) identifies with the second value of the parameter in (8) and indeed the value associated with Icelandic, as in the examples in (6). (9) then introduces three new values, (b), (c), and (e), respectively.

It must be noticed at this point that in the discussion which precedes the values of the parameter in the definition of governing category have been referred to ambiguously as the values associated with particular languages or as the values associated with particular anaphors and pronominals in a language. So value (a) of the parameter in (9) has been referred to as the value associated with English or as the value associated with English *himself* and *he*; and value (d) of the parameter has been referred to as the value associated with Icelandic, or as the value associated with Icelandic *sig*. A close examination of the data, however, leads to the conclusion that the values of the parameter in (9) cannot be associated with particular languages, but rather must be associated with particular anaphors and pronominals in a language.

Consider for example Icelandic again. While the Icelandic reflexive *sig*, as in (6), is correctly accounted for under value (*d*) of the governing category parameter in (9), the Icelandic personal pronoun *hann* gives rise to examples of the type of (10) which are incorrectly accounted for under value (*d*):

(10) a. *Jón* segir að [Maria elskar *hann*]
         Jon says that Maria loves   him

    b. *Jón* segir að [Maria elski *hann*]
        Jon says that Maria loves (subjunctive) him

    c. *Jón skipaði mér að [raka *hann*]
       Jon ordered me to   shave him

Rather, a correct account of Icelandic *hann*, as in (10), requires associating *hann* with value (*c*) of the parameter. If so indeed in (10a) and (10b) the governing category for *hann* is the embedded sentence; for the embedded sentence, being a tensed sentence, obviously is the minimal category which contains *hann* and has a TNS. In (10c), on the other hand, the governing category for *hann* is the matrix sentence; for given that the embedded sentence is untensed, the minimal category which contains *hann* and has a TNS is the matrix sentence. By binding principle B, then, *hann* must be free in the embedded sentence in (10a)—(10b) and in the matrix sentence in (10c). Hence (10a) and (10b), where *hann*, though bound within the matrix sentence, is free within the embedded sentence, are correctly predicted to be well-formed; but (10c) where *hann*, though free within the embedded sentence, is bound within the matrix sentence, is correctly predicted to be ill-formed.

Thus, while English, as in (4)—(5), could be associated with value (*a*) of the governing category parameter as a language, or English *himself* and *he* could be associated with value (*a*) of the parameter as lexical items, Icelandic as a language cannot be associated with any single value of the governing category parameter; rather, Icelandic *sig*, as in (6), and *hann*, as in (10), must be associated with values (*d*) and (*c*), respectively, of the parameter as lexical items. In general, then, one is led to the conclusion that values of the parameter in (9) are associated not with particular languages, but with particular lexical items in a language. This conclusion, extended from the case of the parameter in (9) to the case of parameters in general, we codify informally as in (11), and refer to as the *Lexical Parametrization Hypothesis*:

(11)   Values of a parameter are associated not with particular languages, but with particular lexical items in a language.

3. LEARNABILITY

Consider now the definition of governing category in (9) again. It is relatively easy to see that the values of the parameter in (9) define sets of categories which are subsets one of another; and in particular that the values in (9) are ordered already in such a way that the set of categories defined by each value is a subset of the set of categories defined by the immediately following value. So, concretely, the set of categories which have a subject, as in value (*a*) of the parameter, i.e., all sentences and some small clauses and nominals, is a superset of — i.e., (properly) includes — the set of categories which have an INFL, i.e., sentences, as in value (*b*) of the parameter. Similarly, the set of categories which have an INFL, or sentences, is a superset of the set of categories which have a TNS, i.e., tensed sentences, as in value (*c*) of the parameter; the set of categories which have a TNS, or tensed sentences, is a superset of the set of categories which have an indicative TNS, i.e., indicative sentences, as in value (*d*) of the parameter; and finally the set of categories which have an indicative TNS, or indicative sentences, is a superset of the set of categories which have a root TNS, i.e., root sentences, as in value (*e*) of the parameter.

It is then not too difficult to see that, given any element α, the governing categories for α defined by (9) under the different values of the parameter have the property of being embedded one inside another. Let us in particular call a governing category for α defined by (9) under values (*a*), (*b*), (*c*), (*d*), and (*e*) of the parameter, an A, a B, a C, a D, and an E, respectively. It is not too difficult to show that an A is always embedded inside a B, a B inside a C inside a D, and a D inside an E, in that order.

Consider for example two governing categories for α, A and B. By definition, A is the minimal category which contains α and has a subject; while B is the minimal category which contains α and has an INFL, i.e., is a sentence. But the set of categories with an INFL, or sentences, is a subset of the set of categories with a subject. Hence, in particular B, being a sentence, necessarily is a category with a subject; while A, being a category with a subject, can either be sentence or not. Consider, then, A. If A is a sentence, then A can coincide with B; for A, by definition the minimal category with a subject containing α, being by hypothesis a sentence, can also be the minimal sentence containing α, i.e., by definition B. If on the other hand A is not a sentence, then A obviously cannot coincide with B. But if A is distinct from B, then A can be contained in B; for nothing prevents A, if not a sentence, from being smaller than B, the minimal sentence containing α. However, whether A is a sentence or not, B cannot be contained inside A. For B necessarily is a category with a subject. Hence there can be no category with a subject which is both larger than B and the minimal category with a subject containing α, i.e., A. In other words, the situation in (12) obtains; where A and B can coincide, as in (12a), or not, as in (12b) to (12c), but if A and B do not coincide, B must contain A, as in (12b), and A cannot contain B, as in (12c):

(12) a. $\ldots [_{B\,=\,A} \ldots \alpha \ldots] \ldots$

  b. $\ldots [_{B} \ldots [_{A} \ldots \alpha \ldots] \ldots] \ldots$

  c. *$\ldots [_{A} \ldots [_{B} \ldots \alpha \ldots] \ldots] \ldots$

Similarly, given two governing categories B and C or C and D or D and E, B can coincide with C, C with D, and D with E; but if not, B must be contained inside C, C inside D, and D inside E and not vice versa.

  Now, given any element α again, let us consider the cases in which A, B, C, D, or E is the governing category for α; or indeed α is associated with values (a), (b), (c), (d), or (e) of the parameter in (9). In particular, let us consider the sets of sentences, i.e., the languages, generated in the different cases; and let us call the languages generated, in case α is associated with values (a), (b), (c), (d), and (e) of the parameter, $L(a)$, $L(b)$, $L(c)$, $L(d)$, and $L(e)$, respectively. One can rather easily show that given the nesting properties of the governing categories A, B, C, D, and E the languages $L(a)$, $L(b)$, $L(c)$, $L(d)$, and $L(e)$ ultimately are a subset one of another.

  Consider first the case in which α is an anaphor, such as English *himself,* or Icelandic *sig,* and so on. It is easy enough to show that in this case not only L(*a*), L(*b*), L(*c*), L(*d*), and L(*e*) are a subset one of another, but in particular L(*a*) is a subset of L(*b*), L(*b*) of L(*c*), L(*c*) of L(*d*), and L(*d*) of L(*e*). Consider, for example, L(*a*) and L(*b*). Given that α is an anaphor, L(*a*) obviously contains all and only the sentences in which α is bound in A, its governing category; L(*b*) all and only the sentences in which α is bound in its governing category again, i.e., B. But an A either coincides with a B or is contained inside a B. Hence every sentence in which α is bound by some element β within an A and also is a sentence in which α is bound by β within a B, B coinciding with A or containing A. But not every sentence in which α is bound by β within a B is a sentence in which α is bound by β within an A. In other words, if A and B coincide, then obviously α is bound within A just in case α is bound within B, as in (13a); if B contains A, then if α is bound within A, α is bound within B, as in (13b); but if α is bound within B it can be the case that α is not bound within A, as in (13c):

(13) a. ... [$_{B\,=\,A}$ ... β ... α ...] ...

     b. ... [$_B$ ...]$_A$ ... β ... α ...] ...] ...

     c. ... [$_B$ ... β ... [$_A$ ... α ...] ...] ...

But if all sentences in which α is bound in an A also are sentences in which α is bound in a B, then all sentences which are in L(*a*) also are in L(*b*); while if not all the sentences in which α is bound in a B are sentences in which α is bound in an A, as in (13c), then not all sentences which are in L(*b*) are in L(*a*). Hence, the sentences in L(*a*) are a subset of the sentences in L(*b*), or indeed L(*a*) is a subset of L(*b*). Much in the same way L(*b*) can be shown to be a subset of L(*c*), L(*c*) of L(*d*) and L(*d*) finally of L(*e*).

Consider, on the other hand, the case in which α is a pronominal, such as *he* in English, or *hann* in Icelandic, and so on. Again L(*a*), L(*b*), L(*c*), L(*d*), and L(*e*) are a subset one of another; but in this case L(*e*) is a subset of L(*d*), L(*d*) of L(*c*), L(*c*) of L(*b*), and L(*b*) of L(*a*). Consider indeed L(*b*) and L(*a*). Given that α is a pronominal, L(*a*) obviously contains all and only the sentences in which α is free in A, its governing category; L(*b*) all and only the sentences in which α is free in its governing category again, i.e., B. In other words L(*a*) contains all and only the sentences in which α either is free or is bound outside an

A; L(b) contains all and only the sentences in which α either is free again, or is bound outside a B. But an A either coincides with a B or is contained inside a B. Hence, every sentence in which α is bound by some β outside a B also is a sentence in which α is bound by β outside an A, A coinciding with or being smaller than B. But not every sentence in which α is bound by β outside an A is a sentence in which α is bound by β outside a B. In other words, if A and B coincide, then obviously α is bound outside A just in case α is bound outside B, as in (14a); if B contains A, then if α is bound outside B, α is bound outside A, as in (14b); but if α is bound outside A it can be the case that α is bound inside B, as in (14c):

(14) a. $\ldots \beta \ldots [_{B=A} \ldots \alpha \ldots] \ldots$

b. $\ldots \beta \ldots [_B \ldots [_A \ldots \alpha \ldots] \ldots] \ldots$

c. $\ldots [_B \ldots \beta \ldots [_A \ldots \alpha \ldots] \ldots] \ldots$

It follows that all the sentences which are in L(b) are in L(a); for all the sentences in which α is free are both in L(a) and in L(b), and all the sentences in which α is bound outside a B are also sentences in which α is bound outside an A. But not all the sentences which are in L(a) are in L(b); for not all sentences in which α is bound outside an A are sentences in which α is bound outside a B. Hence the sentences in L(b) are a subset of the sentences in L(a), or indeed L(b) is a subset of L(a). Much in the same way, then, L(c) is a subset of L(b), L(d) of L(c), and finally, L(e) of L(d).

But if the languages L(a), L(b), L(c), L(d), and L(e) are indeed one a subset of another, and in particular each a subset of the following one in case α is an anaphor, and each a subset of the preceding one in case α is a pronominal, the question naturally arises whether this is the case for any reasons at all, and if so, for which reasons.

Obviously, the theory of grammar offers no answers; not only as the theory now stands, no reason exists for the fact that L(a), L(b), L(c), L(d), and L(e) are a subset one of another, but more generally the formal properties and relations of the languages defined by different values of a parameter seem to be no concern of the theory at all. Consider, however, the theory of learnability; obviously, the formal properties and relations of the languages defined by different values of a parameter are a central concern of the theory. In particular, from the point of view of the theory of learnability, is that for any given parameter the learning function selects on the basis of the input data a value i of the parameter such that the input data are compatible with, i.e., a subset of, the language $L(i)$ defined by that value; and that if there are two values i and j of the parameter which define languages, $L(i)$ and $L(j)$, both compatible with the input data, then in case $L(i)$ and $L(j)$ are one a subset of the other the learning function selects that of the two values which defines the smaller language.

Consider indeed the two languages $L(i)$ and $L(j)$ defined by i and j. A first possibility is that $L(i)$ and $L(j)$ are disjoint, as in (15):

(15)
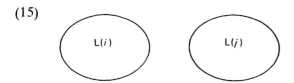

In this case obviously any set of input data is either a subset of $L(i)$ or a subset of $L(j)$, but not of both; hence, on the basis of the input data the learning function can straightforwardly select i or j, respectively. A second posibility is that $L(i)$ and $L(j)$ intersect, as in (16):

(16)
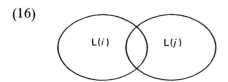

In this case the input data can be a subset of $L(i)$ but not of $L(j)$, or of $L(j)$ but not of $L(i)$, or finally of both $L(i)$ and $L(j)$. Obviously in the first two cases the learning function can straightforwardly select on the basis of the input data values i and j again. In the third case, on the other hand, it can select either i or j; for, whether it selects i or j, it can either stay with the value it has selected or select the other value on the basis of further data belonging to one but not the other language. But suppose finally that $L(i)$ and $L(j)$ are one a subset of another, say $L(i)$ a subset of $L(j)$, as in (17):

(17)

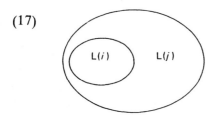

In this case obviously given a set of input data which belongs to L(*j*) but not to L(*i*), the learning function can straightforwardly select *j*. Given, however, a set of input data which belong both to L(*i*) and to L(*j*), crucially the learning function must select *i*. For, if it selects *i*, it can either stay with it or else select *j* on the basis of further data belonging to L(*j*) but not to L(*i*). But if it selects *j* there is no way it can select *i* instead, except on the basis of negative evidence; whereas we assume that only positive evidence exists.

Thus, the theory of learnability is directly concerned with the subset relations between the languages defined by the different values of a parameter; and it requires, in particular, in case two languages defined by two different values of a parameter are one a subset of another, that if the two languages are both compatible with the input data, the learning function selects that value of the parameter which defines the smaller language.

What the governing category parameter in (9) suggests is that a stronger requirement is part of the theory of learnability; and that in fact the theory of learnability requires that for every given parameter and every two given values of it, the languages defined by the two values of the parameter are one a subset of another. For such a requirement forces the languages defined by the values of the governing category parameter in (9) to be one a subset of another; hence, explains the fact that they are.

Let us assume, then, that the theory of learnability indeed includes a restriction to the effect that the languages generated by two values of a parameter are a subset one of the other, for every given parameter and every two values of it. This restriction we can formulate as in (18) and refer to as the *Subset Condition*:

(18)   For every parameter *p* and every two values *i*, *j* of *p*, the languages generated under the two values of the parameter are one a subset of the other, that is, $L(p(i)) \subseteq L(p(j))$ or $L(p(j)) \subseteq L(p(i))$.

Obviously, the most important consequence of the Subset Condition from the point of view of the theory of learnability is that, if indeed any two values of any parameter define languages which are a subset one of the other, then it is true in all cases that the learnability function can map the input data to that value of a parameter which defines the smallest of the languages compatible with the data. We can formulate this principle as in (19), and refer to it as the *Subset Principle*:

(19)   The learning function maps the input data to that value of a parameter which generates a language:
    (a) compatible with the input data; and
    (b) smallest among the languages compatible with the input data.

Thus, summing up, according to the Subset Condition, any two values of any parameter define languages which are a subset one of the other; while, according to the Subset Principle, on the basis of the input data the learnability function selects among the values of the parameter which generate languages compatible with the input data the value which generates the smallest language.

What do we mean when we say that the Subset Condition is necessary? We say that it is necessary in order for the Subset Principle to be always applicable. In other words, if the values that the learning function selects on the basis of data are determined by the Subset Principle and by nothing else, then the values of a parameter must determine languages which form a strict hierarchy of subsets. That is, any two values of the parameter must determine two languages such that one is a subset of the other.

It is important to note that the basis for the derivation of the Subset Condition is the assumption that the Subset Principle determines every value of the learning function. Thus we cannot allow two values of a parameter to yield languages which are disjoint, or intersecting, and not in a subset relation to each other. Of course, this assumption is itself not necessary. If two values of a parameter yield languages which are not in a subset relation, then we can arbitrarily order the two values, it would seem, in terms of the learning function. Then the Subset Principle would only have to apply to those cases of parameter values where a subset relation did hold between the languages. To repeat, the Subset Condition is necessary only in the special case where the Subset Principle is the *only* determiner of learning (or of markedness). Wexler (in preparation) has determined the necessary conditions which must exist for a learning function (markedness hierarchy) to exist when the Subset Condition doesn't hold and there are other determinants to markedness.

Nevertheless, it is intriguing that our studies of parameters in binding theory yield parameters which in fact obey the Subset Condition. Since this fact is not logically necessary, it might indicate that there is indeed some important empirical import to the assumption that the Subset Principle is the only determinant of learning, in at least the case of some parameters. It will take considerably more study of further parametric systems to determine to what extent the Subset Condition in fact holds.

In addition, if the languages defined by two values of a parameter are a subset one of the other as required by the Subset Condition, and as required by the, Subset Principle the learning function selects among two values of a parameter, everything else equal, the value which defines the smaller language, then, it seems evident that any two values of any given parameter can be defined to a more or less marked one than the other on the basis of the subset relations between the two languages they generate.

In particular, one can define an ordering of the values of a parameter to be a markedness hierarchy just in case the language generated by each value is a subset of the language generated by the immediately following value, informally as in (20):

(20)   A given ordering of the values of a parameter is a marked-
          ness hierarchy if and only if the language generated by
          each value is a subset of the language generated by the
          immediately following value in the ordering.

Obviously, then, one can define a value of the parameter to be the unmarked value just in case it is first in the markedness hierarchy; and define a value of the parameter to be marked just in case it is not unmarked. Similarly, a value of the parameter can be defined to be less marked than another value just in case the former precedes the latter in the markedness hierarchy; or vice versa a value of the parameter can be defined to be more marked than another value just in case the former follows the latter in the markedness hierarchy.

Thus in turn the Subset Principle can be revised in terms of marked-ness relations to state directly that the learnability function selects among the values of a parameter which define languages compatible with the input data the least marked value; and indeed the Subset Condition can be revised in terms of markedness relations to require simply that the values of any parameter define a markedness hierarchy.

It must be noticed at this point, however, that even the governing category parameter in (9) accounts only partially for the range of variation in binding theory. So, in particular, while some anaphors simply must be bound within their governing category, some anaphors must be bound within their governing category by a subject; and correspondingly, while some pronominals must be completely free in their governing category, other pronominals must be free in their governing categories only from subjects.

Consider, for example, English *himself* again. In its governing category English *himself* can be bound by a subject, as in (21a), or by an object, as in (21b):

(21) a. *John* told Bill about *himself*
    b. John told *Bill* about *himself*

However, if one considers, rather than English *himself* the Japanese reflexive *zibun*, then a Japanese example corresponding to (21a) can again be seen to be well-formed; but a Japanese example corresponding to (21b) can on the contrary be seen to be ill-formed. Similarly, consider English *he*, as in (22). Within its governing category *he* must be free from both a subject, as in (22a), and an object, as in (22b):

(22) a. **John* told Bill about *him*
    b. *John told *Bill* about *him*

If one considers, however, rather than English *he*, the Icelandic pronominal *hann* once more, one can easily see that the Icelandic example corresponding to (22a) is still ill-formed, but the Icelandic example corresponding to (22b) is now well-formed.

The variation just illustrated can easily be accounted for in the theory of grammar. Suppose indeed that the binding principles A and B, as in (1), are revised to state respectively that an anaphor not only must be bound in its governing category, but must be bound in its governing category by a proper antecedent; and a pronominal must not be free in its governing category, but must be free in its governing category just from proper antecedents, as in (23):

(23) a. An anaphor is bound in its governing category by a proper antecedent

     b. A pronominal is free in its governing category from proper antecedents

Suppose furthermore that a proper antecedent for α is defined to be either a subject or else any element at all, as in (24):

(24)   A proper antecedent for α is
      a. a subject β; or
      b. an element β whatsoever

If so, obviously the theory of binding includes not one but two different parameters: the already familiar governing category parameter, as in (9), and the newly introduced parameter in the definition of proper antecedent, as in (24), with the two values (*a*) and (*b*).

Not less obviously, the version of the binding principles in (23) together with the new parametrized definition of a proper antecedent in (24) correctly accounts for the contrast between English *himself* or *he*, as in (21) and (22), and Japanese *zibun* or Icelandic *hann*. Consider first *himself*. If *himself*, beside being associated with value (*a*) of the governing category parameter in (9), is associated with value (*b*) of the proper antecedent parameter in (24), then by binding principle A in (23), in (21) *himself* must be bound in the matrix sentence by any element. Hence both (21a), where *himself* is bound in the matrix sentence by a subject, and (21b), where *himself* is bound in the matrix sentence by an object, are correctly predicted to be well-formed. Consider, on the other hand, Japanese *zibun*. If *zibun*, contrary to English *himself*, is associated with value (*a*) of the proper antecedent parameter in (24), then by binding principle A in (23) *zibun* must be bound in its governing category by a subject. Hence an example of the type of (21a) is correctly predicted to be well-formed in Japanese, with *zibun* replacing *himself*, as in English; but an example of the type of (21b) with *zibun* replacing *himself* again is correctly predicted to be ill-formed in Japanese, contrary to Englich.

Similarly, consider *he*. If *he*, beside being associated with value (*a*) of the governing category parameter, is associated with value (*b*) of the proper antecedent parameter, exactly as *himself* is, then by binding principle B in (23), in (22) *he* must be free in the matrix sentence from all elements. Hence, both (22a), where *he* is bound in the matrix sentence by a subject, and (22b), where *he* is bound in the matrix sentence by an object, are correctly predicted to be ill-formed. But consider Icelandic *hann*. If *hann*, contrary to English *he*, is associated with value (*a*) of the proper antecedent parameter, then by binding principle B in (23), *hann* must be free in its governing category only from subjects. Hence, an example of the type of (22a) is correctly predicted to be ill-formed not only in English but also in Icelandic with *hann* replacing *he*; while an example of the type of (22b), with *hann* replacing *he* again, is correctly predicted to be well-formed in Icelandic, contrary to English.

From the point of view of the theory of learnability, however, the proper antecedent parameter in (24) faces us with the general problem of the existence of several parameters in the theory of binding and obviously in the theory of grammar as a whole. In the case of the governing category parameter in (9), indeed, in the absence of any discussion about other parameters, the Subset Condition and the Subset Principle were shown to hold very much as if the governing category parameter itself was the only parameter in the theory of grammar. But if there are not one, but several parameters in the theory of grammar and in binding theory itself, can one require that the languages defined by two different values of one such parameter be one subset of the other abstracting away from all other parameters? Or can one still require abstracting away from all other parameters that the learnability function selects a value of a particular parameter on the basis of its defining the smallest language compatible with the data? Evidently if the Subset Condition and the Subset Principle are to apply as before, an additional principle must be introduced in the theory of learnability to the effect that the subset relations between languages generated under different values of a parameter can be established independently of all other parameters, or in other words that the subset relations between languages generated under different values of a parameter remain constant no matter what the values of the other parameters are taken to be. This principle we formulate informally in (25) and we refer to it as the *Independence Principle*:

(25)   The subset relations between languages generated under different values of a parameter remain constant whatever the values of the other parameters are taken to be.

Given the Independence Principle it is easy to show that, as the governing category parameter in (9), the proper antecedent parameter in (24) observes the Subset Condition; hence, the Subset Principle quite straightforwardly applies to it. Consider first the case in which α in (24) is an anaphor. If we call the languages generated when α is associated with values (a) and (b) of the proper antecedent parameter L(a) and L(b), respectively, it is quite easy to see that L(a) is a subset of L(b). Obviously indeed L(a) includes all the sentences in which α is bound by a subject, while L(b) includes all the sentences in which α is bound by any element at all. But since L(b) includes all the sentences in which α is bound by any element at all, it includes in particular all the sentences in which α is bound by a subject, hence all the sentences included in L(a); while conversely L(a) does not include all the sentences included in L(b), notably not the sentences in which α is bound by an object, or an indirect object, or in general a non-subject. Hence, since all the sentences included in L(a) are included in L(b), but not all the sentences included in L(b) are included in L(a), L(a) obviously is a subset of L(b).

Consider on the other hand the case in which α in (24) is a pronominal. Let us call again the languages generated when α is associated with values (a) and (b) of the proper antecedent parameter L(a) and L(b), respectively. Obviously L(b) is a subset of L(a). L(a) indeed includes all the sentences in which α is free from subjects, i.e., all the sentences in which α is free from any element at all and all the sentences which in α is bound by a non-subject; while L(b) includes all the sentences in which α is free from any element at all. But since L(a) includes all the sentences in which α is completely free, it includes all the sentences included in L(b); while conversely L(b) does not include all the sentences included in L(a), specifically not the sentences in which α is bound by a non-subject. Hence, since all the sentences which are in L(b) are also in L(a), but conversely not all the sentences which are in L(a) are also in L(b), L(b) obviously is a subset of L(a).

Finally, it must be noticed that while the governing category parameter in (9) and the proper antecedent parameter in (24) are such that the principles and conditions of the theory of learnability apply to them, these same principles and conditions only apply to them if they indeed are individual parameters. So, from the point of view of the theory of grammar, the governing category and proper antecedent parameter could be one single parameter; but if they were, it is easy to show that the new parameter would violate the principles and conditions of the theory of learnability, in particular the Subset Condition. Hence the governing category and proper antecedent parameter must indeed be two separate parameters for reasons having to do with the theory of learnability once more.

Consider, for instance, the English pronominal *he* and the Icelandic pronominal *hann*. English *he* is associated with value (*a*) of the governing category parameter and value (*b*) of the proper antecedent parameter; Icelandic *hann* is associated with value (*c*) of the governing category parameter and value (*a*) of the proper antecedent parameter. Suppose that the governing category parameter in (9) and the proper antecedent parameter in (24) were one single parameter. English *he* would have to be associated with a value of the new parameter equivalent to the two values (*a*) and (*b*) of the governing category and proper antecedent parameter, respectively; Icelandic *hann* would have to be associated with a value of the new parameter equivalent to the two values of the governing category and proper antecedent parameter (*c*) and (*a*), respectively. Let us call the values of the new parameter associated with English *he* and Icelandic *hann* value (*a,b*) and value (*c,a*), respectively; and let us call the languages generated by values (*a,b*) and (*c,a*), respectively, L(*a,b*) and L(*c,a*). It is easy to see that, for any given pronominal, L(*a,b*) and L(*c,a*) would not be a subset one of the other. Indeed L(*c,a*) would include all the sentences in which the pronominal is bound by a nonsubject, but L(*a,b*) would not include those sentences in which the pronominal is bound by a non-subject within a governing category A, as defined by value (*a*) of the governing category parameter; hence L(*c,a*) would include some sentences which L(*a,b*) would not include. On the other hand, L(*a,b*) would include all the sentences in which a pronominal is bound outside a governing category A, but L(*c,a*) would not include those sentences in which the pronominal, though bound outside A, is bound by a subject inside a governing category C, as defined by value (*c*) of the governing category parameter; hence, L(*a,b*) would include some sentences which L(*c,a*) would not include. But if some sentences were in L(*c,a*) and not in L(*a,b*) and some sentences were in L(*a,b*) and not in L(*c,a*), neither L(*a,b*) would be a subset of L(*c,a*), nor L(*c,a*) a subset of L(*a,b*).

Similarly, one can consider instead of pronominals, anaphors: the result remains the same. If the governing category parameter in (9) and the proper antecedent parameter in (24) are made into one single parameter, the values of the new parameter define languages which are not a subset one of another. But if so, the Subset Condition is violated; hence, the governing category and proper antecedent parameters must indeed be two separate parameters. Note, however, that if we adopted a weaker form of the theory, as discussed after (19), in which the Subset Condition did not hold, then the two parameters *could* be reduced to one parameter. The natural interpretations of the parameters, from a learning point of view, however, would be lost. Once again, it is important to discover to what extent the Subset Condition is empirically true.

4. ACQUISITION

4.1. *The Acquisition of Anaphors and Pronominals*

Let's start with the simple cases first. Assume that binding theory is not subject to variation, applying to all pronominals and all anaphors in all languages uniformly. Also, for simplicity again, we will consider only lexical anaphors and pronominals, ignoring for the moment empty categories. All that has to be learned about an item under these circumstances is whether it is referential (an *R*-expression) or not and in case it is not, whether it is a pronoun or anaphor.

It seems natural to assume that a child first decides whether an item is referential or not. How does he or she do this? Along with most contemporary language acquisition theorists (e.g., Wexler and Culicover, 1980; Pinker, 1984; cf. also MacNamara, 1972), we assume that the learner has the 'cognitive' capacity to derive some of the interpretation of some sentences, even when he or she does not understand the full set of grammatical properties of the sentence. Included in this interpretation is the reference of the noun phrases in the sentence. There appears to be a number of mechanisms by which a learner can conclude that an item is 'non-referential'. For a pronoun, for example, consider the 'deictic' use of a pronoun, in which it is not co-referential (co-indexed) with anything else in the discourse. For example, somebody points to a toy and says, "It's broken." How is the child to distinguish *it* from a referential item, like 'toy'? One possibility is that the child realizes that the things to which *it* refers, over a variety of sentences are very varied, with their features varying wildly, as compared, say, with the things to which *toy* applies. If this proposal is to be correct, it is clear that it involves cognitive abilities which go beyond syntax. Another possible mechanism, more syntactic, is that a child might realize that, if he or she takes a certain item (really a pronoun) to be a referential item, then there are violations. Chomsky's (1981) Binding Principle C or whatever other principle of grammar (see Higginbotham, 1983) accounts for the fact that *R*-expressions cannot be bound. For example, in the sentence, "*Mary* thinks that *she* is ill," since *Mary* and *she* are co-indexed, the child can derive from Principle C that *she* is not a referential item (otherwise it couldn't be co-indexed with a *c*-commanding item). We assume, as we mentioned earlier, that the child has knowledge of which items in a sentence are co-referential. Or perhaps he or she has this knowledge only for some sentences, but this will be sufficient (cf. Wexler, 1981). There are likely a variety of other particular mechanisms which will allow the child to decide that an item is non-referential. We will simply assume for now that the child can decide this first, before he or she has to decide whether a non-referential item is a pronoun or anaphor.

4.2. *The Ordering of Pronouns and Anaphors*

So we assume that the learner knows that a particular lexical item *w* is non-referential. Therefore he or she knows that *w* is a pronoun or an anaphor. How does he or she decide which it is? For example, how does the child learning English decide that *him* is a pronoun and *himself* is an anaphor?

Following the general consensus in the field, we assume that only 'positive data' are available to the learner. That is, the learner is not corrected for ungrammatical sentences; in general he or she receives no direct information about ungrammaticality. (See Brown and Hanlon, 1970; Wexler and Hamburger, 1973; Baker, 1979; see Wexler and Culicover, 1980, Section 2, for a discussion of the input that is available to the child.) The assumption of only positive data creates obvious problems for the theory of language acquisition. For example, the linguist can use the ungrammaticality of sentences like "*Mary* hates *her*" to infer (from Principle A) that *her* is not an anaphor. But this negative information is not available to the child learning a first language.

In the absence of negative information, it is often suggested that some kind of markedness theory will allow values of parameters to be learned. Jakubowicz (1984) has suggested such a solution in the case of anaphors and pronominals. She suggests that the Subset Principle may be used to construct a method of learning whether a non-referential item is an anaphor or a pronominal.

As we saw above, the Subset Principle, along with Binding Principle A, predicts that locally bound anaphors are unmarked with respect to non-locally bound anaphors. Jakubowicz, however, concentrates on what she claims is the following prediction from the Subset Principle: There will be a stage (in English, say) in which the child takes pronouns to be anaphors. This means that pronouns will be locally bound for the child at this stage, whereas for the adult, pronouns are never locally bound. Jakubowicz's argument seems to be the following: Anaphors are locally bound. Pronouns can be non-locally bound. Because of this if a non-referential item is an anaphor, a smaller language is obtained than if the item is a pronoun. Therefore, the Subset Principle predicts that (locally bound) *anaphor* is unmarked with respect to *pronoun*. Therefore, the child will first analyze a non-referential item as a (locally bound) anaphor. This will be true even for items that are actually (in the adult language) pronouns. Therefore, there will be a stage in child language in which (adult) pronouns are interpreted by the child as (locally bound) anaphors. Jakubowicz reports that she has run experiments in which such results are obtained. Presumably positive evidence will eventually lead the child to reinterpret these items as pronouns.

Putting aside the empirical question in child language (to which we will return), we believe that there is an error in Jakubowicz's analysis. The Subset Principle does *not* imply that anaphors are unmarked with respect to pronouns. This is because the Subset Principle doesn't apply: The language with respect to a locally bound anaphor is *not* a subset of the language with respect to a pronoun. Consider (26):

(26)   *John* shaved *w*

If *w* is a (locally bound) anaphor, then (26) is grammatical. Let's say that (26) is in $L(p(i))$. Suppose *w* is a pronoun. Then, since *w* is locally bound in (26), Principle B implies that (26) is ungrammatical. Let's say that (26) is *not* in $L(p(j))$. Therefore, $(26) \in L(p(i))$ and $(26) \notin L(p(j))$. From this it follows that $L(p(i))$ is not a subset of $L(p(j))$, since there is at least one element of $L(p(i))$ which is not in $L(p(j))$: $L(p(i)) \nsubseteq L(p(j))$. Therefore, the Subset Principle does *not* imply that a locally bound anaphor is unmarked with respect to a pronoun. If there is an empirically attested stage in which pronouns are taken to be anaphors, then this stage is not derivable from the Subset Principle.

In fact, it is clear that neither the (locally bound) 'anaphor' language nor the 'pronoun' language are subsets of each other. For "John likes *w*" is in the pronoun language, but not in the anaphor language, with *John* and *w* not co-indexed, and this shows that $L(p(j)) \nsubseteq L(p(i))$. Therefore, the Subset Principle makes no prediction about markedness or order of acquisition for a pronoun versus an anaphor. The basic intuition is that Principles A and B of the Binding Theory define complementary domains in which sentences with pronouns and anaphors are grammatical. Therefore, the languages defined by these principles are not subsets of each other.

4.3. *Indexed Languages*

Note that in order to analyze the potential subset relations, we had to make particular assumptions about what 'language' means in this case. Consider again (26). Let *w* be *him* in (26), yielding (27).

(27)   *John* shaved *him*

(27) is ungrammatical, by Principle B, since *him* is locally bound. But, if we ignore indices (or assume that *John* and *him* are disjoint in reference), (27) becomes grammatical, as in (28):

(28)   John shaved him

(28) is grammatical, under the assumption that *him* is somebody else, not John. Therefore, if 'language' means "set of (unindexed) strings," (26) is in $L(p(j))$, in the same way that (28) is grammatical. In general, if 'language' is taken to have this meaning, since a pronoun disjoint from other noun phrases can appear in any noun phrase position in a sentence, it is clear that the pronoun language contains the anaphor language. Hence, $L(p(i)) \subseteq L(p(j))$. In this case, the Subset Principle will apply, with anaphors taken to be unmarked relative to pronouns.

However, it is clear that this definition of language as a set of unindexed strings is wrong. We have to take language to mean an indexed set, that is, a set of indexed strings, a set of strings with referential indices. First, it is our general assumption that the input to the child consists of interpreted strings, with referential properties being part of the interpretation. (More strictly, the child derives the interpretation; see Wexler, 1981, for discussion.) Second, if the language is not taken to be an indexed set, then the Subset Principle can't apply in other cases. In particular, there seems to be no way for the learner to discover that a pronoun that he or she has mistakenly taken to be an anaphor is indeed a pronoun. Suppose the child has decided that *him* is an anaphor. According to the Subset Principle (for example, in Jakubowicz's analysis), there will be a sentence which will show the child that *him* cannot be an anaphor. Such a sentence is (28), under the assumption that *John* and *him* are disjoint. Since *him* is not bound in (28), Principle A implies that it cannot be an anaphor.

But the input to the child in this case is taken to be an indexed sentence, with the index of *John* different from the index for *him*. Suppose that (28) is taken to be a string of words, with no referential indices. In that case the child can't conclude from (28) that *him* is unbound. One might think that a sentence like "Mary likes him" would be sufficient for learning that *him* was unbound, even if unindexed, but this assumes that the learner knows features which imply disjoint reference, which is what we want to derive. It might also be thought that a local sentence without another noun phrase in it besides the pronoun would be sufficient to show that the pronoun was unbound, and therefore not an anaphor. In other words, the deictic uses of pronouns (the uses in which the pronoun is made to refer by ostension — pointing — and does not have a linguistic antecedent whether local or not) might be used against the assumption that pronouns are anaphoric. In what follows we will discount this possibility as well.

From Jakubowicz's earlier papers it is not clear whether she intends 'language' with regard to the Subset Principle to mean indexed languages or not. We have just argued, of course, for the Subset Principle to work at all, languages must be taken to be indexed. In her latest (1984) paper, Jakubowicz does seem to imply that she means indexed language as the relevant concept. She writes, "One can then see that the set of output type sentences where pronouns may appear is larger than the one where anaphors may appear (in an extended sense, determined by co-indexing)."

It thus seems that to make the Subset Principle work at all, it is necessary to take the input as indexed sentences, and the 'language' as an indexed language. It thus follows that the Subset Principle does not imply that anaphors are unmarked with respect to pronouns. It does follow, however, as we showed earlier, that the Subset Principle implies that locally bound anaphors are unmarked with respect to non-locally bound anaphors.

4.4. *Do Children Treat Pronouns as Anaphors?*

We have shown that under the appropriate assumptions the Subset
Principle does not imply that children will first treat non-referential
items as if they were anaphors and not pronouns. In particular, the
Subset Principle does not imply that children will first treat (adult)
pronouns as anaphors. But, of course, our argument does not show that
children do not treat pronouns as anaphors. We have only shown that
the Subset Principle does not imply this result. All learning does not
necessarily take place according to the Subset Principle. In fact, as we
showed in the last section, the Subset Principle does not apply to the
relative ordering of pronouns and anaphors.

A different question yet is whether there are cases of parameter
setting where the Subset Principle does not apply. One such case would
be the acquisition of the 'pro-drop' parameter in Hyams' (1983)
important analysis. It is clear that the Subset Principle does not apply,
since null subject languages have sentences without subjects which non-
null subject languages don't have, and, as Hyams points out, non-null
subject languages have sentences with expletive subjects, which null-
subject languages don't have. Hyams' solution is to order the parameter
values in terms of built-in markedness hierarchies thereby predicting an
acquisition order for which she gives evidence. Whether this is in fact
necessary, or on the contrary the pro-drop parameter can be reanalyzed
so as to define languages which are in a subset relation and whether this
would have any consequences for binding theory, is the open question.

Now it could logically be that children first treat pronouns as
anaphors, even though this does not follow from the Subset Principle.
But this possibility seems to run up against an overwhelming empirical
fact. This is that a child's first use of pronouns seems to be a completely
free use, where the pronoun is not co-indexed with any other noun
phrase in the sentence. Thus a child at an early age could say, "It gone,"
where *it* is free. If a pronoun is taken by a young child to be an
anaphor, as Jakubowicz claims, how would the free use of a pronoun be
possible? An anaphor must be bound. If *it* is an anaphor in "it's gone,"
then the sentence is ungrammatical.

Therefore, it seems to us extremely implausible that pronouns are
first taken to be anaphors. It seems to us that Jakubowicz is not
sufficiently separating out two properties of non-referential items. The
first is the crucial, defining property, which separates anaphors from

pronouns. This property has to do with whether the item necessarily has an antecedent or not. If yes, the item is an anaphor. If no, the item is a pronoun. A second question has to do with the domain in which an anaphor has to be bound and a pronoun has to be free. Jakubowicz's evidence is that, in her experiments, there is a stage at which children prefer a reading for pronouns in which they are locally bound as opposed to locally free. If such a stage existed, it would certainly violate the second property for pronouns — that they are free locally. However, the evidence does not relate to the first crucial property of pronouns — that they can be (completely) free.

One possible position that Jakubowicz might take is that she is only concerned with bound uses of pronouns, that free uses are to be explained in some other fashion, as a separate piece of development. Indeed Jakubowicz (1984) might be taking this position. In Footnote 1 she writes, "Throughout I am concerned with sentences in which either an anaphor or a pronoun co-occur with one or more definite noun phrases, and the question is whether or not it is possible to establish a referential link between them." But it does not seem to be a reasonable position. From the standpoint of linguistic theory, and especially of binding theory, it does not make sense for the free use of a pronoun to be unrelated to a bound use. One of the major achievements of Binding Theory is, in Principle B, to integrate structures underlying the bound and free uses of a pronoun. To inquire into the development of the bound uses of the pronoun, while ignoring the development of the free uses, is to say, in fact, that Principle B is irrelevant to the development of pronouns. A theory that assumes that Principle B is present at a particular stage of the child's development (for example, from the beginning of linguistic development) cannot say that free uses of pronouns are not relevant data, for such free uses are in fact part and parcel of Principle B.

So far we have argued: (1) that the Subset Principle does not imply that pronouns will be learned first as anaphors and (2) that the child does not treat pronouns as anaphors early on, since the free use of pronouns is quite early. The question remains, Why does Jakubowicz obtain certain results in her experiments? Her main claim seems to be that at a certain age, children take a sentence like (29) in such a way that Peter is understood to wash Peter.

(29)   John said that Peter washed him

In other words, Jakubowicz claims that children at a certain age (around 3 to 4 years old) co-index *him* with *Peter* and not with *John* in (29). Thus, she argues, in (29) *him* is bound locally for the child. She further argues that the child takes *him* to be an anaphor, consistent with the local binding.

It is instructive that Otsu (1981) did studies quite similar to Jakubowicz's using sentences like (29). Otsu's summary of his results is not clear in this regard, and Jakubowicz (1984, Note 12) claims that "a more careful analysis of Otsu's results shows that children made fewer errors involving binding in sentences containing anaphors than in those containing pronouns." However, there is really no evidence in Otsu's experiment that children are treating pronouns as reflexives. In fact, there are more cases of children treating reflexives as pronouns than there are of them treating pronouns as reflexives. In recent experimental studies by Wexler and Chien (to appear), it is clear that there is no stage in which children treat pronouns as anaphors.

In summary, the Subset Principle does not imply that pronouns will be treated as anaphors, children's early use of pronouns as free indicates that they are not anaphors, and what experimental evidence is available does not indicate that pronouns are treated as anaphors.

ACKNOWLEDGEMENTS

* This paper reports research we developed and presented in the 1983–84 UC Irvine Linguistic Theory and Language Acquisition Seminar. For very helpful comments, we wish to thank Hagit Borer, Noam Chomsky, Neil Elliott, and Nina Hyams. We also wish to thank Bob Berwick, Yu-Chin Chien, Kyle Johnson, Ed Matthei, and Edwin Williams. This research was partially supported by National Science Foundation Grant #BNS 78–27044–05 to UC Irvine. Rita Manzini was supported by a grant for Cognitive Science from the Alfred P. Sloan Foundation to the University of California, Irvine.

REFERENCES

Baker, C. L.: 1979, 'Syntactic theory and the projection problem', *LI* **10**(4).
Berwick, R.: in press, *The Acquisition of Syntactic Knowledge*, MIT Press, Cambridge, Massachusetts.
Borer, H.: 1984, *Parametric Syntax*, Foris Publications, Dordrecht.
Brown, R. and C. Hanlon: 1970, 'Derivational complexity and the order of acquistion of child speech', in J. R. Hayes (ed.), *Cognition and the Development of Language*, Wiley, New York.

Chomsky, N.: 1980, 'On binding', *LI* **11**(1).

Chomsky, N.: 1981, *Lectures on Government and Binding*, Foris Publications, Dordrecht.

Chomsky, N.: in press, Knowledge of Language: Its Origins and Use, MIT Press, Cambridge, Massachusetts.

Higgenbotham, J.: 1983, 'Logical form, binding and variables', *LI* **14**(3).

Hyams, N.: 1983, *The Acquisition of Parameterized Grammars*, Ph.D. Dissertation, CUNY.

Jakubowicz, C.: 1984, 'On markedness and binding principles', *NELS* **14**.

Johnson, K.: 1984, 'Some notes on subjunctive clauses and binding in Icelandic', ms., MIT.

Koster, J.: 1984, 'On binding and control', *LI* **15**(3).

MacNamara: 1972, 'Cognitive basis of language learning in infants', *Psychological Review* **79**(1).

Manzini, R.: 1983, 'On control and control theory', *LI* **14**(3).

Manzini, R.: in preparation, 'On control and binding theory', paper presented at the conference on *Mental Representations and Properties of Logical Form*, London, April 12–14, 1985.

Manzini, R. and K. Wexler: 1984, 'Parameters, learnability and binding theory', ms., Irvine (in press, *Linguistic Inquiry*).

Otsu, Y.: 1981, *Universal Grammar and Syntactic Development in Children: Toward a Theory of Syntactic Development*, Ph.D. Dissertation, MIT.

Pinker, S.: 1984, *Language Learnability and Language Development*, Harward University Press, Cambridge, Massachusetts.

Wexler, K.: 1981, 'Some issues in the theory of learnability', in C. L. Baker and J. J. McCarthy (eds.), *The Logical Problem of Language Acquisition*, MIT Press, Cambridge, Massachusetts.

Wexler, K.: in preparation, 'A representation theorem for the learning of linguistic parameters', Irvine.

Wexler, K. and Y.-C. Chien: in press, 'The development of lexical anaphors and pronouns', in *Proceedings of the 1985 Child Language Research Forum*, Stanford University.

Wexler, K. and P. Culicover: 1980, *Formal Principles of Language Acquisition*, MIT Press, Cambridge, Massachusetts.

Wexler, K. and H. Hamburger: 1973, 'On the insuffiency of surface data for the learning of transformational languages', in K. J. Hintikka, J. M. E. Moravcsik and P. Suppes (eds.), *Approaches to Natural Language*, D. Reidel, Dordrecht.

Williams, E.: 1981, 'Language acquisition, markedness and phrase structure', in S. Tavakolian (ed.), *Language Acquisition and Linguistic Theory*, MIT Press, Cambridge, Massachusetts.

Yang, D. W.: 1983, 'The extended binding theory of anaphors', *Language Research* **19**(2).

KEN SAFIR

COMMENTS ON WEXLER AND MANZINI*

1. INTRODUCTION

The development of a parameterized theory of Universal Grammar is still a very young idea, and so some fundamental questions are still very close to the surface: What counts as a parametric theory? What should such a theory explain? Wexler and Manzini (henceforth, W & M) provide us with a new approach to these issues, one which is sure to engender much worthwhile research and discussion. In the commentary that follows, I limit my discussion to some of the contrasts and consequences that emerge when the W & M approach is compared to what has come to be the standard account of parameters.[1]

Let us begin by recalling how the theory of parameters was presented in Chomsky (1981), a version I will call the Standard Parameter Theory (SPT). According to SPT, the success of acquisition can be accounted for by the ability of a child to 'fix' the value n of some formal grammatical parameter P so that Pn, once fixed, results in greater knowledge than might be expected from induction on whatever data triggers the parameter setting. Pn, moreover, will interact with other value-fixed parameters and with grammatical principles invariant across languages (i.e., universal principles of grammar — hereafter, UPGs). The resulting interaction between value-fixed parameters and UPGs results in a 'core grammar' — one of the particular grammars made possible by the innate schema of parameters and the innate universal principles. The project of research that emerges from this account is to (A) identify the relevant parameters that distinguish one language from another, (B) seperate these parameters from one another and from the UPGs and (C) to give a plausible account of how these parameters are fixed.

Matters are not, however, quite so straightforward. While the unification of two sorts of inquiry — stages of acquisition and language typology — seems highly desireable, our assumptions about what counts as a 'possible parameter' or a 'learnable parameter' remain very weak. One constraint on formulation of parameters from the acquisition side

77

Thomas Roeper and Edwin Williams (eds.), Parameter Setting, 77–89.
© 1987 *by D. Reidel Publishing Company.*

is the requirement that the child must have positive evidence in order to set a parameter in the appropriate way, though in practice it is often too easy to formulate a parameter so as to make it sensitive to some sort of positive data trigger. No formal property was proposed that delimited the class of possible parameters either. If the positive evidence restriction is too easily circumvented (and I am overstating the case to make a point) then what is to prevent us from describing any sort of language difference in terms of some *ad hoc* parameter? In short, how can we prevent SPT from licensing mere description?

The issue did not arise in the latter form right away, however, as Chomsky's (1981) primary example of a parameter, the pro-drop parameter, was supposed to account for properties of surface word order, 'missing subjects' in tensed sentences, and extraction patterns all by means of the same formal statement that held for Italian but not for English or French. As long as it appeared that the actual number of parameters might turn out to be relatively few, each accounting for a whole set of superficially unrelated syntactic distributions, it appeared that the explanatory force of proposing a parameter might be great indeed. It has since been disputed, however, that the pro-drop parameter is the unique agent in the set of syntactic properties found in Italian (cf. Chao, 1980; Safir, 1985; Hyams, 1983, among others) although the matter is still very much in debate. As individually proposed parameters have come to correspond to narrower differences between languages, the problem of promiscuous descriptiveness has become more apparent.

The first study to address these weaknesses of SPT was Borer (1984) who suggested that parametric variation might be confined to the lexicon, more specifically to lexical properties of the inflectional system. While I believe the more specific proposal to be too descriptively limited,[2] restricting interlanguage variation to the lexicon is a very appealing step, as no one disputes the fact that children must learn properties of lexical items. A parsimonious theory of what must be acquired must begin by assuming this minimum, and Borer's contribution holds out hope that under a properly conceived account of the lexicon, it might not be necessary to assume language learning of any other sort.

The point of presenting this (selective) recent history is to provide a context for some of the novel proposals put forth by W & M, especially as a central strategy of their approach is to sharpen our notion of 'learnable parameter' while at the same time assuming that parametric variation is confined to the lexicon. W & M's paper thus presents a principled theory of parametric acquisition, perhaps the most explicit one currently available. I shall concentrate my discussion on three closely related issues, namely, (A) the sorts of generalization that may be achieved if parameters are stated for individual lexical items, (B) the claim there exists a separate 'learning module' which derives a markedness hierarchy for parameter settings, and (C) the force of the Lexical Parametrization Hypothesis.

2. OVERGENERALIZATION AND UNDERGENERALIZATION

One of the most striking novelties of the W & M approach is the assumption that parameters may be set for individual lexical items. Thus they raise the possibility that a given language may have, say, five lexical anaphors, each with a different domain within which its binder must be present. The child does not have to construct the various domains by induction, rather a class of possible domains (parameter settings for governing category) are provided by UG, and the child can arrive at the proper setting without overgeneralization. The key problem, from the perspective of the W & M theory, is that the child should not be faced with a situation wherein it can conjecture an inappropriate parameter setting for which there is no positive evidence to act as a corrective.

From the perspective of SPT, however, a central goal is to state parameters that have the widest possible range of syntactic effects within a language. In the W & M approach, not only does a parameter fail to generalize across the language, it may fail to generalize across as many as two lexical items, even though the range of parameter settings is still determined by UG, and the markedness relations between the parameter settings is determined by the Subset Principle.

What is emerging here is a conflict between the SPT notion of parameters, wherein the parameters were few and their effects pervasive within a language, and the 'possible parameter' reasoning which limits the possible form of parameters while devaluing the generalization achieved within a language. I must hasten to add that W & M present a range of cases which seem to argue against generalizing in this way in a number of languages (e.g., it is claimed that the different anaphors within one language have differing binding domains, exactly as predicted), but the issue here is only partially one of fact. Rather I would prefer to focus on a methodological consequence: If lexical entries within a language L can have different parameter values for different lexical items in L, then parametric theory does not compare L and another language L', but rather the lexical items of L' are compared with lexical items of L. To put it another way, it is not so meaningful to talk about a language typology so much as a cross-linguistic lexical typology.[3]

For example, within the W & M theory, it is not natural to say "L is a left-headed language" insofar as for any particular lexical entry, it is possible that the directionality parameter could be set the other way. Thus a child cannot even assume this as an initial setting in light of hearing complement final phrases, indeed the child could conclude nothing general at all. Rather it would be necessary to set the parameter separately for each lexical item, which results in undergeneralization — one of the sorts of problems that SPT was supposed to overcome.

The latter limitation, however, is not so surprising in that the W & M theory is crafted with the avoidance of overgeneralization in mind. This is not to say that the W & M theory cannot be adjusted or modified to deal with potential undergeneralization, but the key point to be kept in mind is that confining parameters to settings for individual lexical entries, while it alleviates the overgeneralization problem, is confronted with a potential undergeneralization problem as a result.

Another respect in which the 'possible parameter' reasoning developed here contrasts with the spirit of SPT is that the Subset Condition, together with the Independence Principle may conspire to force an atomization of parameters — it becomes difficult to link more than one grammatical property to a single set of parameter settings. The general idea of the Subset Condition is that the set of parameter settings (values) $V_1 \ldots V_i$ for a given parameter P must form a subset relation, such that each setting would contribute to forming a language L which either properly contains, or is properly contained by, the language formed as a result of setting any other value for P, other things being equal. Other things are insured to be equal (for the determination of subsets) by the Independence Principle. The whole complex of ideas, as well as the issue I wish to raise, is best presented in terms of a specific example.

Recall that W & M assume that the parameter setting that is preferred by the learning module will be the one that results in the smallest language (the Subset Principle and the learning module are discussed in the next section). Thus the setting for the binding domain of anaphors that is conjectured by default is the one where they must be bound as locally as possible, as this defines the smallest language (consisting of possible indexed strings).[4] It has been suggested from time to time, however, as W & M note, that long distance anaphors are often, if not always, associated with the property that they must be bound by subject NPs and not by object or indirect object NPs.

More concretely, suppose we contrast a language like Japanese, which permits the largest possible domain for a reflexive anaphor and requires that the anaphor must be bound by a subject, with a language like English, where non-subject NPs can be anaphor antecedents, but the relation is relatively local. Within the assumptions of SPT, these two languages might correspond to the two possible settings of a single parameter, and the linkage between antecedent type and domain size would be seen as a simplification of what a child must master in order to set the parameter (a non-subject antecedent would provide positive evidence for the English-type, and a long distance anaphor would indicate that non-subject antecedents are not possible).

As W & M note, however, it is not possible in their system to formulate a parameter for anaphors which links the 'long distance' property with the 'only subject antecedent' property, as this does not satisfy the Subset Condition: A language that allows non-subject antecedents for anaphors is larger than one that only allows subjects, but a language that allows a long distance anaphor domain is larger than one that limits the anaphor to a small domain, i.e., no subset relation holds.

Now the fact of the matter with respect to the case just mentioned is not so important — antecedent and domain properties may indeed turn out to be independently fixed — but the illustration is intended to show how the Subset Condition could significantly limit any attempt to link more than one grammatical property to a single parameter or parameter setting. Thus while the W & M approach provides a more restrictive theory of 'possible parameter', the result could be an acceleration of the atomization of parameters that might render their role more descriptive.

Just one more example of this sort of concern is worth mentioning, as it is one that involves the proposed contrast in markedness properties between anaphors and pronouns. Consider the W & M account of the binding domains for Icelandic *hann* and *sig*. Now suppose the antecedent and domain size properties are set separately even in SPT. It would then be expected that the domain size for *hann* and *sig* would be the same with respect to the 'long distance' factor, and W & M show that this is false. On the other hand, however, it would still be expected in SPT that if anaphors require subject antededents, then pronouns would only be disjoint from potential subject antecedents (within the relevant long or short domain), as the antecedent parameter setting would be general across lexical entries. Thus W & M, while they accomodate the failure of generalization across domain size (distance), render accidental the potential generalization concerning the role of subject antecedents in Icelandic, i.e., that all binding domains in Icelandic are only sensitive to subject antecedents. As the consequences of a constant subject antecedent determinant across pronouns and anaphors is not subject to the 'smallest language' calculation (for pronouns it is smaller, for anaphors, larger), this generalization is unstateable for principled reasons in the W & M approach. Once again, an accomodation to avoid overgeneralization leads to the possibility of undergeneralization.[5]

Similar sorts of issues will come up again in different forms in the discussion to follow, but it is worth pointing out here that the W & M proposals make a very significant contribution by focusing on the overgeneralization problem rather than the more commonly addressed undergeneralization problem. A better balance between these considerations is likely to result from careful consideration of the W & M conceptualization of this issue.

3. THE LEARNING MODULE

One of W & M's more striking innovations is their proposal that the usual markedness assumptions may be derived from their Subset Principle, which requires a preference, in the absence of positive counterevidence, for the parameter setting that would result in the smallest language. Once again, the motivating goal is the attempt to avoid overgeneralization that could not be corrected by positive evidence. In this section I will focus on the Subset Principle and the proposal that it is located in a separate cognitive module that W & M call the 'learning module'.

One might immediately ask why we should need another module, and why we should narrow the realm of linguistic theory by removing markedness from it. It seems to me that W & M have plausible answers to these questions. Typically, generative grammar has taken a Cartesian "divide and conquer" approach to its subject matter, constantly abstracting away from contingent phenomena to focus on answerable questions about linguistic knowledge. For example, insofar as the 'garden path' sentences (e.g., the horse raced past the barn fell) are grammatical, but simply hard to process, it is reasonable to suppose that there is a parsing operation that is not simply the automatic function of the system of linguistic knowledge. Nonetheless, one would want to say that the parsing mechanism or module has at least some access to the system of linguistic knowledge. The same view is possible with respect to the learning module, which presumably has some access to linguistic knowledge, though it is not obvious that markedness plays any role in the adult grammar after the parameters have been set, marked or not. Thus it is quite conceivable that the principle that underlies markedness might be isolable from linguistic knowledge proper.

We may then ask how autonomous the learning module really is. Does this module interect in interesting ways with non-linguistic learning tasks? W & M make this suggestion at least, and, even if they are right about this module, it may be that the question is premature. Notice, however, that the same question about parsing seems bizarre, as there is no other activity that is like parsing but clearly non-linguistic. Indeed the latter fact leads some to question the parsimony of an approach that sets up a separate parsing module altogether. Supposing, nonetheless, that the parsing mechanism exists and is somewhat separate, notice that we have two ways of conceiving of the learning module — either as an autonomous component of cognitive ability that is relevant to other realms of knowledge, or as a component with special properties that is parasitic on linguistic knowledge, i.e., on Universal Grammar.

I believe that the W & M idea more closely resembles the latter sort of component as it seems to require rather complex linguistically specific computation on the part of the language learner. This is clearly necessary with respect to the parameter settings that determine governing category, since the same set of parameter values is supposed to hold for both anaphors and pronouns. A small domain means a larger language with respect to pronouns, but a smaller one with respect anaphors, and so the child must be able to compute this difference in establishing the markedness hierarchy for a given lexical item. After all, the Subset Condition only insures that the values of any given parameter will be nested for language size, while it is the learning module and the Independence Principle that result in the markedness ordering. Thus the learning module must know the difference between linguistic entities like pronouns and anaphors, compute the smallest language for each lexical entry of this type, and allow for the translation of possible structures (governing category size) into a computation of possible indexed strings for a given parameter setting. Perhaps this computation, repeated for each lexical anaphor or pronoun, will seem implausible to some, as it does to me, but the fact of the matter is we know nothing for certain about this realm of computational ability, and we cannot rule it out.

The latter computation, however, would be a lot more complex were it not for the the Independence Principle which allows the determination of the markedness hierarchy abstracting away from how other parameters are set. If the computation of language size were not limited in this way, then the problem raised with respect to linking subject-antecedent and domain size arises in a slightly different form; Even if domain size and subject-antecedent properties are parameters fixed separately, the 'smallest language' computation will not be able to determine a markedness hierachy, as language that allows non-subject anaphors in small domains is neither smaller nor larger than a language that requires subject antecedents in large domains.

Notice, however, that the only requirement for the existence of an Independence Principle is in fact the Subset Principle, since the latter is assumed to require a computation that cannot be carried out without the former. In a theory like SPT, it is stipulated that the parameter values and markedness values are provided by Universal Grammar, and so the independence of parameters, at least in theory, does not itself have to be stipulated. Thus the appeal of the Independence Principle is thrown back on the success of the Subset Condition.

The scope of the Subset Condition seems challengeable on the basis of a number of types of variation that do not appear to involve subsets. For example, a language that takes its complements to the right is no larger or smaller, other things being equal than a language that takes its complements to the left, and yet somehow the language learner must make the systematic distinction. Many other word order variations might be problematic for the Subset Condition in similar ways. Also it is not obvious that languages that allow missing subjects in tensed sentences are any larger or smaller than languages that do not allow subjects to be missing, especially because the missing subject languages often do not allow pronominal subjects in such cases (i.e., the missing subject sentences correlate one-one with sentences in non-missing subject languages that have pronominal subjects — compare French and standard Italian). This suggests that the scope of the subset properties is limited as a restriction on possible parameters.

It is suggested by W & M themselves, in fact, that the Subset Condition may simply be superfluous if it has exceptions, as the Subset Principle will then only regulate the setting of parameter values that happen to have the appropriate subset property. While this retreat does not undermine the force of the Subset Principle where it applies, it does raise the issue of how values are set for the parameters that do not fall under the Subset Principle. Is there another determinant of markedness for these cases, and is this determining factor a part of UG or part of the (semi-)autonomous learning module?

We must also ask if other forms of lexical acquisition, forms that are irrelevant to the subset property, but sensitive to the positive evidence assumption, should also be conditioned by the learning module. For example, consider the generalization of inflectional paradigms, such as the -ed ending in English. Children typically overgeneralize the application of this ending (forming *goed instead of went) before eventually settling on the suppleted form. English will have just as many past tense verb forms either way, and the number of possible indexed strings is irrelevant, so the Subset Principle is irrelevant too. Yet it is assumed that the child adjusts to the adult lexicon on the basis of positive evidence that is available to correct the overgeneralization. Perhaps it is an advantage of the Subset Condition that it applies only to parameter values, as it then predicts that this sort of lexical learning is not to be confused with parameter setting. On the other hand, this sort of learning is just as irrelevant to the adult grammar, once it is formed, as the parameter setting ability is. Should the learning module have additional structures to determine how positive evidence is to be interpreted in the case of morphological overgeneralization as well? Perhaps this is another direction that a more developed theory of the learning module might be able to exploit.

4. THE LEXICAL PARAMETRIZATION HYPOTHESIS AND
THE SUBSET CONDITION

In Section 2 it was suggested that setting parameters for individual
lexical items might lead to insufficient breadth of generalization. In
effect, it was pointed out that confining the class of parameters to the
lexicon would direct the study of adult grammars away from language
typology to the typology of possible lexical properties. What exactly
may then be taken to be a 'lexical property?'

While the question is an obvious one, it is not so easy to answer, as
the correct characterization of lexical properties is currently an area of
considerable theoretical debate. Moreover, the statement of the structural properties of governing categories that determine binding domains
as parameter values conditioning lexical entries moves a property
thought to be quintessentially syntactic into the realm of lexical
specificity. Is any syntactic property exempt from reinterpretation as a
lexical property?

Syntacticians might fill volumes disputing the answer to this question,
and so I will only indicate here what is at stake. As long as we have no
theory of 'possible grammatical principle' or 'possible parameter' any
invariant property across languages might be a grammatical principle. A
syntactician whose primary study is adult grammars must be wary that a
supposed grammatical principle is not simply abandoned in the face of
some recalcitrant lexical properties. Within the W & M approach, there
is a descriptive way out of this difficulty by moving the grammatical
principle to the lexicon and giving it parameter values that will
accommodate the recalcitrant case. Moreover, given that it appears that
some parameters are irrelevant to the Subset Principle, as mentioned
above, it could not be guaranteed that a parameterization of this type
would have the subset properties that would, within the W & M
perspective, otherwise tag it immediately as a parametrically determined phenomenon.

While the danger of overdescriptiveness just described is perhaps
emphasized within the W & M approach, neither is this form of descriptiveness ruled out within the SPT approach, and so it is not quite fair to
see this problem as unique to W & M's theory. Indeed what this shows
is that there is a great deal more to be said about what a theory of
parameters should contain.

One possibility which might tighten the W & M approach would be to tighten the notion of possible parameter by systematically distinguishing the class(es) of parameters that do not appear to be regulated by the Subset Principle. Notice, for example, that the direction of complement-taking is not only non-formulable in terms of subsets, it also does not fit well with the Lexical Parameterization Hypothesis. If a verb takes its complements to the left (independently of how it assigns or governs Case) in L, we do not expect to find other verbs in L that take their complements to the right, or that this property would have to be set for each lexical item in L.[6] There is no obvious lexical property that would account for this general property. Notice also that this is just another version undergeneralization problem described in Section 2. Moreover, there seems to be no reason at all to assume that a parameter for direction of complement-taking, assuming there is one, would involve any unmarked setting. Perhaps these three properties of the direction of complement-taking are typical of all parameters that do not fall under the Subset Principle.

The suggestion that parameters inconsistent with the subset properties have no marked value would fit well with the idea that the learning module is only relevant to those parameters for which there is a danger of overgeneralization that could not be corrected by positive evidence. Direction of complement-taking is obviously a domain where there is a great deal of available positive evidence, and so no markedness hierarchy need be assigned. The failure of the Lexical Parameterization Hypothesis for this sort systematic language internal generalization remains obscure, but at least there would be systematic criteria for diagnosing parameters that do not obey the Subset Principle, and this particular undergeneralization problem would be overcome.

Whatever the fate of the subset idea, it may be necessary to articulate the notion of 'parameter' somewhat. One reason this has not been attempted so far is that research on parametric variation is that the range of proposed parameters has only recently begun to appear extensive and diverse. Often such apparently uncontrolled diversity turns out to be manageable once a few subregularities are discerned, and so more principled notions of 'possible parameter' may still be hidden behind some unmade distinctions between classes of parameters.

5. CONCLUSION

In developing one of the first relatively explicit parametric theories of language acquisition and variation, W & M have broken much new ground and have advanced our conceptual sophistication about the consequences of the positive-evidence-only assumption. Even should the particular mechanisms and computations they propose turn out to be untenable, their approach to the overgeneralization problem in terms of subsets is sure to be influential. It appears that this theory might be less successful at dealing with the undergeneralization problem, though this drawback might partially be overcome if our analysis of parameters and parameter types is further articulated.

The proposal that a separate learning module accounts for a markedness hierarchy that plays no role in adult grammar is an especially interesting idea, as it would provide a way to break down a complex problem into what are hopefully simpler subparts. Moreover, the possibility that such a module exists is an idea that is potentially independent of the 'smallest language' calculations that W & M claim are to be regulated by it.

But perhaps a more important contribution of the W & M paper is that it focuses attention on the key issue that must be faced if we are to arrive at an explanatory parametric theory, namely, what is a possible parameter? The descriptive flexibility of the parameters permitted by SPT, for example, may prove too convenient to be explanatory, and if so, only a principled theory of possible parameters can save the parametric approach from vacuity. W & M have made an impressive attempt, and one of the first, to grapple with this issue.

NOTES

* I would like to thank Robert Matthews for useful discussion of some of the issues involved. He does not necessarily share my views. I would also like to thank Tom Roeper and Edwin Williams for their patience and editorial help.
[1] In so doing I will all but ignore the more detailed empirical and analytic issues, except for some brief notes. I have also passed over the acquisition studies discussed by W & M and their dispute with Jakubowicz (1984), to which I have nothing to add.
[2] The reason for this conclusion will be discussed specifically in Section 4 with regard to the somewhat less narrow "Lexical Parametrization Hypothesis" of W & M.
[3] Notice that the assumption that NP-trace is 'anaphoric' now becomes less interesting, in that the properties of the domain in which it must be bound do not necessarily follow from anaphorhood. In a language in which a child heard sentences like "Mary$_i$ was

requested that John like e," meaning "it was requested that John like Mary," pre- sumably the domain of NP-trace could easily be set for the first S containing non- subjunctive tense. If indeed all of the elements classed as anaphors by W & M differ only in terms of how their binding domain is determined, then one of the more striking properties of NP-trace — that it always appears to take the smallest domain — is rendered unexplained.

[4] It may be better to express this in terms of possible indexed LF representations, as it appears to be necessary to predict the distribution of anaphors for VP deletion structures, as in "The men knew each other and the women said the children did too" where *the children* must know each other and not the women. Thus the antecedent of the 'missing' *each other* in the VP-deletion context must be determined on the basis of the reconstructed VP at the level of LF.

[5] Within the W & M theory, it is always a coincidence if the domain for anaphors and the domain for pronouns should coincide. This coincidence of domains, long assumed (e.g., Chomsky, 1981) has been recently disputed for English (e.g., Huang, 1983), but any tendency for even close coincidence of domains should be accidental.

[6] It is worth noting, however, that this sort of lexical variation is indeed attested for languages that have both postpositions and prepositions, such as Dutch.

REFERENCES

Borer, H.: 1984, *Parametric Syntax*, Foris Publications, Dordrecht.

Chao, W.: 1980, 'PRO drop languages and non-obligatory control', in W. Chao and D. Wheeler (eds.), *University of Massachusetts Occasional Papers in Linguistics Vol. 7*, University of Massachusetts, Amherst.

Chomsky, N.: 1981, *Lectures on Government and Binding*, Foris Publications, Dordrecht.

Huang, J.: 1983, 'A note on binding theory' *Linguistic Inquiry* **14**(3).

Hyams, N.: 1983, *The Acquisition of Parameterized Grammars*, unpublished CUNY Ph.D. dissertation.

Jakubowicz, C.: 1984, 'On markedness and binding principles', in *NELS* **14**.

Safir, K.: 1985, *Syntactic Chains*, Cambridge University Press, Cambridge and New York.

Wexler, K. and R. Manzini (this volume) 'Parameters and learnability in binding theory'.

TAISUKE NISHIGAUCHI AND THOMAS ROEPER

DEDUCTIVE PARAMETERS AND THE GROWTH
OF EMPTY CATEGORIES

1. INTRODUCTION AND OVERVIEW

The parametric model is extremely simple. An innate set of grammars presents a child with highly limited choices: two or three possibilities exist. A piece of input data shows unambiguously which is correct. How does the model connect to the reality of acquisition?

We will pose a number of questions about the parametric model which lie beyond this essay to answer, but which the field of acquisition must address. Then we will make a proposal which we entitle the Modularity Principle. It states, in brief, that acquisition steps occur only within a single module. It follows naturally, though not logically, that temporal stages will arise that reflect steps in acquisition. We will illustrate the Modularity Principle with several examples, although the proposal has implications far beyond the domains under consideration.

Three problems stand out: (1) Why are expletives (it, there) identical to referential pronouns?, (2) Why are complementizers (for, to) identical to prepositions?, and (3) Why do children appear to begin with an empty pronominal as their first empty category and not with trace? Our answer to each of these questions follows from the Modularity Principle. Children first learn lexical items as referential objects (it = a reference to context) within the unmarked syntactic category of N, V, A, or P. In a second step, they acquire special features within the syntactic model (it = expletive). The same argument will be made for the acquisition of the complementizer *for*.

Finally we provide an independent argument for the claim advanced by Hyams, (this volume) that children begin with small pro as their first empty category.

1.1. *The Parametric Model and the Evaluation Metric*

The parametric model has dramatically reduced the language acquisition problem. An abstract problem has been rendered concrete. Two

Thomas Roeper and Edwin Williams (eds.), Parameter Setting, 91—121.

features of acquisition, which had been originally seen as involving infinite dimensions, have not only finite but deterministic origins:

(1)   the set of grammars is finite and small,
(2)   the triggering data is deterministic.

The first claim is possible when one sees grammars as a set of substantive modular features which are not the output of transformational combinatorix. The second claim is that certain pieces of prominently available data (short sentences, frequently uttered) dictate grammatical decisions unambiguously.

Such a theory stands in stark contrast to a model which involves an Evaluation Metric (Chomsky, 1965). The evaluation metric has two consequences. (1) No piece of data makes a direct choice of grammar. (2) All the data must be examined simultaneously to guarantee the simplest common grammar for all sentences.[1] Under the parametric model, no calculations are implied.

Nevertheless the parametric approach, though it simplifies the acquisition problem in principle, remains a model, in effect a metaphor, whose viability must be tested along various deductive paths.

1.2. *An Enriched Parametric Model*

Parametric models, thus far, offer an exact acquisition procedure at a few choice points, but leave the overall pattern of growth unarticulated. For instance, how do empty categories grow? Particular grammars show intricate variation in the projection of anaphors, pronominals, and the domains where they can occur. We will focus on this question.

In general, we will argue that the theory of parameters must be enriched to account for the following three, putative facts:

(1) Parametric implications are not instantaneously fixed. In effect subparameters exist, with independent data requirements, each of which must be separately set.

(2) Eliminated features recur in later phases of acquisition. For example, a rejected parametric option continues to function as an elsewhere condition.

(3) The grammar fails to have a deductive structure where it should have. For example, it could have unique lexical items for expletives but it does not.

Our basic argument is quite simple, although the details are rather complex. The child faces three tasks in his effort to associate sound and meaning. (We ignore the problem of fixing the contents of the sound stream itself.) He must:

(4) Connect a word to a feature of the environment: reference.

(5) Connect the word to a syntactic environment: lexical subcategorization.

(6) Connect syntactic positions with other positions and determine content: anaphoric relations.

These decisions each have a separate character. We suggest that an acquisition mechanism functions more efficiently if these decisions can be independently fixed. For instance, a child will first associate *give* with an action and the unmarked syntactic category of verb. Then he will learn special subcategorizations (*give* allows two objects). Finally he will determine that there can be an empty NP in a sentence like *John gave (NP) money*. The empty NP, moreover, is disjoint from *John*.

1.2.1. *Explanation of the temporal decision*. It is important to observe that there is no reason why the sequence (4—6) should be reflected in a temporal domain. Logically dependent operations can occur simultaneously. Conversely, logically independent decisions can also all occur simultaneously when rich data appears. However it might be natural, for neurological reasons, for an organism to divide its labors temporally; therefore we should look for temporal differentiation. In brief, we claim that a child may not instantly reach all of the conclusions which the data he absorbs dictates; that is, acquisition does not occur instantaneously and stages exist for which ample counterevidence in the environment is present.

The consequence of this perspective is that we predict the presence of grammatical stages in acquisition, however short-lived. For instance, a classic case of a grammatical stage is children's use of uninverted questions "What I can do". Although children receive hundreds of counterexamples each week and there is no obvious parsing difficulty or cognitive problem with the sentence *what can I do*, they may continue to use the uninverted form for years.

There are, of course, pre-grammatical performance stages which cause the greatest differences between adult and child language. Inability to remember or parse longer sentences restricts both the realization of Universal Grammar and its modification by new inputs.

1.3. *The Role of Primary Linguistic Data*

The parametric theory has other challenges to confront. It ignores a fundamental prior question: how does a child acquire the language structure needed before she can set a parameter? As it stands, the theory presupposes that the child has correctly analyzed the language data which serves as the input to the parametric decision. Incorrectly analyzed input data could, in principle, fix a parameter in a way opposite to the adult language. If the child analyzed "find it" as a clitic, she could incorrectly conclude that she was in a clitic language, which could lead to a mis-analysis of binding relations.

In effect we may have simply shifted the true acquisition problem to an earlier phase: fixation of the primary linguistic data. Unless a step by step system can be devised whereby a child acquires vocabulary and rudimentary syntax without having to decide every issue of his particular grammar beforehand, the parametric model leaves the acquisition problem unsolved. In other words, determination of the features of the input data that have 'epistemological priority', in Chomsky's terms (1981), becomes the primary problem. (See also Pinker's 'bootstrapping model' (1984).)

In addition we can ask: does the child actually use the deductive structure that is available? The question is an important one to ask although it may be difficult to answer. There may be several deductive paths or there may be a possible deductive path but the child prefers an *ad hoc* representation. An analogy lies in the lexicon: one can specify a rule relationship between two words (*expect* and *expectation*), but the child could learn them independently. Likewise there could be a logical relationship between NP-structure and VP-structure (i.e. *X*-bar theory), but the child might not make use of that logical relationship. In effect, parts of the deductive structure may be epi-phenomena.

2. THE DEDUCTIVE APPROACH TO COMPLEMENTIZERS

We will look at deductive structure more closely now. Deductive structure follows from the stipulated interaction of modules. For instance, two theses of UG are:

(7) a.   Every NP requires case
          Verbs, Prepositions, and Tense provide Case
    b.   Verbs have Subjects

Now suppose a child heard a sentence like (7c) and he knew all the words except *rof*:

(7) c.   rof Bill to go is good

The deductive logic (and meaning from context) could provide him with these conclusions:

(8) a.   *to* marks an infinitive (with no tense) and therefore does not assign case,
   b.   *Bill* is the subject of the verb *go* (from context), and needs case,
   c.   *rof* cannot be a verb because it would require a subject,
   d.   therefore *rof* must be a complementizer preposition which assigns case to *Bill*, the subject of the infinitive.

In other words, the deductive logic is powerful enough to identify unique functional lexical items (like *rof*). Why, then, does a child use a complementizer *for*, which is lexically identical to the purposive preposition? The result is that the following sentence is ambiguous. The *for* phrase is either a benefactive of the matrix verb or the subject of the lower verb:

(9)   It is good for the children to be on time

(9) can mean either that the children should be on time or that it is good for the children for unspecified people (like the parents) to be on time. If we had a unique complementizer preposition it would select only the former reading:

(10)   It is good rof the children to be on time.

What we must conclude is this: the grammar does not seem to utilize its own deductive potential.

In fact the same argument can be made with reference to every functional or non-referential element in the language. Suppose a child heard (11)

(11)   Bill decided ot go.

He could infer that *ot* was a complementizer because *go*, lacking a subject and lacking a tense marker, must be an infinitive. Why should *to* be homophonous with a preposition? The same relation holds in divergent languages (French, German, Hebrew).[4]

The same logic applies to the acquisition of expletives. UG provides the child with the assumption that expletive is a possible NP. Therefore if the child were to hear:

(12)   *plet* is a good idea to go

then he should have expletive as an available analysis of *plet*. But the language uses the expletives *it* and *there* which each have independent referential value. If the child hears the expression *it*, then he must be certain that it does not have any referential value. This, in turn, is complicated by the fact that children appear to allow abstract referents before the age of three. Therefore a child cannot simply survey his/her environment and decide that *it* has no reference, because the reference could be abstract. If one hears *it rains*, the *it* could be an agent in the sky.

The argumentation holds in various domains of grammar. The emphatic form of *himself* can violate all of the anaphoric restrictions that hold for anaphoric *himself*. For instance one might hear a sentence of the form: *John hates his torturers. But you can't expect retribution to be carried out all by HIMSELF.* If the child hears such sentences, they will contradict his presumed decisions about binding theory and the scope of reflexives.

There are three paths whereby we can confront these deficiencies of the deductive model. We can

(13) a. attribute the interactions to historical accident,
     b. revise the deductive model,
     c. adduce independent acquisition principles.

Alternative (a) in essence argues that the complementizer preposition is *rof*, following the logic we enunciated, but *rof* happens to be identical to *for* because of the evolution of subject PP's from purpose PPs in English. But the child does not recapitulate the history of English in his recognition of complementizer PP's. Instead, he is occasionally burdened with an unnecessary ambiguity from the historical residue.

Alternative (b) would require us to search for a feature of complementizer PP's that is identical to purpose PP. Although a notion of purpose is often compatible with infinitives, it is not necessary. In the sentence *for it to happen is unusual* the *for* gives case to *it* but there is no sense of purpose that can be associated with *it happen* or *unusual*. Strategy (b) requires us to find a logical connection that cannot be envisioned within current grammatical theory.

Alternative (c) seeks an explanation in the fashion in which a child passes from one stage to another in the acquisition of grammar. Under (c) it is quite plausible that the history of English might be recapitulated if it entailed natural acquisition steps. We will pursue this strategy. One might incorporate such acquisition principles into the adult UG; then (b) is apparently equivalent to (c). However such formulations obscure the true dynamic which lies in the acquisition process and not in the properties of the adult grammar.

3. ACQUISITION CONSTRAINTS

We propose two constraints which should undergo refinement as our grasp of acquisition processes deepens:

(14) a. Parametric choices are linked to lexical items
b. Lexical items are learned via reference

We can project the operation of these principles in the following fashion:

(15) a. Reference ⇒ identification of lexical items.
b. Lexical items *trigger* syntactic functions
c. Syntactic functions *trigger* deletion of reference
d. Syntactic functions *trigger* parametric choices

(15) states that a child begins with the acquisition of words. (See Wexler and Manzini (this volume) for a similar conclusion derived from a completely independent source.) Words then trigger innate syntactic knowledge which is not logically entailed in the referential knowledge. The referential trigger may then disappear or become optional. In effect, a trigger, once in force, disappears. Under this scheme, *for* is learnable and *rof* is not.

The logic of disappearing triggers can be seen in a simple example (see Roeper, 1978, 1982). Suppose a child makes the initial assumption: *noun = concrete object*. This allows him to differentiate nouns from verbs. However the assumption is false since expressions like *the hope* do not involve a concrete object. A second trigger says: articles appear with nouns. When the article is located, then the trigger *noun = concrete object* is dropped (i.e. may or may not be true).[5] In effect, then, the original trigger disappears. (The disappearance of the trigger does not, of course, prevent nouns learned in the future from referring to things.) This approach is in the spirit of what is known about triggers

in biology. All of the examples mentioned above (expletives, complementizers, reflexives) may begin with a referential feature that is then
dropped (i.e. becomes optional, therefore not criterial.) The referential
feature is then a disappearing trigger.

How is (15) simpler than the fictitious deduction leading to knowledge of *rof*? In the deduction which produces knowledge of *rof* several
modules are simultaneously invoked. In effect, in (8) the child must
perform a kind of quadratic equation to find the answer: case-marking,
semantics, X-bar theory are all simultaneously involved. In the model in
(15) we can posit a strong constraint.

(16)   The Modularity Principle (MP):
        Acquisition steps occur only within a single module.

Each change occurs within one module in (15), although the trigger
comes from a different module. If it can be sustained, (15) will place
sharp limitations on patterns of growth and upon UG itself.

3.1. *Two Ontological Predictions*

Our rudimentary model of triggering makes two predictions. The first is
very straightforward: purpose prepositions will precede complementizer
prepositions. A child will say *this is for you* before he will say *for me to
hit is bad*. That is, a word with a new meaning is added to the existing
syntactic class of prepositions, before a new syntactic class (complementizer preposition) is added to the definition of the word. This
sequence can be seen in virtually any acquisition transcript.[6]

A second prediction is subtler: we predict a stage during which
complementizers have only a purposive reading. In other words, the
evolution should follow this sequence, which allows a change in one
module at a time:

(17)   Stage I: for NP, + purpose [fix reference, unmarked
                    syntactic role (PREP)]
        Stage II: for NP, + purpose, + complementizer [add
                    syntactic role (COMP)]
        Stage III: for NP, + complementizer [Purpose → Optional]

This prediction fits an observation made by Slobin in the late 1960s:
"new functions are expressed by old forms".[7] In effect, the purpose
preposition *for* becomes the complementizer prepositon without pur-

pose. A function is added in the syntactic module and then meaning becomes optional in a semantic module. The Modularity Principle prevents a child from adding a complementizer function and deleting the purpose reading simultaneously.

3.2. *Acquisition Evidence*

We turn now to a corpus of data from a child between the ages of 2 and 3 and 1/2:[8]

(18) a. "I got some water for Lola to come back now"
    (= for the purpose of inducing the dog to return)
  b. "grandma has a present for me to blow on"
  c. "some berries for the birds to eat"
  d. "it's for the birds to eat"

(19) a. "these are matches for make a fire"
  b. "this is for I can put some light on, so you won't be cold"
  c. "move it closer for you can get in there"
  d. "I need some more for when my friends come back"
  e. "it's for fix things"
  f. "that's for wiping these off"
  g. "I want for you hold it" ("for you" is benefactive)
  h. "it's too big for you eat"

(20) a. "let's bring a bench for to jump in" (three times)
  b. "I have a place for to put my girls, right here"
  c. "You can have a pocket for to put them in, Dad"
  d. "(What do you want to get in there for?)" "for to eat"
  e. "I can draw something, but I need a pencil for to:
  f. "This milk is for to drink"
  g. "There's one for Mom for to brush he's too"
  h. "These buttons are for to sew on you"
  i. "Toys are for to play with"
  j. "Vitamin C is for to grow"

What is notable about these examples is that they all express *purpose*. There are many other infinitival expressions in the corpus which do not involve purpose ("I want to eat"). No expressions occur of the form *"I want (very much) for you to come*" or the forms:

(21) a. *"I hope for you to win"
     b. *"let's hope for a good day"

The verb *hope* is very common. It is natural for a parent to say *let's hope for a sunny day*. Why do we have no evidence (thus far, lacking a systematic study) that children use *hope for*? Our prediction is that the *for* here does not express purpose but rather it is a part of a complex verb and therefore it will not be learned early. It runs counter to a child's hypothesis (a) that every word should have a referential value and (b) that *for* carries a purpose interpretation. In the same fashion we predict that the acquisition of non-purpose *for* in sentences like *I love for you to carry me* or *for me to jump is fun* will only appear in a later phase.

In sum we have found another instance of a disappearing trigger. In addition we have developed a principle, the Modularity Principle, to explain the existence of grammatical stages in acquisition. The MP is a strong principle and may require modification or it may fail to be true for all combinations of modules.

The MP, at the minimum, has a clarificatory value. It contrasts with the opposite extreme, the instantaneous model: all possible changes, in every module, are instantaneously computed for every new input. The simple fact that acquisition takes time means that evidence is not instantly analyzed. We should therefore seek acquisition principles whose natural execution, if not by logical necessity, produces a temporal dimension.

4. THE MODULARITY PRINCIPLE AND EMPTY CATEGORIES

Now we turn to a far more complex domain: the growth of empty categories (EC). The problem of learning how EC's work resembles the problem of learning pronouns (*she*) and anaphors (*each other*). The acquisition of pronouns involves both (a) the fixation of *reference* and (b) the fixation of *syntactic domains*.

Current Binding Theory (see Chomsky, 1981, 1982) collapses reference and binding into single formulations. The typology of EC's is commonly represented in a feature matrix. The features anaphoric and pronominal are independently applicable. The distinction, seen outside the dynamic process of acquisition, provides little insight into the problem that the child faces. Linguistic theory is able to state two principles in parallel fashion, Principles A and B.

(22)   Principle A says that anaphors are bound in sentences,
         Principle B says that pronominals are free in sentences.

This formulation expresses a parallelism in UG which a child must
eventually fix in his own language. However the formulation obscures
the presence of two distinct modules. In reality, the essence of
pronouns is that they require a referential connection to context. The
essence of anaphors is that they are syntactic in character. In fact, it has
often been suggested that *reference* involves connections to context,
while binding indicates indices or links within syntax. (See Reinhart,
1986; Higginbotham, 1985.) From this perspective, reference and
sentence-internal anaphora should be seen as independent modules.
(See Lust, 1986.)

4.1. *A Brief Look at the Acquisition of Pronouns*

This view of modularity in acquisition has a radical component: the
referential definition of pronominal does not fully correspond to the
UG concept of pronominal. It is a phenomenon within a child's
grammar that is a precursor to the adult grammar. (Note that if
pronominals are initially demonstratives (it = this), then they would be
lexically misanalyzed, but fall within UG (Ken Wexler (pc)).) The UG-
violation perspective differs from the Continuity Hypothesis (see
Roeper, 1981; Klein, 1982; Hyams, 1986; Pinker, 1984):

(23)   All features of UG are unchanged in the acquisition process.

Strictly speaking, we do not argue that the child does not possess some
features of UG. Instead we argue that the MP prevents them from being
instantly applied. Many accounts seek to define a child's initial uses of
pronouns as completely within UG (see Lust, to appear; Manzini and
Wexler, to appear; Jacubowicz, 1984, and Lasnik and Crain, to
appear). Their approach, implicitly or explicitly, is to redefine features
of UG such that child grammar is necessarily expressible in it. This is a
worthwhile strategy but not an inevitably correct one.

Our approach defines the child's notion of pronoun as involving an
'extra-linguistic' dimension (contextual reference without a syntactic
domain) which is not at first expressed within UG. The syntactic
domain specification of Principle B is not present. This approach fits
suggestions by Solan (1983) and Chomsky (1981). They suggest that

'precede' is a possible extra-linguistic dimension which is not stateable as a part of UG, but participates in triggering coreference. It is clearly compatible with the Maturation Hypothesis proposed by Borer and Wexler (this volume). Our approach, therefore, makes a prediction, which in essence (too broadly) says:

(24) a.   Children fix the referential module first.
       b.   Then they fix sentence-internal modules.

This predicts that children will be initially insensitive to (at least some) syntactic constraints on pronouns.

This prediction, in fact, pertains to a current mystery in the acquisition literature: why do children, until the age of six, persistently fail to obey Principle B? They allow *him* to refer to *John* in *John likes him*. The mystery is solved (in part) if our proposal is correct. Children cannot fix both the referential and syntactic character of pronominals simultaneously, therefore their initial use of pronouns does not require them to be "free in their sentences", but 'free' altogether.

A large body of experimental acquisition evidence indicates that children do not obey Principle B. Otsu (1981), Jacubowicz (1984), Manzini and Wexler (this volume), using a wide range of experimental designs, all provide evidence that children do not initially know that *John likes him* cannot be coreferential.[9] Initially, children learn to use pronouns as pointers to context (at a very early age): "that", "gimme it", "throw it" appear in the first word stage. Next children acquire anaphoric expressions like *himself* and *each other*. Positive data readily occurs for anaphors. Only later do they learn that their original pronouns have syntactic as well as contextual definitions.[10]

4.2. *The Substructure of Empty Categories*

What predictions follow for the acquisition of EC's? Let us first consider how a child located an EC. An EC has a lexical dimension. UG generates an EC if a lexical item has an unfilled case-marked position. (This follows what is called the Projection Principle.) If a verb or a preposition requires an object but none is present, then an EC is projected. The child's task is to discern the difference between intransitives and transitives. For instance, he must recognize the difference between *let's play around* and **put it under*. (Most adults would reject "put it under" as ungrammatical although it occurs easily in explicit contexts and in the language of children.) The sentence *let's play around* has an intransitive preposition, while *put it under* [*NP*] is a transitive preposition with an EC. In sum, the child uses the lexicon to determine where EC's occur. This is logically prior to hypotheses about the content of EC's.

The content of EC's is commonly represented with a feature matrix (Chomsky, 1982):

(25) a. *Wh*-trace: = −anaphoric, −pronominal (What did he do trace)
b. NP-trace = +anaphor, −pronominal (John was hit trace)
c. small pro = −anaph, +pronominal (Spanish: John thinks pro went)
d. PRO = +anaph, +pronominal (I want PRO to go)

It is quite possible that a child has a primitive notion of an EC which is less differentiated. Our argument, thus far, makes a distinct prediction: the pronominal characteristics should occur first with free reference. Free reference will allow children to arrive at all adult interpretations. But also it fails to exclude the domain-sensitive readings which are enunciated in the Binding Theory. Therefore the principle overgenerates and allows some readings not found in the adult grammar. Traces should be more difficult to acquire. They require a second act of module-setting in the syntax because they are anaphoric.

4.3. *EC's and Parameters: Unmarked Small pro*

There is another reason why children may not correctly project EC's initially: they exhibit parametric variation across languages. There exists one family of languages, called pro-drop languages, which allows empty subjects in tensed sentences. In Spanish one can say *went*, while in English we must say *he went*. The child requires subtle data to know precisely how EC's behave in a particular language.

In the feature matrix, the small pro is +*pronominal*. This means that it has a definite, contextual reference. Hyams has advanced the claim that all children begin with small pro. She adduces extensive evidence that until children learn to use expletives, they will allow empty subjects in sentences ("Yes, is toys in the kitchen").

Current theory has provided no independent reason to predict that either PRO or pro would be the unmarked case. It is also possible that there is no unmarked case.[11] Our theory provides an explanation for why the pro-drop should be the unmarked case:

(26) a. The reference module is fixed first
     b. +pronominal is triggered by the reference module

Since pro is pronominal and not anaphoric, it should appear first. It is also possible that the EC for pro and PRO are undifferentiated at this point. Both are defined as +pronominal. At a later point PRO also acquires +anaphoric. If EC's in general are +pronominal, then Hyams' prediction follows.[12]

Let us now return to the evidence that we have presented in (19). A number of examples have the form: "let's bring a bench for to jump in". The child allows *for* to appear without an object. The preposition *for* is transitive; therefore an object is obligatory and case-marked. An EC is possible only if the child allows small pro which can appear in case-marked environments. Therefore we have independent evidence in behalf of the Unmarked pro Hypothesis.

There are some alternatives which deserve attention. If a child generates an *S-bar* after *for*, then case-assignment would be blocked:

(27)   for $[_{\text{S-bar}}$ $[_{\text{S}}$ to grow

In effect, the *for* would function as a conjunction (as in archaic forms "For he's a jolly good fellow"). There are three reasons to argue against this hypothesis, although they are not conclusive.[13]

I. We find that the *for* can assign case in examples like "grandma has a present for me to blow on". If S-bar were present, then we would have "for I . . .".

II. Phinney (1981) has evidence that children below three do not generate an S-bar. For instance, they delete *that* in sentence repetition tasks.

III. The assumption that the child uses *for* as a conjunction does not confront a central issue: how does the child eliminate the *for to* sequence? For adults, the sentences cited are clearly ungrammatical. The child must have some principle which allows their elimination from his/her grammar. We argue that if small pro is present then the child can eliminate the *for to* sequence as a consequence of the decision that English is not a pro-drop language.

4.4. *The Argument for Grammar Narrowing*

The elimination of a feature of grammar has been called 'delearnability': (Klein, 1982), or 'Retreat' (Randall, 1982). We shall call it grammar narrowing (GN). Our choice of words reflects a particular emphasis: the new grammar is smaller than the earlier ones. In effect it violates the subset principle (Berwick, 1982). Grammar changes that are motivated by GN refer to parametric variation rather than the logical necessity that positive data expand the grammar. We can illustrate the difference. The Positive Data theory can account for expansion of a child's grammar:

(28)   The grammar is expanded to include a piece of input data

The GN Principle uses input data to set a parameter which then eliminates a structure. The elimination of data means that the grammar is *prima facie*, smaller.

(29)   A structure in a child's grammar is eliminated to fulfill parametric implications.

The parametric implication in binding theory is that Principles A and B are in complementary distribution. The parametric implication for EC's is that where expletives are present small *pro* is eliminated. All of the data we have adduced above represent structures that must be eliminated in the adult grammar. Therefore the GN approach is neces- sary. For the data at hand, it means the elimination of structures which allow *pro* from a language which does not allow pro.

We wish to introduce here the notion that GN can be a decisive feature in a choice of representation for a child. If we could use either trace or pro to represent the child's grammar, then pro is superior if the structure must eventually be eliminated. We turn now to the domain of Object EC's where these arguments play a role.

4.5. *The Representation of Missing Objects*

Many of the sentences in (20) contain a second EC. We repeat them here with additions:

(30) a. "toys are for to play with _____"
     b. "these buttons are for to sew _____ on you"
     c. "this milk is for to drink _____"
     d. "you can have a pocket for to put them in _____ Dad"

(31) a. "I want my something to drink to hold _____"
  b. "I want something to eat on the way to bring _____"
  c. "I want a paper to cut with _____"
  d. "Mommy will you help me with my brocoli to eat _____"
  e. "I'm making some for you to pull _____" (= to pull you)
  f. "I forgot my pants to pull up _____"
  g. "let's make a list ice cream to get _____"

These sentences do not occur in the adult language. They involve an object gap in an infinitive with the object pre-posed within the infinitive ("ice cream to get", "my pants to pull up", "something to drink to hold") or subject control from a higher clause ("toys$_i$ are for to play with _____ $_i$). The former must be excluded in the adult grammar while the latter remain perfectly grammatical. We will outline three approaches to these sentences within GB; we treat each approach in some depth because we do not believe that any of them can be definitively rejected without a greater wealth of data and the resolution of theoretical issues.

Two possible analyses come to mind. One possibility is that these sentences involve what has been called 'free adjunction' of an infinitival *with a gap in it*, in effect a pro. The gap within the infinitival would be base-generated. Possibly there would be co-indexation between the gap and the NP or the relation could be determined pragmatically.[14] A second possibility is that the sequence *NP to VP EC* originates in a clausal expression where the NP originates in the EC position. This possibility entails the use of Move-alpha and the interpretation of EC as trace.

4.5.1. *Free adjunction*. The notion of adjunction has to be differentiated from lexically controlled subcategorization. Adjunction is possible with a loose relation to a clause. It is possible that adjunction is replaced by subcategorization in the grammar of children as their knowledge of lexical entailments increases. In any case, there appears to be evidence for some free adjunction:

(32) a. "I got some water for Lola to come back now"
      (= for the purpose of inducing the dog to return)
  b. "I am strong to do that"
  c. "It is priddy to do that here"

In the adult grammar adjectives are variously subcategorized or not subcategorized for a complement, but free adjunction is not possible. Therefore we have a contrast between *it is possible to sing* and **it is probable to sing*, where the latter is disallowed in the adult grammar because *probable* does not subcategorize for a clause.

We can represent these facts with adjunction to either S or VP.

(33) a.

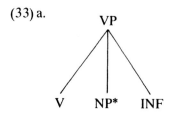

b.

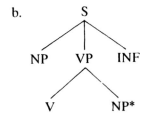

The grammar under consideration must permit adjunction of the infinitival complement to either VP (33a) or to S (33b), as proposed by Tavakolian (1981).[15] Takahashi (1983) presents arguments that the kind of data previously dealt with in the literature should better be treated in terms of Chomsky-adjunctioin of complements to VP.

How can we integrate the object EC cases into this analysis? In effect they have a representation of the following form:

(34)   I forgot [$_{NP}$ my pants] [$_S$ EC$_1$ to pull EC$_2$ up]

The use of the adjunct analysis for infinitives with an object EC is superior under the VP analysis because it allows the EC to be *c*-commanded by a coreferential NP.[16]

Expressions like (34) could then be regarded as a precursor to purpose clauses, which, in adult grammar, are considered to be VP-adjuncts with an object EC[17].

(35) a.   John bought it [EC to read EC]
     b.   The dean is here [EC to talk to EC]

This analysis is satisfactory for sentences of the form "toys are for to play with". But it will not account for (34) of "Help me with my broccoli to eat EC" for a simple reason: the latter sentence fails to conform to the semantics requirements of purpose clauses (Bach, 1982). They require that the verb should denote positive transition, creation, or existence, of a certain object or individual. Similarly, *forget* does not have this character so it cannot be used in these environments.

(35) c. *I forgot it to read

The only way to sustain a purpose clause analysis for (30) is to claim that the child *learns* the subtle semantic restrictions on purpose clauses, which leads to the elimination of the (ultimately) ungrammatical sentences. It is very unclear how this could be done.

   The purpose-clause analysis also fails to meet the c-command criterion for those sentences where the EC$_2$ controller (NP$_2$) is within a PP.

(36)

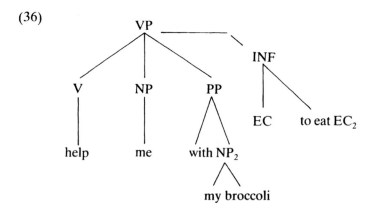

Goodluck (1981) has shown that young children are aware of PP as being a branching node preventing c-command. Therefore the purpose-clause analysis fails syntactically.

   In sum, we have found that purpose-clause analysis fits a portion of the data from a young child. However it fails both semantically and syntactically to account for another portion.

4.5.2. *The movement analysis.* A fundamental precept of modern grammar is the notion of preservation of information in a 'deep' structure. The preservation of information can take various avenues. It can be construed in a syntactic sense to mean that if a verb takes an object in one structure, the object must be invisibly represented in all structures. A current version of that claim is that both the syntactic position and the thematic content are fixed at deep-structure. It is called the Projection Principle. Chomsky (1981) has argued that it constitutes a natural constraint on acquisition.[18] The child knows that a particular verb must have an object and therefore seeks an NP to fill that thematic role.

Under the adjunction theory, a sentence of the form "I forgot my pants to pull up" would have *my pants* as the object of *forget*. It is obvious, though, that the sentence does not entail the meaning *I forgot my pants*. That is, *forget* does not assign a thematic role to *my pants*. The meaning of the sentence is : forgot [$_s$ my pants to pull EC up]. This representation is unobtainable — "my pants" has no thematic home — unless it acquires its thematic interpretation from the object position of *pull up*. The adult representation of such a sentence would capture the relation with a trace in the object position:

(37)   [my pants [to pull trace up]

Now we must confront a new range of questions about the plausible syntactic structure in which to embed a trace.

There are two related questions to address: what position does *my pants* occupy and what kind of trace is involved. There are two possible structures: adjunction to the subject S (38) or S-bar (39):

(38)   I forgot [$_s$ EC to pull (my pants) up]
(39)   I forgot [$_s$ COMP [$_s$ EC to pull (my pants) up]

We shall examine arguments for each structure. Phinney (1981) provides evidence that children may not have S-bar, which would rule out (39). In addition, it is important to remember that our goal is to find a structure whose elimination is natural. The primary defect with (38) is that it involves a violation of the Projection Principle (PrP) which projects an AGENT role onto the subject position.

We could argue that the PrP is not always effective, but this is an unnatural move. The primary disadvantage with this proposal is that it eliminates the connection between the lexicon and the syntax. If syntax can be projected from lexical items via the PrP, then we have a direct connection between the syntax and the lexicon.[19]

Another possibility is that the object occupies subject position under a primitive version of middle formation. Keyser and Roeper (1984) have argued that the structure of a middle like *bureaucrats bribe easily* involves a trace in the object position after *bribe*. Note that it is possible to have forms like: *bureaucrats seem to bribe easily*. Nonetheless this analysis of our data seems remote because children in this age range (a) do not use simple middle constructions[20] (b) do not use an adverb like *easily*, and (c) there is no trace of the generic in the semantics of these sentences.

In addition, movement to subject position in (38) is a form of NP-movement. The noun moves from one theta-position to another. Borer and Wexler (to appear) have argued that all forms of NP-movement are subject to maturation and are not within a child's grammar.

Finally, none of these solutions offers a means whereby a child could eliminate such structures. Therefore this apporach seems less promising. We turn now to an argument that Wh-movement is involved.

4.5.3. '*Wh*'-*movement.* The operation of *Wh*-movement moves a constituent to a non-argument (A-bar) position. The COMP node, introduced by S-bar, constitutes an A-bar position. There are two other logical possibilities: a TOPIC node and adjunction to S in pre-subject position.

The TOPIC option is generally excluded for subordinate clauses. However if we assumed that the infinitive was not subordinate, but instead there was an S freely adjoined to the topmost S, we might have a viable way to generate a TOPIC position. When the child learned that the infinitive was subordinated, then the TOPIC position would be eliminated and therefore topicalization would be eliminated. It constitutes a more radical departure from the adult grammar, and it does not contribute to our argument naturally, but it remains a tenable hypothesis. We will argue instead for adjunction to S.

4.5.4. *Trace or pro in theory.* Before we proceed, let us digress to consider the appropriate linguistic analysis. Chomsky analyzes these strucures with an Operator and a *Wh*-trace:

(40)   I bought it$_i$ [O_i [to sell t_i]]

We can also represent these examples in the same fashion:

(41)   "toys$_i$ are for [O_i [to play with t_i]]"

In addition, it is evident that children have a *Wh*-movement in single clause sentences from an early age ("What you are doing").

Cinque (1984) has proposed, using a wide range of facts, that purpose clauses should be represented with a small pro. The indexing mechanism that operates between *Wh*-trace and Operator can also index pro to perform what is called the Identification function. The use of small pro explains the absence of long-distance (successive cyclic) movements in purpose clauses. Cinque presents a wide range of other arguments to support a small pro analysis of parasitic gap constructions and *that* relative clauses.

Chomsky (p.c.) offers a critique of Cinque's approach. He observes that long distance movement exists with purpose clauses and parasitic gaps (and moveover it observes subjacency):

(42)   I want something [$_S$ to get Bill [$_S$ to play with _____]]

Therefore trace rather than pro should fill the EC. The facts from acquisition, we argue, reveal the virtues in both approaches.

The presence of "toys are to play with" in the grammar of a two-and-a-half year old stands in stark contrast to the demonstrable inability of 6—7 year olds to process successive cyclic *Wh*-movement correctly. In work by Roeper, Rooth, Akiyama, and Mallis (1984) experimental evidence from over 160 children ranging in age from 3—10 years, it was found that children to age 7 persistently failed to observe strong crossover in sentences of the form:

(43) a.   who$_i$ does he$_i$ think _____ $_i$ has a hat
     b.   who$_i$ thinks he$_i$ has a hat

Whereas adults do not allow a bound reading for (43a), only for (43b), children up until the age of 7 permitted bound readings in both structures. This result is compatible with the view that the children allow the *Wh*-word to *c*-command the gap and therefore assign coreference. In a word, the children are very slow to master successive cyclic *Wh*-movement. What is the content of the gap if it is not a trace that moves into COMP and successive cyclic movement? Since the subject position of the tensed clause is case-marked, once again we must argue that it is small pro.

There is some explicit evidence in behalf of this view. In work by Nishigauchi, Otsu, and Takahashi (1984) they report that in an experiment with ten children between 4 and 8, there were nine instances where children would respond to the question "A car is to ...?" with the answer "drive it", rather than simply *drive*. Four children were involved and they were in the 5—6 age range. Their responses suggest that, predictably, the small pro can appear as a residual pronoun.

Our argument thus far supports Cinque's analysis. However we must take a further step: explanation of the shift to a grammar where *for to* and preposing in infinitives is excluded, and successive cyclic movement is possible. This shift correlates exactly with the introduction of long-distance *Wh*-movement.

Introduction (or possibly modification) of an S-bar COMP node should suddenly license successive cyclic movement. The child has a position through which successive cyclic movement is possible. When a child confronts the fact that successive cyclic rules are necessary, he must convert all *pro* to *trace* in those environments.

4.5.5. *S-adjunction.*
Our argument has seized upon a correlation at the moment of attainment of the adult grammar: the child replaces pro with trace and adds an S-bar COMP node. Suddenly we have an instance of parametric growth: successive cyclic movement is possible (through COMP), strong cross-over restrictions appear on coreference (because *trace* replaces *pro*), and it is no longer possible to prepose objects in infinitives ("I forgot my pants to pull up") because the S-bar blocks case-assignment. This is just the kind of growth we expect: a small shift in the abstract features of a language has widespread, apparently disconnected results in the new set of grammatical sentences. The results, moreover, include the narrowing of the grammar as well as its expansion: sentences like those we have cited, which were grammatical, are rendered ungrammatical.

Two major questions remain unaddressed: first, what does the pre-final node structure look like? The pre-final structure must have two characteristics: (1) it must account for the data within UG, and (2) it must provide a basis for re-analysis, that is, for what has been called 'delearnability' or 'retreat' in the literature. We will suggest a minimal difference between the child's grammar and the adult grammar. The second question is: why does the child project these structures? We suggest that the child's extra adjunction rule is a primitive form of QR (quantifier raising) in the sense of May (1977). This instance of Move Alpha, which applies in the syntax, will disappear in a later stage with the introduction of the variable, which constitutes a 'chain' together with the moved element, on one hand, and S-bar, which blocks case-assignment of the moved element, on the other. This analysis roughly coincides with recent work by Chomsky (1986) on 'barriers'.

We argue that the preposed NP occupies an A-bar position defined by an extra S node rather than an S-bar node. In effect the following structure exists:

(44)

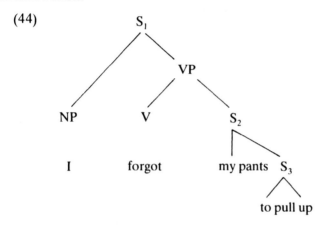

the S_2 is not an S-bar but a simple projection of S in the manner of X-bar projections for NP and VP. The node S_2 differs from S-bar precisely in not being a barrier to case-assignment and not defining a COMP node escape hatch for long-distance movement.

The projection of a higher S-node will allow "my pants" to receive case from a higher verb although it receives a theta-role from a lower verb. In order for it not to receive case, the NP must not be moved by Wh-movement but rather must be directly projected in pre-subject position. In order to prevent the NP from having two cases, one from the higher verb and one from the trace, we must argue that no movement has taken place. Instead there is a small pro in object position. In short, everything conspires to argue for the child's initial use of pro and initial absence of S-bar.

We can also imagine what the eventual stimulus to re-analysis may be: the attempt to provide a grammatical representation for long-distance movement. Children will find themselves in situations where they understand what the following sentence means: *what did you say you wanted.* They then seek to make an adjustment in their grammars to allow such sentences. The adjustment is to allow the existence of a COMP node that serves as an escape hatch: $[_{COMP}$ what$_i$ $[_S$ did you say $[_{COMP}$ t_i $[_S$ you wanted $t_i]]$. The escape hatch must also function as a barrier to case-assignment if *Wh*-words are to retain case-marking from their origin.

Then, in turn, the S_2 could not continue to function if an S-bar is present, since the S-bar would always block case-assignment from the higher verb. We find no instances of the data in question in later protocols taken from the same child. We are currently seeking to substantiate our analysis with the analysis of other children, but there is little spontaneous data available from older children.

Our evidence contains a further instance of S-projection.

(45)   Help me with my broccoli to eat
        This is for dinner to eat (= a spoon, i.e. to eat my dinner
        with)

The prepositions in question subcategorize for an NP but not for an S. The child has projected a sentential subcategorization by herself. This projection is predictable on the basis of a feature of universal grammar uncovered by Grimshaw (1981) (see also Pesetsky, 1982):

(46)   If a verb is subcategorized in such a way that it governs NP,
        it may also govern a clause.

The child therefore can hear "with Bill" and project the grammaticality of "with to eat broccoli". It is notable that, once again, where UG dictates the presence of S-bar, the child projects an S which is transparent to case-assignment, such that the subject of the clause receives case from the preposition. (We expect that the unpreposed version "with to eat broccoli" can also occur.)

In sum, once again, when the child is ready to incorporate long-distance movement in his grammar, the S-bar is forced into existence to prevent case-assignment. The fact that this requires evidence for instantiation correlates with the putative fact that there exist languages in which there is no long distance movement and therefore in which no S-bar is necessary.

4.5.6. *Summary.* Let us review the phenomenon. We have argued that there is an absence of a COMP node which serves as a barrier to case-assignment. Then we have been confronted with the presence of fronted objects in children's language. In addition, the PRO subject position is controlled in cases like *I forgot my pants to pull up*. Were a middle to occur in the embedded clause, as in *John prefers pants to pull up easily*, then the agent-subject position would receive a generic interpretation and not a controlled interpretation. If the COMP position is not present and the PRO subject is controlled, then there is no position into which to put the fronted object. We therefore projected an additional S-node.

A complex argument about linguistic theory and a claim about children's syntactic immaturity (absence of S-bar COMP node) conspire to predict the possibility that the fronted NP receives case. Consequently movement (or indexing between an NP and pro) is possible just at this moment of language growth. In fact, we find that indeed NP's are adjoined to the dominating S. This possibility disappears in the adult grammar with the introduction of S-bar, blocking case-assignment, and therefore such sentences are ungrammatical in the adult language. It is precise and subtle predictions which make a theory robust.

The evidence in our discussion is admittedly slim. It would be advantageous to receive further confirmation from different diary studies. The importance of the data at hand should not, however, be minimized. It is often observed that in tightly constructed scientific domains, for example physics, very small amounts of evidence are sufficient to confirm or deny strong hypotheses.

4.6. *Parameters and Time*

We have provided a number of environments in which small pro is arguably the content of a child's EC. They make a coherent argument with one exception: the temporal dimension. Hyams' version of how the pro-drop parameters is set would eliminate all pro's in the grammar of three-year-olds. Our evidence suggests that children continue to use pro until the age of seven.[21]

This sequence is explainable if we make two assumptions:

(1) subparameters exist which require their own evidence

(2) an excluded parameter can function as an 'Elsewhere' condition

The expletive fixes English as a non-pro-drop language. However, small pro will not be excluded from *Wh*-environments until the child revises his grammar to include successive cyclic movement. Although *Wh*-environments remain compatible with both pro and trace, the child will prefer trace to achieve parametric harmony (i.e. elimination of all small pro's consistent with the pro-drop parameter).

We can distinguish the notions of parameter from subparameter through the notion of compatability. Fixation of a parameter introduces, in effect, a new unmarked case. Until the parameter is fixed either there is no unmarked case or one possibility is unmarked. When the parameter is fixed, producing a new unmarked case, then all ambiguous instances are interpreted with reference to the unmarked preference. When the parameter is fixed against small pro, then although it remains an Elsewhere option, the child will always favor trace or big PRO because it is compatible with the parametric setting. In the case of successive cyclic movement, it is trace.

The notion that small pro is available as an Elsewhere condition is equivalent to a suggestion by Cinque that the appearance of residual pronouns constitutes a predictable feature of the small pro approach. In effect, where performance conditions cannot be met, the child or adult can revert to the pro analysis. Then simple contextual reference is possible and no indices must be computed. The definition of English as a non-pro-drop language gives the speaker the intuition that residual pronouns are semi-grammatical or substandard.[22]

5. CONCLUSION

Our argument has some major thrusts which should be seen separately from the intricate analyses in which they play a role.

We have argued for a number of acquisition principles.

(1) The Modularity Principle predicts that children will make single changes within a module. Therefore grammatical stages in language growth will appear.

(2) There is a primitive EC which is pro. It is the natural primitive because it is initially defined within a referential module and not a binding module. The child's version of reference and binding decomposes the Binding Theory in a way that is not obvious from an instantaneous perspective.

(3) A large range of evidence including subjectless sentences, "for to" sentences, object preposing sentences, *Wh*-movement sentences, all point to pro as a primitive EC.

(4) After the pro-drop parameter is set by the presence of expletives, there are a series of subparameters, sensitive to their own evidence, which must be set. The presence of successive cyclic long-distance sentences forces the child to substitute trace for pro in a variety of *Wh*-contexts. The result is that parameter-setting is not instantaneous.

In sum, we have developed an account of the course of language acquisition which fits both the theory of empty categories and the Binding theory. Our strategy has been to decompose these theories into modules which fit natural acquisition principles. In effect we argue that UG principles exist in a slightly different form in earlier stages of acquisition.

NOTES

* Thanks to N. Chomsky for comments on an earlier draft. Also we would like to thank G. Cinque, and audiences at GLOW, MIT, Irvine, and UMass for comments. This work was supported in part by a grant from the Sloan Foundaton and an NSF grant to T. Roeper and E. Williams.

[1] There is a literature on this topic which reveals how these two consequences follow. In particular, Chomsky (1965), Wexler and Culicover (1981) and references therein, Roeper (1978), Pinker (1984) and references. In effect if grammars can be formulated in infinite sets of ways, then the order of exposure will determine the nature of the grammar, since each new sentence will modify the old grammar. The only way to guarantee the same grammar for all people is to project a set of possible grammars for a representative set of sentences and then choose the simplest. Since the child hears sentences in virtually random order, he must have a mechanism which orders the input (and hence ignores most sentences) if all people have the same grammar. All of this reasoning becomes unnecessary in a parametric model.

[2] See Matthews (to appear), Wexler and Manzini (this volume) for a discussion of the role of Independence in parameter setting.

[3] See Sells (1984) for an extremely interesting differentiation of resumptive pronoun languages.

[4] Fabb (1984) and also Roeper and Vergnaud (1981) have argued that verbs must also receive case under government. The child might then learn *to* as a general case-assigner. The child can learn *to* as a preposition with a particular meaning, then delete the meaning but keep the case-assigning function in complement structures. This would provide an alternative deductive path, though not necessarily a superior one, to the recognition of *to* as a case-assigning complementizer.

[5] Grimshaw (1981) takes a related but crucially different point of view. She claims that the notion of thing continues to be a part of the core definition of noun. It is not clear that the notion of 'core' here has any effects in the adult grammar, i.e. that *the car* has a status as a noun different from *the hope* for an adult. See also Stowell (1984, lecture Amherst).

[6] It is very clear in the transcripts that T. Roeper has collected from his daughter.

[7] See Slobin (1973).

[8] Collected by T. Roeper. Informal discussion with other acquisition researchers reveals that the phenomena occur with other children. Obviously it would be valuable to study it in several children. A diary study rather than occasional tapes is necessary because crucial sentences may not appear in a random sampling of a few hours.

[9] The constraint holds in an absolute sense only for quantifiers: *everyone likes him*. It remains an open question whether children will also make errors of coreference on quantifiers. There is a substantial literature on this topic. See Otsu (1981), Manzini and Wexler (this volume), Jacubowicz (1984), and the papers in Lust (1986).

[10] We think the answer follows from the MP together with a feature of how UG is instantiated. If we assume that UG features must be instantiated, then there must be evidence for them. In effect, a child does not receive direct evidence that pronouns cannot be referential within a single domain. He does receive evidence that anaphoric pronouns are coreferential within a sentence. In a sense, then, the child does not receive positive evidence about Principle B. The fact that he hears cases where pronouns refer outside the clause does not prove that they cannot refer inside the clause. He must learn the restrictions on pronouns as a reflex of an independent piece of data together with the effort to achieve 'parametric harmony' (see Principle (29) herein). That is, after he learns Principe A, his acquisition device chooses to make Principle B operate in complementary distribution.

[11] Rizzi (1986) has suggested that PRO may be the unmarked case. There is a natural learnability argument in behalf of this view. There exists positive evidence to indicate that subjects are optional, but there can be no positive evidence that something is obligatory. Therefore obligatoriness is a natural first assumption. However, a powerful concept of parameters could introduce the notion of obligatoriness. For instance, the parameter might read: if an expletive is present, then subjects are obligatory. It is only in a non-parametric system that the concept is underivable.

[12] See Roeper *et al.* (1984), and Wexler and Manzini (this volume) for relevant discussion.

[13] Thanks to G. Cinque for suggesting this perspective.

[14] In either case, the connective could be *thematically* linked. See Nishigauchi (1984) and Jones (1985)

[15] See a variety of papers arguing for S-adjunction in Tavakolian ed. (1981).

[16] By this phrase some of the syntactic constraints seem to have been instantiated, in particular the *c*-command feature. (The domain specifications apparently take longer, and are subject to language variation.) See literature on *c*-command, particularly Solan (1983), also Lust (to appear). It would be natural to seek an explanation using the MP for the observed bias towards forwards anaphora in child language. (See Roeper, 1985, forthcoming.) In fact such a system is readily imaginable.

[17] See Faraci (1973), and Jones (1985), who offers extensive discussion of the 'free adjunct' option.

[18] Finer and Roeper (to appear) have argued for it as a constraint on lexical derivations as well.

[19] The evolution of the subject position and its thematic properties is an interesting topic by itself. (See discussion by Anne Vainikka, 1985). It is possible that the comple-

ment subject position in children's grammars may be optionally non-thematic. Consider the following utterances from one child (but found among others as well):

(i)   "help my eat it"
        "see my ride it"
        "I want Ria's get it"
        "see my do it backwards"
        "I want do my rake"

If Williams (1982) is correct that nominalizations allow a free interpretation of possessives, then this could be true for children as well.

[20] There seem to be a very few examples like "it fixes by glue", but not many.

[21] See Van Riemsdijk comments in Lust (to appear) for an interesting discussion of the typology of EC's and their development. See Sells (1984) for an extremely interesting discussion of residual pronoun languages and binding.

[22] In addition the *for to* dialect, though not fully explained, is not a mystery under our account. In some dialects in the South and Ontario, the *for* present in child language is not eliminated with the demise of pro. How could it be retained? One possibility is that there is some pragmatic interpretation which attaches to the *for to* sequence. Therefore this structure resists parametric harmony. However it is defined as exceptional and therefore will not generalize.

REFERENCES

Bach, E.: 1982, 'Purpose clauses and control', in P. Jacobsen and G. Pullum, *On the Nature of Syntactic Representation*, D. Reidel, Dordrecht.

Berwick, R.: 1982, *Locality Principles and the Acquisition of Syntactic Knowledge*, MIT dissertation.

Borer, H. and K. Wexler (this volume), 'The maturation of syntax'.

Chomsky, N.: 1965, *Aspects of a Theory of Syntax*, MIT Press.

Chomsky, N.: 1981, *Lectures on Government and Binding*, Foris Publications, Dordrecht.

Chomsky, N.: 1982, *Some Concepts and Consequences*, MIT Press.

Chomsky, N.: 1986, *Barriers*, MIT Press.

Cinque, G.: 1984, 'A-bar bound vs. variable', Universita di Venezia.

Fabb, N.: 1984, *Syntactic Affixation*, MIT dissertation.

Faraci, R.: 1974, *Aspects of the Grammar of Infinitives and For-phrases*, MIT dissertation.

Finer, D and T. Roeper: to appear, 'From cognition to thematic roles: The projection principle and the lexicon.'

Goodluck, H.: 1981, 'Children's grammar of complement subject interpretation', in Tavakolian *op. cit.*

Grimshaw, J.: 1981, 'Form, function, and the language acquisition Device', in *The Logical Problem of Language Acquisition* (1981), MIT Press.

Higginbotham, J.: 1985, 'On semantics', *Linguistic Inquiry* **16**(4), MIT Press.

Hyams, N.: 1986, *Language Acquisition and the Theory of Parameters*, D. Reidel, Dordrecht.

Jacubowicz, C.: 1984, 'On markedness and binding principles', *NELS* **14**.

Jones, C.: 1985, *Syntax and Thematics of Infinitival Adjuncts*, University of Massachusetts dissertation.

Keyser, S. J. and T. Roeper: 1984, 'On the middle and ergative constructions in English', *Linguistic Inquiry* **15**(3), MIT Press.

Klein, S.: 1982, *Syntactic Theory and the Developing Grammar*, UCLA Dissertation.

Koopman, H.: 1985, *The Syntax of Verbs*, Foris Publications, Dordrecht.

Lasnik, H. and S. Crain: to appear, 'Review of "On the acquisition of pronominal reference" by L. Solan', *Lingua*.

Lust, B.: 1986, 'Introduction to *Studies in the Acquisition of Anaphora*', D. Reidel, Dordrecht.

May, R. and R. Matthews: to appear, *Proceedings of Ontario Conference on Learnability*, D. Reidel, Dordrecht.

Matthei, E.: 1981, 'Children's Interpretations of Sentences Containing Reciprocals', in S. Tavakolian, *Language Acquisition and Linguistic Theory*, MIT Press.

Matthews, R.: to appear, 'Introduction', to R. May and R. Matthews.

Nishigauchi, T.: 1984, 'Control and the thematic domain', *Language* **60**(2).

Nishigauchi, T., Y. Otsu, and M. Takahashi: 1984, 'The acquisition of tough and related constructions in English', Paper read at Kobe University.

Otsu, Y.: 1981, *Universal Grammar and Syntactic Development in Children*, MIT dissertation.

Pesetsky, D.: 1982, *Paths and Categories*, MIT Dissertation.

Phinney, M.: 1981, *Syntactic Constraints and the Acquisition of Embedded Sentential Complements*, University of Massachusetts dissertation.

Pinker, S.: 1984, *Language Learnability and Language Development*, Harvard University Press.

Randall, J.: 1982, *Morphological Structure and Language Acquisition*, University of Massachusetts dissertation (to appear), Garland.

Randall, J.: 1985, Boston University talk on Retreat Strategies.

Reinhardt, T.: 1986, 'Center and periphery in the acquisition of grammar', in Lust *op. cit.*

Roeper, T.: 1978, 'Linguistic universals and the acquisition of gerunds', in H. Goodluck and L. Solan (eds.), *Language Acquisition: The State of the Art*, Cambridge University Press, Cambridge.

Roeper, T.: 1982, 'Linguistic universals and the acquisition of gerunds', in L. Gleitman and E. Wanner, *Language Acquisition: The State of the Art*, CUP.

Roeper, T. and J. R. Vergnaud: 1981, 'On the government of infinitives', University of Massachusetts ms.

Roeper, T., M. Rooth, L. Mallis, and A. Akiyama: 1984, 'The problem of empty categories and bound variables in language acquisition', University of Massachusetts ms.

Roeper, T.: to appear, 'Theory, process, and mechanism in language acquisition', Proceedings of Conference on Mechanisms in Language Acquisition, Carnegie-Mellon University (1985).

Sells, P.: 1984, *Syntax and Semantics of Resumptive Pronouns*, University of Massachusetts dissertation.

Slobin, D.: 1973, 'Cognitive prerequisites for the development of grammar', in D. Slobin and C. Ferguson, *Studies in Child Language Development*, Holt.

Solan, L.: 1983, *On the Acquisition of Pronominal Reference*, D. Reidel, Dordrecht.
Stowell, T.: Paper presented at Amherst Conference on Parameter setting.
Takahashi, M.: 1984, *The Acquisition of Embedded Clauses*, M.A. thesis, Osaka University.
Tavakolian, S.: 1981, ed. *Language Acquisition and Linguistic Theory*, MIT Press.
Vainikka, A.: 1985, 'A theory of default rules', University of Massachusetts ms.
van Riemsdijk, H.: to appear, 'Comments on *Anaphoric Binding*', ed. by B. Lust.
Wexler, K and P. Culicover: 1981, *Formal Principles of Language Acquisition*, MIT Press.
Wexler, K. and R. Manzini (this volume), 'Parameters and Learnability'.
Williams, E. S.: 1982, 'The NP cycle', *Linguistic Inquiry* **13**(2).

HAGIT BORER AND KENNETH WEXLER

THE MATURATION OF SYNTAX*

1. THE ROLE OF MATURATION IN THE EXPLANATION OF LINGUISTIC DEVELOPMENT

1.1. *Continuity or Maturation?*

In recent years there has been a good deal of effort devoted to the problem of the development of linguistic representations. An active group of investigators is attempting to simultaneously figure out how linguistic representations can be attained given the limited data available to the child (the problem of learnability) and to understand why the course of development takes the actual form that it does. Needless to say, these problems interact. While concentration on both problems expands the goal of study, thereby making the ultimate solution more difficult to attain, the double concentration also has the effect of bringing a greater body of evidence to bear on the fundamental problem of the growth of language, thereby aiding in attempted solutions.

It is now accepted among a body of investigators that there are innate formal principles of grammar in the child's mind, and that these innate principles play a substantial role in the development in the adult of a particular grammar. Thus the innate principles contribute in a major way to the solution of the problem of learnability. At the same time it is clear that the innate principles are guiding the construction of the child's grammar. Thus the innate formal principles also play an explanatory role in the study of the time course of linguistic development.

The basic picture that has emerged is that the child is equipped at birth with a set of principles (called Universal Grammar, UG), a variety of places where variation can occur (for example, parameters that can be set, a lexicon that can be filled in), and a learning procedure (usually a fairly simple procedure based on fitting evidence to principles) which indicates how the possibilities for variation are to be fixed. (We intend here to be very general, capturing a variety of linguistic-based approaches.) A fundamental feature of these theories is that UG, the set

123

Thomas Roeper and Edwin Williams (eds.), Parameter Setting, 123–172.
© 1987 *by D. Reidel Publishing Company.*

of principles, is fixed and unchanging. For the most part, the learning procedure is also considered to be fixed and unchanging. This hypothesis — that the principles that the child uses to fix her/his grammar are constant over the course of development of the child — has been called the 'continuity hypothesis' by Pinker (1984).

The purpose of this paper is to challenge the continuity hypothesis. In particular we will propose a theory for the development of certain aspects of linguistic competence. This theory is in contradiction to the continuity hypothesis. It does not assume that the formal principles available to the child are constant through development. Rather, the assumption is that certain principles mature. The principles are not available at certain stages of a child's development, and they are available at a later stage. We definitely and clearly hypothesize that the principles are *not* learned. That is, the principles do not depend for their development on the child's obtaining evidence. Rather, the principles mature. Like any other instance of biological maturation, the principles take time to develop, but the particular character of experience during this time is not what makes the principles develop. As analogy, we have in mind, for example, the maturation of secondary sexual characteristics, which do not develop until adolescence. Nobody would argue that, in essence, these characteristics are 'learned'. Of course, there may be some effect of experience. Thus onset time of puberty might be related to nutrition. But the actual experiences do not guide the essential structure of the development of these characteristics. Rather, the underlying biological program guides this development, taking time to unfold. In the same way, we are suggesting that linguistic principles might mature. Extensive experience with language might have some effect on the exact time that the principles develop and, perhaps, on certain less basic details. But we are proposing that the biological program underlying the formal principles guides their development over time.

The maturational hypothesis is in no way an argument for 'learning' or an argument against the existence of innate linguistic universals. The claim that certain linguistic properties mature is consistent with what is known about many innate biological systems — that they mature. Thus the analogy to the development of biological systems is even stronger under the maturational hypothesis. It is well-known that many aspects of the brain mature after birth. On the assumption that linguistic properties are situated in the brain, it is quite plausible that linguistic properties mature.[1]

In fact, it is quite clear that the maturation hypothesis is a stronger innateness hypothesis than the continuity hypothesis. This is because a child is not born with fully developed language. Rather, language develops over time. Suppose that the continuity hypothesis holds. Then the child has a fixed set of linguistic abilities, together with a developing language. The only way to explain this conjunction is to assume that new pieces of language are learned. In short, the only way for language to change in the child over time, according to the continuity hypothesis, is for the child to learn. According to the maturation hypothesis, however, the underlying biological program can guide not only the details of the development of linguistic structures, but also the time course of this development. Thus, to the extent that maturational principles operate, there is no need for learning to take place. Thus it is clear that the maturation hypothesis provides for a stronger theory of innateness than the continuity hypothesis.

1.2. Maturation and Linguistic Theory

We have concluded that, from the viewpoint of general biological considerations, there seems to be no reason to assume the continuity hypothesis. What about the viewpoint of linguistic theory? Although many scholars seem to believe that the continuity hypothesis is to be preferred in linguistic theory, it seems to us that linguistic arguments lead to exactly the opposite conclusion.

Part of the problem in the study of language acquisition is to explain why certain constructions develop at a certain time, or why certain constructions precede other constructions. Suppose construction A precedes construction B. What can explain this? Within linguistic theory, which has (usually implicitly), assumed the continuity hypothesis, there have been two kinds of possible explanations. The first is the assumption of some kind of extrinsic ordering. For example, it is assumed that A is 'unmarked' with respect to B. Often there is no linguistic motivation for the markedness assumption. An example is Hyams' (1983) important hypothesis that the mechanism underlying the possibility of null subjects has an unmarked value which allows null subjects (Italian, Spanish) and a marked value which disallows null subjects (English, French). This hypothesis is used to explain the early existence of subjectless sentences in English-speaking children. Optional subjects (construction A) precede obligatory subjects (construction B) because A is unmarked with respect to B.

The second kind of possible explanation given in linguistic theory for order of development is the assumption of some kind of intrinsic ordering. The degree-2 theory (Wexler and Culicover, 1980) provides an example. Following the standard theory, transformations have structural descriptions. It may turn out that T' can only apply if T has applied, creating a context for it. So T' can only be learned if T has already been learned. In other words, intrinsic ordering of constructions insures that one must be learned before the other. However, linguistic theory has moved further and further away from ordering (extrinsic or intrinsic). For example, there are no longer structural descriptions of transformations, simply Move α. There *is* ordering between modules, but there seems to be no evidence that the relative development of modules is explanatory for the order of development of constructions. It is an empirical question, of course, but we see no reason to assume that, say, Move α develops late, because the whole categorical component must first develop. Or that phonetics can't develop until the categorical component develops. Given the assumption of modularity, one would look for independent principles governing the development of modules, rather than a linguistic theory-dependent relation among them.

In sum, *linguistic* explanations of ordering in development, based on the continuity hypothesis, involve the assumption of some kind of ordering in linguistic theory (extrinsic or intrinsic). And we have suggested that there is no *linguistic* motivation for the ordering. So according to these acquisition accounts, linguistic theory has to make linguistic assumptions (e.g., markedness or intrinsic ordering) which have no linguistic motivation. This is not a demonstrative *a priori* argument against such accounts. But it *does* suggest that there is no general argument from linguistic theory for the continuity hypothesis. To repeat, suppose, as we have suggested, that the continuity hypothesis necessitates the existence in linguistic theory of linguistic assumptions which have no linguistic motivation. Suppose, also, that linguistic theory itself seems preferable when it contains no assumptions that don't have internal linguistic motivation. We then conclude that linguistic theory might be preferable without the continuity hypothesis, if the alternative allowed the non-principled assumptions to be removed from linguistic theory.

Another way of looking at the continuity hypothesis and its effect on linguistic theory is that it represents an attempt to model within an instantaneous theory processes which are clearly non-instantaneous. Suppose construction A actually precedes construction B in development. Linguistic theory based on the continuity hypothesis attempts to capture this within an instantaneous system by making an ordering assumption (markedness or intrinsic ordering). But if, in fact, these are time-dependent processes, they may not fit very naturally into the instantaneous model. In fact, they may distort the large number of real insights of the instantaneous model. In short, it may be that one should not attempt to model certain time-dependent processes within the instantaneous idealization.

1.3. *Ordered Input and the Triggering Problem*

There have been attempts to capture time-dependent processes outside of the instantaneous idealization. These have mostly had to do with making special assumptions about the linguistic input to the child. Suppose that a parent provides examples of construction A before construction B. Then, on certain common assumptions, A should develop before B. Let's call the assumption that the input to a child is systematically varied in such a way as to account for particular development, the Hypothesis of *Ordered Input*. The best evidence, both empirical and theoretical, seems to support the view that Ordered Input, in this sense, does not exist. (For a review and analysis of the literature, see Wexler and Culicover, 1980, Section 2.7.3.) In short, there seems to be no reason to believe that parents or others order linguistic input to children in such a way that the order of input can be looked upon as causal with respect to the order of development.

The lack of ordered input, together with the continuity hypothesis, leads to the assumption of markedness relations among the values of a parameter. There have been many proposals to this effect within linguistic theory. For example, Hyams (1983) postulates a parameter which controls Pro Drop (we are simplifying). The plus Pro Drop value is unmarked. Thus the child starts out believing that under many conditions subjects are optional in the language (like Spanish, but unlike English). The Spanish-speaking child is correct, and this value doesn't change. The English-speaking child is incorrect. Since Hyams (following the general consensus in acquisition theory — see e.g., Baker, 1979; Wexler and Culicover, 1980, and Maratsos, 1983, among many others) assumes that there is no negative evidence given to the child (no evidence telling the child that a particular sentence is ungrammatical), there must be positive evidence which shows that the plus Pro Drop value is incorrect. Hyams suggests what this evidence may be (it can't be simply the presence of subjects, since these are optionally possible even in Pro Drop languages). One possibility that Hyams suggests is the existence of expletive subjects in non-Pro Drop languages. And Hyams provides evidence from child language that the first value is plus Pro Drop, even in non-Pro Drop languages.

But there is a problem, as Hyams explicitly acknowledges. Namely, why isn't the 'triggering' data (the data that the child uses to switch the value of the parameter) available at an earlier age? Why does it take a considerable period of time for the data to become active for the child? Why does the English-speaking child not have the triggering data available at an earlier age so that she or he can reset the parameter's value? This is an example of what we are calling the 'triggering problem'.

There are many examples of triggering analyses in the literature, where it is considered what kind of data can lead from an unmarked to a marked value. Many are to be found in Pinker (1984). And Roeper also has many triggering analyses. But the same basic problem seems to exist in many cases. Why isn't the triggering data available earlier? The problem is that constructions often seem to follow a clear developmental ordering, with quite a bit of time between the different values of a parameter, say. But, if input to the child isn't ordered, there seems to be no explanation for the developmental delay. Sometimes Pinker seems to suggest that the data simply aren't available earlier — that the data are somehow 'ordered'. But, as we have already pointed out, the empirical evidence, to the extent that it exists, seems·to not agree with this hypothesis. Basically, it seems that input isn't ordered in any way that will cause constructions to develop at one time rather than another.

It seems to us that most scholars who are pursuing theory in this field (including Pinker and Roeper) want to agree that input isn't ordered. This is especially so since there has been no demonstration that input is ordered and that this ordering predicts order of acquisition. Also, there are many conceptual and theoretical problems with a strong assumption of input ordering. Why, then, is ordering used?

The answer seems to be that strong ordering of input is assumed because the continuity hypothesis necessitates it. Pinker (1984) has written very clearly about the continuity hypothesis as the simplest hypothesis. It might be reasonable to follow Pinker (and pretty much all other scholars in this field, including Wexler and Culicover, 1980) in saying that the continuity hypothesis is therefore to be preferred, everything else being equal. But the continuity hypothesis leads to the following dilemma. If it is true and if some constructions develop before others, why? The only answer within this framework seems to be to assume that input data trigger the development of later constructions. Why don't these data trigger the constructions earlier? The only answer seems to be that the data are strongly ordered (and in significant relation to the acquired constructions). Therefore it seems to us that it is reasonable to question the continuity hypothesis, whose main advantage seems to be a certain kind of simplicity, but which seems to lack theoretical and empirical justification.

The natural alternative to the continuity hypothesis is the assumption that certain linguistic abilities mature as the child grows older. It is aspects of such a 'maturation hypothesis' that we will pursue in some explicit detail in this paper. By 'maturation' we mean, in general, that certain linguistic abilities simply grow over time, in contrast to learning, in which specific evidence is used by the child to create a grammar. Of course, there is some learning (it is obvious, for example, that specific properties of individual lexical items have to be learned). One of the things that is relatively unique about the theory to be proposed in this paper is the assumption of an important element of grammatical maturation. Of course, a complete theory will also have to account for various kinds of learned competence, which will interact with maturation. The presented theory will also contain instances of this kind of learning.

1.4. *The Maturation of Non-Linguistic Capacities*

We have not presented every possible kind of response to the triggering problem. Somebody might suggest that certain data in the input aren't available to the child at certain times for various reasons. Roeper (1983) has made suggestions of this kind. Certain data, for example, might demand an analysis that is beyond the child's capabilities at certain times. But then the question is: why are these data beyond the child's capabilities at certain times, but not later? Maturation might underlie *this* ability.

Although maturation of explicit, specific pieces of grammatical competence has not been suggested or studied, as far as we know, there *have* been maturational suggestions in the literature which have to do with maturation of non-linguistic abilities which interact with linguistic abilities. It has often been suggested, for example, that memory capacity of various kinds matures, becoming larger with a child's age. The maturation of non-linguistic abilities such as memory might be the underlying cause of the efficacy of data at certain times and not at others. For example, suppose certain data were only manifest in complex sentences. And suppose that, because of a limited memory, a young child could not process complex sentences. Then the data would not be available to the child until her or his memory matured.

We do not want to rule out maturational effects of this kind, in which non-linguistic competence matures. There is no reason to believe that such maturation doesn't exist. For some reason, this kind of non-linguistic maturation seems to be much more accepted in the literature than the maturation of specific aspects of grammar. Perhaps the reason is that such an assumption — of a completely fixed set of linguistic abilities together with maturation of non-linguistic abilities — seems, on the surface, more consonant with an instantaneous linguistic theory. But we have already argued that this is not the case. It is, naturally, an empirical question. Our own view is that it would be surprising if the richness of detail involved in ordering in linguistic development could follow from some general principles of cognitive development acting in concert with a fixed linguistic substrate. From a more general point of view, why should the linguistic system be the only system which is fixed at birth and which doesn't mature?

There is one general kind of claim in the field of language acquisition that may be related to maturational claims about grammar development. This is the notion that early child language can best be described in 'semantic' terms, while later stages are more 'grammatical' or 'formal'. Gleitman (1981) has provided a well-known argument concerning the semantic to formal shift. She argues that, if the shift exists, then it makes the problem of language learning even more of a mystery, since there is no way to account for this learning. Therefore, she argues, the process of language learning must be like a tadpole growing into a frog. It is this sense of maturation that we will study in this paper. However, we do not propose a semantic to formal shift (at least with respect to the phenomena and aspects of grammatical abilities that we are studying). Rather we propose the maturation of specific aspects of grammatical competence. The learner, in our theory, starts off with certain aspects of grammatical competence and adds other pieces of competence.

1.5. *Feasibility*

There are many important conditions to be put on a theory of language acquisition besides the correct prediction of order of development. Many of these are discussed in the learnability literature (e.g., Wexler and Culicover, 1980; Wexler, 1981, 1982; Pinker, 1979; Gleitman and Wanner, 1982), and we do not have the space to review them here. Basically they are instances of 'feasibility' (Chomsky 1965), the criterion which says that a correct theory of language acquisition not only has to predict that language can be learned but that the learning takes place in the fashion in which the child actually accomplishes it. Thus, on the basis of empirical evidence we demand of our theory that it meet the following conditions:

(1)   There is no negative data (no correction of ungrammatical sentences).

(2)   Children are not explicitly taught rules of grammar.

(3)   To the extent that grammar is learned, the relevant data are simple (and thus available to a young child).

Here we want to mention one other criterion which has not been the subject of extensive discussion. We want the acquisition mechanism to exhibit the following characteristic:

(4)   Learning is Deterministic.

This means that the child's options in constructing a grammar are so restricted that there are not many options from which the child can choose. Why is Determinism plausible? First, because it seems to be roughly correct empirically. If it were not correct we would expect to see lots of incorrect grammatical features constructed by children. In general we do not see these. Second, Determinism makes the grammar acquisition process more efficient. Third, the notion of Determinism seems to fit in with what is known about other natural processes in cognitive science at which humans are particularly good. Determinism is to be contrasted with hypothesis-testing, in which there are many possible choices of hypotheses, and correction (back-up) when an error is made. Marr (1982) suggests that all processes at which humans are good have the characteristic of Determinism (he argues it in detail for vision). Marcus (1979), Berwick (1982) and Berwick and Weinberg (1984) make the same argument for on-line language processing.

Within the kind of maturational theory that we are proposing, the child can change his or her grammar without going through a correction process based on new data. Suppose that a child has created a grammar at a certain maturational point. At a later point, new linguistic abilities grow. Based on these new linguistic abilities, plus the principles that he or she already has, the child reinterprets the earlier principles, in accordance with the new abilities. This reinterpretation is not a process based upon correction for which external evidence is responsible. The child is not hypothesizing and correcting. Rather, the child's underlying biological program, by bringing forth new principles, is allowing for a process of reinterpretation of already acquired knowledge.

In the remainder of this paper we present a maturational theory of the growth of certain aspects of grammatical competence. We argue why a learning account seems not to work and that the maturational system has advantages. It is suggested that a particular piece of grammatical competence matures. We further conclude that various particular constructions, which are not related on the surface, should develop at the same time because the same piece of competence, which matures, underlies them. The maturation hypothesis also seems to account for a variety of learnability puzzles. Furthermore, there is data from the field of language acquisition which appear to support aspects of the maturational theory.

2. A PRESENTATION OF THE PROBLEM AND THE THEMATIC INFERENCE PRINCIPLE.

Maratsos *et al.* (1983) observe that children at a certain age perform better on passive constructions which involve actional verbs before passives which involve verbs which are not actional. These children show difficulties in comprehending and producing sentences such as (1a—b), but fewer difficulties with respect to sentences such as (2a—b):

(1) a.   the doll was seen (by Mary)
    b.   the doll was liked (by Mary)

(2) a.   the doll was combed (by Mary)
    b.   the doll was torn (by Mary)

Somewhat similar facts are observed by Pinker (1983), who claims that children show difficulties comprehending and producing passive constructions which involve spatial relations, while the comprehension and the production of other passive constructions is less problematic. See also discussion in De Villiers *et al.* (1982), Maratsos *et al.* (1983) and Berwick and Weinberg (1984) who offer an account of these facts. As will become clear, our account follows different lines. Yet another observation concerning the acquisition of passive is the fact that *by* phrases seem to be acquired later than short passives. While the literature on this topic is somewhat complicated, the consensus seems to be that long passives are at least as late as short passives (Maratsos, 1983). Thus the short version of (2) in which the *by* phrase is omitted is likely to be comprehended and produced earlier than the longer version, including the *by* phrase.

A third observation concerning passive constructions which is problematic from the viewpoint of acquisition is the well-known fact that in short passive constructions the thematic role of the subject is not lost. Rather, it is implicit in the interpretation. It is further clear that the θ-role assigned to the implicit subject is not an unmarked uniform role, but rather, it is precisely the role which would be assigned to an overt subject, had one been present in the structure. Thus in the examples in (4) the θ-role assigned to the implicit subject corresponds to the θ-role assigned to the overt subject in the examples in (3):

(3) a. Bill received the letter
    b. Mary heard the song
    c. Jake pushed the ball

(4) a. the letter was received
    b. the song was heard
    c. the ball was pushed

How is knowledge of this fact achieved by the child? From the learnability perspective, the problem is as follows. It is a fair assumption that a child learns lexical entries (say, the lexical entries for verbs) by hearing simple sentences spoken in contexts from which the child can infer the meaning of the utterance. It is these contextual clues which enable the child to infer the thematic roles assigned by a particular verb. For example, if the child hears, "Daddy kicked the ball", while watching Daddy kicking a ball, it seems plausible to assume that the child can infer from the situation that 'daddy' is an *agent* and 'the ball' is a *patient*. We assume, of course, that the categories *agent* and *patient* are universal categories available to the language learner, and that the child has the ability to make an inference with respect to such thematic roles. Such an assumption is made by practically every contemporary approach to the theory of language learning (MacNamara, 1972; Wexler and Culicover, 1980; Pinker, 1984; among others).

Now suppose that the child hears a short passive, such as "the ball was dropped". By hypothesis, the child can tell that 'the ball' is *patient*. What can s/he infer about the *agent*, which adults know is implicitly present? Suppose we were tempted to say that the child in many cases can infer that there is an agent in this sentence because s/he sees an agent, i.e., when the child hears the sentence s/he actually sees Daddy dropping the ball and infers that Daddy is an agent. On such an account we could claim that the child is given semantic information by the context, and that computing it, s/he concludes that there is an *agent* in the sentence and hence that the verb in question assigns an *agent* role.

But there is a problem with this account. In practically every situation there will be many possible semantic relations which *could* be inferred on the basis of contextual cues and thus mistakenly related to the verb in the sentence. Thus suppose that the child sees Daddy throwing or dropping a ball, and hears somebody describe the situation as "the ball dropped slowly", or "the ball fell slowly". No *agent* is mentioned in this sentence, but there is an *agent* in the interpretation of the situation, as determined by contextual factors. Thus the child would assume that there was an *agent* in the sentence "the ball dropped/fell slowly" just as in "the ball was dropped". Such an hypothesis would result in inferring that the verb 'drop' in sentences such as "the ball dropped" assigns two thematic roles, a hypothesis that is incompatible with the structural properties of that verb. In short, there are too many possible thematic roles that can be computed if there are no structural constraints on the possible roles which any lexical item may assign, and which are entirely independent from contextual cues. In fact, there are almost always time and space relations which could be inferred on the basis of the context, and mistakenly assumed to be part of the sentence structure. Thus as a first approximation of the basic principle utilized by the child to compute thematic roles from situations, we will assume a *Thematic Inference Principle*, (discussed by Wexler, 1982) which can be stated roughly as (5):

(5)   *The Thematic Inference Principle*:

> When a learner is computing thematic roles from situations, s/he assumes a thematic role only if it can be related to an appropriate phrase in the sentence.

The Thematic Inference Principle, or something similar to it, is necessary to any adequate learnability account. Such a principle will rule out correctly the inference of an agent in "the book dropped/fell slowly". However, such a principle will also rule out the child's inferring an *agent* in "the ball was dropped", although the adult intuition clearly indicates that an *agent* exists in this sentence. Thus the question of how the child learns that short passives contain implicit subject thematic roles remains a problem.

In this paper, we would like to supply an answer to the questions which these observations give rise to, while adhering to the theoretical considerations discussed above. We will first suggest a linguistic account for the passive constructions, from which some of the properties of the acquisition of passive fall out. We will then suggest how the remaining properties are acquired by means of a maturational step, and test the empirical predictions which our system makes.

Note now that the distinction between (1) and (2) observed in the early grammar, as well as the absence of *by* phrases, correspond to a valid distinction in the adult grammar. The participles in (1)—(2) are potentially ambiguous between a verbal passive reading and an adjectival passive reading. Interestingly, it turns out that the passive forms which are excluded in the early grammar are precisely those passive forms which are never homophonous with adjectival passives in the adult grammar. Put somewhat differently, in the grammar of English the participles of non-actional verbs rarely make good adjectives. This contrast (with respect to the examples in (1)—(2)) is exemplified in (6)—(7).[2]

(6) a. *the doll appears seen; *the seen doll; *seen though the movie was, John decided to go again.

   b. *the doll appears liked; *the liked doll; *liked though the doll was, John did not keep it.

(7) a. the doll appears combed; the combed doll; combed though the doll was, Janie recombed her.

   b. the doll appears torn; the torn doll; torn though the doll was, John decided to keep her.

It is further a well known fact that constructions which are unambiguously adjectival and not verbal do not admit very easily of *by*
phrases:[3]

(8) a.   the fact was unknown (*by Peter)
    b.   the uninhabited island (*by the British)
    c.   the closed door (*by Peter)
    d.   the torn doll (*by Peter)

As a first approximation, then, we may say that in the early grammar,
the operation which generates adjectival passives has been acquired,
but not the operation which generates verbal passives. Since the passive
constructions in (1) cannot be generated by this adjectival passive
operation, they are missing from the early grammar. Once the child
learns to derive verbal passives, the expansion of the passive constructions to the sentences in (1) is natural and expected. Note, however,
that the early operation, deriving adjectival passives, is not discarded:
it is present in the adult grammar, and is responsible for the facts
illustrated by (6)—(7).

Independent evidence for the acquisition of adjectival passives prior
to verbal passives is found in Hebrew. In Hebrew, the distinction
between adjectival and verbal passives is reflected by distinct morphological marking. While verbal passives are verbs, which display the
distribution and the properties of verbs (e.g., they are inflected for tense
and exhibit agreement markers similar to those of verbs), adjectival
passives display the typical distribution and properties which one
expects from adjectives: they do not take tense markers, and agree only
in gender and number (but not in person). Tense marking on adjectives
is achieved by the copular verb *haya* 'to be', similar to English. As in
English, only verbal passive allows *by*-phrases, while adjectival passive
does not. Thus consider the following paradigm:

(9) a.   ha-yalda   sorka   ('al-yedey 'ima   shel-a)
          the-girl   combed-pass. (by   mother of-her)

          'the girl was combed by her mother'

    b.   ha-yalda   tesorak   ('al-yedey 'ima   shel-a)
          the-girl   will-comb-pass. (by   mother of-her)

          'the girl will be combed by her mother'

(10) a. ha-yalda hayta   mesoreket (*'al-yedey 'ima shel-a)
    the-girl was   combed-adj.

   b. ha-yalda tihiye   mesoreket (*'al-yedey 'ima shel-a)
    the-girl will-be combed-adj.

In Hebrew, we further have a strong implied θ-role in short verbal passives, vs. its complete absence in adjectival passives. Thus in (10) it is not implied that anybody combed the girl. We only get the reading that the girl's hair is in a combed state.

On the other hand, there are clear morphological relations between the verbal and the adjectival passive paradigms in Hebrew. The adjectival passive is, in effect, the passive participle form, as found in the present tense of the verbal passive (in general, present tense forms in Hebrew are the participial forms). Thus the following sentence, which is in the present tense, is ambiguous between adjectival and verbal reading, and may be disambiguated by a '*by*'-phrase:

(11)   ha-yalda mesoreket
       the-girl combed

          'the girl is being combed'
          'the girl is combed'

It is thus clear that the morphological complexity of adjectival passives and of verbal passives is equal, and that morphologically they are on a par. Nevertheless, adjectival passives precede verbal passives in development in children speaking Hebrew. Berman and Sagi (1981) report that verbal passives do not emerge in Hebrew-speaking children until school-age. On the other hand, adjectival passives are not only used, but are used productively, i.e., children coin adjectival passives from verbs and from nouns freely, sometimes exhibiting clear cases of overgeneration. Berman and Sagi (1981) report the following cases of overgeneration from children ages 4;5—5;0:

(12) a. ki   hayom 'ani *meshu'elet* ve-ani gam *mecunenet*
    because today I   coughed   and-I also cold

    ve-gam   cruda
    and-also   hoarse

       'because today I am coughing and I have a cold and I am hoarse'.

  b. 'ani kvar *me'uyefet* legamrey
    I already tired   entirely

    'I am already very tired'

  c. 'ani 'od pa'am *mefura'at*
    I again   disheveled

    'I am disheveled again'

  In example (12a), the child coins the adjectival passive *meshu'elet* (having a cough), on par with the well-formed *mecunenet* (having a cold), following an appropriate morphological pattern. The adjectival pattern here is the passive participle of the verbal pattern of *KiTeL-KuTaL*, which is *meKuTaL*. Well-formed adjectives formed in this pattern are, for instance, *melubash* 'dressed', *meluxlax* 'dirty', *mekupal* 'folded', *mevushal* 'cooked', etc. In (12b) and (12c), the child is substituting for existing adjectives ('*ayefa*, 'tired'; *pru'a*, 'disheveled') an innovative form, based on the passive participle form *meKuTaL* of the verbal pattern *KiTel-KuTaL* given above. We thus conclude that the child at the relevant age clearly has the morphological ability to derive complex forms and use derivational morphology productively (and see also below, Section 4, for more examples of the morphological ability mastered by Hebrew-speaking children of that age). Nevertheless, we find that verbal passives are missing from their speech. As this cannot be attributed to morphological complexity, we must conclude that verbal passives are excluded in the early grammar due to a non-morphological factor.[4]

  On the other hand, the fact that in Hebrew adjectival passives precede verbal passives lends support to our conclusion that the distinction which underlies the performance differences uncovered by Maratsos is not between actional vs. non-actional passives, but rather, between adjectival and verbal passive. To the extent that it can be shown that the processes deriving adjectival passives in English and in Hebrew pattern together, and are different in a principled way from the processes involved in the derivation of verbal passives in both languages, then whatever explanation is given for the late development of verbal passives will be useful in explaining the order of behavior in both languages.

  Before we proceed, one more point deserves mentioning. Note that not all actional verbs give rise to well-formed adjectives in the adult grammar. Thus the adjectives formed by verbs such as *kick* or *hit* are not felicitous. It should be noted, however, that context seems to improve those, but it does little to improve non-actional adjectives:

(13) a. ?the kicked ball landed in front of the referee
     b. ?this child very often appears hit
     c. *the seen movie was applauded by all critics
     d. *this bell very often seems heard

Our claim is, however, that at the stage of the early grammar discussed in this paper, the factor involved in rendering (13a—b) marginal is not present. Concretely, we claim that adjectival constructions involving actional verbs of the kind illustrated in (13a—b) are in fact attested — and are thus 'grammatical' in the stage discussed here. Some evidence that this is in fact the case comes from studies done by Horgan (1975), which we cite in Section 3.2. below. Horgan's data strongly indicates that at an age at which children produce adjectival passives, they do so disregarding the fact that certain actional verbs do not give rise to well-formed adjectival passives. Thus in the early grammar, the rule which forms adjectival passives operates on all actional verbs, and an independent constraint, not discussed in detail here, later indicates to the child that adjectives such as the ones in (13a—b) are not well-formed.

In what follows we will make our proposal more precise. We will start by sketching the properties of verbal passives and adjectival passives respectively, drawing on the distinctions made by Wasow (1977) and Williams (1981). We will then proceed to show that in the absence of a certain grammatical apparatus, which matures later, an adjectival analysis of passive sentences is all that is available to the child. However, once maturation occurs, the derivation of verbal passives becomes possible. The addition of the missing component makes it possible for the child to acquire verbal passives alongside adjectival ones. We will then show that in a crucial respect, Hebrew passive constructions are similar to English ones, thus predicting the same order of acquisition. The analysis will be further extended to ergative constructions in Hebrew, showing them to display the same behavior as passive verbs from the point of view of both syntax and acquisition.

In Section 4 we address the predictions made by our maturational system with respect to yet one more mystery of language development. Bowerman (1982) observes that children overgenerate the causative-

intransitive construction, producing, alongside the (adult-wise) grammatical sentences in (14) the sentences in (15):

(14) a. the ball dropped; John dropped the ball;
     b. the ball moved; John moved the ball;

(15) a. the doll giggled; John giggled the doll;
     b. the dog went; John goed the dog;

Similar cases of overgeneration are observed by Berman and Sagi
(1981) in Hebrew speaking children. Thus the children use productively the *hiKTiL* form, which is the standard causative morphological
pattern, to derive causative verbs from non-causative ones in the
KaTaL form, producing forms such as the ones in (16), which do not
exist in the adult language:

(16) a. *mashte*   from   *shote*
         make-drink   drink

     b. *mashin*   from   *yashen*
         make-sleep   sleep

     c. *magir*   from   *gar*
         make-dwell   dwell

     d. *maclil*   from   *colel*
         make-dive   dive

Two important questions are involved in offering an explanation for
the overgeneration exemplified in (15)–(16). First, as this overgeneration clearly reflects the incorporation of a wrong rule in the early
grammar, how did that mistake come to happen? And even more
puzzling: as positive evidence is not available, and as there is no
negative evidence, it is not clear what leads to the elimination of the
ungrammatical overgenerated transitive variations from the early grammar. As we will show below, the maturational step which will enable
the child to derive verbal passive constructions will account for the
elimination of such overgeneration in English without any additional
machinery. It will be further shown that in the grammar of Hebrew this
very same maturational step will make slightly different predictions,
which are verified by the acquisition process.

3. THE ACQUISITION OF PASSIVE

3.1. *A Syntactic Analysis of Passive*

It would be useful to start this account by making explicit our assumptions about the nature of passive in the adult grammar. Our account is embedded in the grammatical framework of the Government-Binding model, as in Chomsky, (1981) and references cited there. Some of our specific assumptions require elaboration. Chomsky (1981) proposes that the following principle holds in the grammar:

(17)   *The Projection Principle*:

Lexical features must be represented at every syntactic level.

In other words, the Projection Principle prevents rules which apply in the syntax from changing lexical specifications. Now consider in light of the Projection Principle the respective properties of adjectival and verbal passives. Wasow (1977) argues that while the former is lexical, the latter is syntactic. Consider first adjectival (= lexical) passive. Some of the typically lexical properties of adjectival passives which Wasow names are the categorial change (V → A), and the elimination of the thematic subject, attested, e.g., in (8a—d). Thus consider an adjectival passive construction, as in (18):

(18)   the island was uninhabited

There is no reason to assume that in (18) *uninhabited* is different from standard adjectives, such as *blue* and *little*. (We refer the reader to Siegel, 1970 and Wasow, 1977, for morphological support for the claim that forms such as *uninhabited* are lexically derived). As a first approximation, then, it seems plausible to assume that the adjectival passive morpheme, attached lexically, accomplishes the following tasks:[5]

(19) a. [+V, −N] → [+V, +N], resulting in the elimination of the accusative Case assigning feature.

b. The elimination of the subject θ-role

c. The externalization of the internal θ-role

Following Williams (1980, 1981), we refer to the subject as the *external argument*. Following Williams we also assume that a process of *externalization* is involved in the derivation of adjectival passives. The externalization of the internal (object) θ-role in (19c) means that the θ-role that was previously assigned to the internal argument, the object, is now assigned to the external argument, i.e., the subject. Following the accomplishement of the tasks specified in (19), and given a sentence such as (18), we must also assume that the post-verbal position subcategorized originally by the verb has been eliminated. This follows from the fact that if such a position were generated, it could not be assigned a θ-role. We assume, with Chomsky (1981), that D-structure is GF_θ, and hence the generation of a position which may not be assigned a θ-role at D-structure would result in ungrammaticality. Thus, following the application of the rule of passive, the thematic role (θ-role) that would have been assigned in the [NP, VP] position is now assigned directly in the subject position, as is the case in regular adjectival constructions. Now consider the passive constructions generated by (19). Since the constructions are adjectival in nature, and since the post-verbal subcategorized position has been eliminated, the base-generated version of these constructions is similar to their surface string. Concretely, the D-structure of a sentence such as (18) is identical to its S-structure in all relevant respects, as it is identical to the D-structure of (20):

(20) $[_S [_{NP} \text{the island}] \text{ INFL } [_{VP} \text{was } [_{AP} \text{large}]]]$

Crucially, no movement is invoked in the derivation of (18). Recall now that adjectival passives are restricted semantically in a way which does not constrain verbal passives, thus accounting for the ungrammaticality of (6) in the adult grammar of English. Since this contraint applies only to adjectival passives, but not to verbal passives, we will assume that it is a constraint on adjectives in general, specified lexically. We tentatively notate this semantic property SR, and we may now say that adjectives must be [+SR], and that the adjectival passives derived by (19) are well-formed only if they are +SR. It is observationally correct that most actional verbs (i.e., verbs which assign *agent-patient* relations) give rise to derived adjectives, while verbs which do not assign these relations do not. (Note, incidentally, that forms such as *unseen, unknown, much-liked* etc. are possible. We assume that in these cases the +SR feature comes from the prefixed elements, rather than from the stem, rendering the adjective well-formed and see Note 2 for some discussion). However, it is clear that the verbs which give rise

to well-formed +SR adjectives without further affixation are a subset of
actional verbs, and we will assume this to be a valid generalization,
leaving aside the precise nature of the SR feature. Possibly, SR is a
reflex of a universal semantic property, giving rise to no further
problems of learnability. Alternatively, it could be acquired earlier,
again, enabling the child to sort out proper adjectival forms according
to their semantic properties.

Now consider the list in (19) from the viewpoint of the Projection
Principle. As stated, properties (a,b) violate the Projection Principle. (a)
involves a change in categorial status and the subsequent elimination of
a lexical feature (the Case assignment property), and (b) involves the
elimination of a lexical feature (subject θ-role). Property (c) entails a
violation of the Projection Principle if the latter is perceived as a
condition on assignment, as well as a condition on features.[6] But even if
the Projection Principle is perceived as a condition on features, the
externalization of the internal θ-role without the elimination of the
subcategorized [NP, VP] position would result in ungrammaticality, as
shown above. On the other hand, elimination of the subcategorized
position would violate the projection principle. To conclude, (19) is
incompatible with a syntactic rule application. Such application would
inevitably violate the projection principle.

Consider now the analysis of verbal passives. Following assumptions
advanced in Chomsky (1981), in Jaeggli (1981) and in other work, we
assume that in the derivation of verbal passives the following factors are
involved (and see also (3)—(4) and related discussion):

(21) a. $[+V, -N] \rightarrow [+V]$, resulting in the absorption of the accusative Case.

b. the passive morpheme absorbs the external θ-role (and may
optionally transmit it to the object of *by*).

Crucially, it is assumed in the GB literature that the internal θ-role is
preserved as an internal one, resulting in the obligatory maintenance of
the subcategorized VP-internal NP position. A preservation of the
internal θ-role without the subcategorized position would result in a
violation of the θ-criterion, in that it would give rise to a θ-role which
may not be assigned. The preservation of the internal θ-role and the
subcategorized position, coupled with the fact that accusative Case may
no longer be assigned in that position result in the obligatoriness of

movement in verbal passive constructions. This follows from the Projection Principle in (17) in the following way. The Projection Principle entails that the D-structure of a sentence such as (22) would be as in (23a). This is due to the fact that the verb *hit* assigns a θ-role in the [NP, VP] position, and hence that position must be occupied at D-structure by an argument. As that property may not be changed during the syntactic derivation, there must be an element in the [NP, VP] position at S-structure as well as at D-structure, so as to allow such an assignment. On the other hand, Case assignment is not possible at the [NP, VP] position, and the post-verbal NP must move to the [NP, S] position in order to get Case; and since the [NP, VP] position may not be eliminated, a trace must be left behind. This trace, in turn, forms a *chain* with its antecedent in the [NP, S] position (see below for further discussion of this last point). It is that chain which is in turn assigned the objective θ-role at S-structure by the participle *hit*, thus rendering the derivation well-formed from the viewpoint of the Projection Principle.

(22)   John was hit

(23) a.   e was hit John
    b.   John$_i$ was hit [e]$_i$

By absorption, as in (21), we specifically mean that the property was not eliminated (as is the case, e.g., in adjectival passives), but that it was realized as a morphological marker on the verb. In that, we follow the spirit of the operation of absorption proposed for cliticization processes by Aoun (1979), Jaeggli (1982) and Borer (1984). Thus it is clear that such absorption as well does not give rise to a violation of the Projection Principle.

It is worthwhile at this point to compare the properties of the adjectival passive rule, as illustrated by (19), and the properties of the verbal passive rule, illustrated in (21). It is easy to see that they bear non-trivial similarities to each other. In essence, the difference can be summarized as follows:

(24) a.   (19) changes [−N] to [+N]; (21) renders the [N] feature unspecified.

    b.   (19) triggers elimination of the subject θ-role; (21) absorbs it.

    c.   (19) externalizes the internal θ-role; (21) does not.

Note, now, that from the viewpoint of the Projection Principle, the changes which are produced by (19) constitute a violation of the Projection Principle, while the changes which are produced by (21) do not: we see that (19) performs a category change and an elimination of a lexical feature: the subject θ-role. Further, we noted above that the externalization of the internal θ-role (property (c) of (21)) entails an elimination of the subcategorized position, again, a violation of the Projection Principle. On the other hand, the changes which occur following the application of (21) do not result in a violation of the Projection Principle: (21) renders the [N] feature unspecified, hence not allowing any positive change in the category type of the participle, and further, (21) does not eliminate the subject θ-role: rather, it absorbs it and may transmit it to the object of *by*, if a *by*-phrase is present. Following Borer (1983) and Borer and Wexler (1984) we will assume that rules of morphology may apply at any stage of the derivation (concretely, both in the lexicon and in the syntax) and that their application in the syntactic component is constrained by the Projection Principle.[7] Specifically, rules of morphology may apply in the syntax up to the violation of the Projection Principle. If one considers now the distinction between adjectival passives and verbal passives, it is easy to see that the affixation rule in question may be the same one, and that the different output is exactly what we would expect, given that the rule may apply in the lexicon as well as in the syntax. A lexical application would result in category change and in the elimination of a θ-role. However, a syntactic derivation cannot perform these tasks, as they would result in a violation of the Projection Principle. Hence we have a neutralization of the category type and an absorption of the external θ-role, instead.[8]

To summarize, we assume that there is one passive morpheme, whose affixation to verbal stems yields both verbal and adjectival passives. The affixation process has a set of properties, which are interpreted somewhat differently, depending on the level at which affixation takes place. If affixation takes place in the lexicon, the full range of changes may take place, and in particular, category change and the elimination of lexical features. Syntactic affixation, on the other hand, results in a narrower range of changes, as it is constrained by the Projection Principle. Thus we have, instead of a category change and a θ-role elimination, a catgory neutralization and a θ-role absorption. As a result of the application of the affixation process in two separate levels, we also have different syntactic representation for sentences in which the affixed form appears. If lexical affixation took place, the participle is projected into D-structure having the structure in (25), which is identical in all relevant respects to its S-structure. If syntactic affixation took place, the D-structure projected is as in (26a), a syntactic representation which necessitates the application of movement, and which results in the S-structure in (26b). Crucially, a chain is formed between the antecedent in the [NP, S] and its trace in (26b), to which a θ-role is assigned by the participle. No such chain is formed in (25).

(25)   the doll is torn

(26) a. e is torn the doll
    b. the doll$_i$ is torn [e]$_i$

3.2. *The Acquisition of Verbal Passives*

Some features of our account of passive in the adult grammar are worth emphasizing before we turn to the acquisition fo verbal passives. First note that the presence of an implicit thematic subject in verbal passives follows immediately from their syntactic derivation. In particular, it is a 'side effect' of the level at which the rule applies, and as such, is not a factor about the rule or the construction which needs to be learned. It follows from the innate knowledge of the Projection Principle, coupled with the (learned) meaning of the passive morpheme and the application of the passive morphological rule in the syntax, an operation licensed by Universal Grammar. As the affixation which leads to the formation of verbal passives applies in the syntax, and as no θ-roles may be eliminated in the syntax due to the Projection Principle, the presence of such (implicit or assigned) θ-role follows immediately. Second, notice that the extention of verbal passive to forms such as *seen* and *liked*, which are not possible as adjectival passives need not be learned either. Rather, the application of SR to adjectival passives follows from the fact that lexical affixation results in the formation of adjectives, and that adjectives in general are thus constrained. The disappearance of SR in verbal passives follows from the fact that in verbal passives no adjective is formed. The formation of an adjective under syntactic affixation would, again, result in a violation of the Projection Principle, as it would involve changing the value of [N] from [−] to [+].

Let us now turn to the child. We will assume here that the child knows the semantic properties of adjectives, leaving undiscussed the question of whether these are innate (and thus must be true in any language) or learned at a previous stage. If we assume now that in the early grammar only adjectival passives are present, the absence of the subject θ-role, the +SR semantic restriction on passives, and the preference for short passives follows immediately. We thus expect the adjectival use of passive participles in accordance with the +SR restriction, excluding non-actional passives. The adjectival use of passive participles derived from actional verbs exclusivly is, in fact, attested in very young children, as is recorded by Horgan (1975). The following examples were produced in an elicited production task, i.e., the child was induced to talk about pictures presented to him/her. Ages of tested children range from 24—48 months:

(27) a. tree is blowed down
     b. tree is broken
     c. a ball be kicked
     d. the car's parked
     e. lamp got kicked
     f. the tree's smashed
     g. that was colored
     h. the window's breaked again

Several points should be made with respect to the data in (27). Horgan, referring to the passives in (27) as 'truncated passives', makes the following statement with respect to their use:

The children's use of truncated passives differs in important ways from the adult's use ... all the truncated passives have inanimate logical objects (grammatical subjects). ... *truncated passives were especially common in pictures with the agent deleted ... Truncated passives seemed to be almost exclusively* an after-the-fact observation on the state of things. *Most of the passives used the verb 'broken', which children also used as an adjective, or a stative, as well as a verb.* (Emphasis ours)

From Horgan's description little doubt may be left that the children producing the sentences in (27a—h) are producing adjectival passives. Particularly suggestive in this respect is the absence of agent and the "after the fact" nature of their observations. It is also worth pointing out that the evidence in (27a—h) clearly points out that the children are deriving the participles from verbs (rather than using adjectives that

were acquired as independent, unrelated lexical items). This is clear
from the overgenerated participles *breaked* and *blowed*. On the other
hand, at the same age at which children are producing the truncated
passives in (27), their performance in producing 'full passives' (i.e.,
passives including *by*-phrases, which are unambiguously verbal passives) is considerably poorer. The following are the percentages of
children who use the constructions quoted from Horgan (p. 48):

(28)   Construction   Boys   Girls
        truncated passive   48.40   65.40
        full passive   6.45   19.20

Horgan's data thus confirm our analysis.

It is worthwhile at this stage to point out some of the utterances in
(27) which are not well-formed adult adjectival constructions: (27a) and
(27c). Recall that we assumed a well-formedness condition on adjectives which ruled out adjectives derived from non-actional verbs. We
did point out, however, that in the adult grammar of English the class
of well-formed adjectival participles is a subset of the participles
formed from actional verbs. Thus in the adult grammar of English
participles such as *kicked* and *blown down* are not well-formed adjectives. Notice, however, that they are well-formed in the early grammar.
We conclude from this, that the additional restriction in the adult
grammar which rules out adjectives such as *kicked* and *blown down*
does not enter the child's grammar until a later stage, and does not
interact with the acquisition of passive. In other words, the acquisition
of passive proceeds along the assumption that all participles of actional
verbs are well-formed adjectives, whereas participles of non-actional
verbs are not. The array of facts described by Maratsos *et al.* (1983)
now follows in its entirety. Further, to the extent that Horgan is correct
in assuming that utterances such as (27a–h) reflect the children's
ability to construct adjectival passives, then precisely the overgeneration
predicted by our system (i.e., that the non-actional vs. actional gap is in
actuality for the children a verbal vs. adjectival gap, and that children
will thus form adjectives from all actional verbs) in fact takes place,
strongly supporting our analysis.

Turning now to the extension of the grammar so as to include verbal
passives, note that once the derivation of verbal passives is made
possible, by what we assume to be an independent factor, the actual
properties of that construction follow immediately without the need for

any further learning: the implicit θ-role for the subject, the extension of the rule to other semantic verb-types and the availability of *by*-phrases all snap into place by the mere availability of the syntactic affixation.

How is the extension of the rule from adjectival passives to verbal passives made possible? Intuitively, it seems that in the early grammar the possibility of moving the post-verbal NP, as in the derivation depicted in (22)–(23) above, is somehow impossible.

Consider again the S-structure illustrated in (23b). It follows from the θ-criterion of Chomsky (1981) that the NP in the subject position, *the doll*, is assigned a θ-role. On the other hand, no θ-role is assigned directly in the subject position, as that θ-role was absorbed by the passive morphology. It is clear that the θ-role assigned to the subject in (23b) is the θ-role of the post-verbal argument. Within the Government-Binding system this correlation is captured by assuming that the subject, *the doll*, forms an argument-chain (A-chain) with its coindexed trace. This chain serves, in a sense, as a discontinuous element, and the θ-role assigned to it in the post-verbal position, in the position of the trace, is the θ-role assigned to the entire chain. In this way, the subject receives the post-verbal θ-role, as required.

In order to account now for the absence of verbal passives in the early grammar we would like to invoke the Maturation Hypothesis. Concretely, we would like to propose that in the early grammar it is not possible for the child to accomplish non-local assignment of lexical features, or in other words, given a structure such as (23b), the child is not capable of forming an argument-chain, an A-chain. In essence, the absence from the early grammar of A-chains means that while the child utilizing that grammar is capable of executing movement operations (e.g. *Wh*-movement is possible), nevertheless if that movement is into an A (= argument) position (unlike *Wh*-elements, which do not move into an A-position) the child will not be able to combine this moved NP and its trace into an A-chain. As a result, s/he will not be able to assign a θ-role to the moved NP, and would be driven to rule out the derivation. The child, then, knows that all referential NPs must be assigned a θ-role: s/he knows the θ-criterion, which we assume to be innate. On the other hand, s/he is not equipped with the machinary that will enable him/her to assign that θ-role non-locally, utilizing an A-chain. This machinary matures at a later stage, bringing about a reinterpretation of the passive rule.

Consider how that would take place. For the sake of simplicity we assume that the only thing which matures is the machinary which allows the formation of A-chains. Now let us consider the passive rule again. The child knows that all morphological rules may be applied in the syntax as well as in the lexicon. We assume this knowledge to be part of Universal Grammar. So far, however, s/he was only applying the passive rule in the lexicon. The reason for this is obvious: a syntactic application, as illustrated above, would require movement and would result in the representation in (23b). In the early grammar, however, the representation in (23b) is ungrammatical, since no θ-role may be assigned to the moved subject. Once A-chains are possible, however, the extention of the rule to the syntax follows immediately, and the relevant properties follow as well, as described above.

A few comments are in order before we move to the description of the acquisition of passive in Hebrew. First, note that the learning attributed to the child here does not involve any back-tracking. At no point does the child infer that an earlier rule was wrong, and hence must be discarded. Rather, what we have here is an extention of an already existing rule, so as to apply it in an additional domain, to a larger set of data. Thus this analysis meets the criteria posited in section 1: learning must not involve the abandonment of a rule formulated in an earlier stage of the grammar. Further, no special extrinsic ordering (such as markedness rules or triggering events) is assumed. The child matures and a range of constructions follows.

Note further that the system suggested here predicts that at the age at which a child cannot form A-chains, and thus cannot produce syntactic passives, s/he can nevertheless produce instances of *Wh*-movement, as the latter does not involve the formation of A-chains, i.e., it does not involve non-local assignment of θ-roles. As far as we know, this is correct, and *Wh*-movement does enter the child's language considerably earlier than verbal passives. On the other hand, the child at such an age should not be able to perform movement operations which involve A-chain formation, i.e., instances of NP-movement. Thus we predict that, e.g., raising would not be available. Again, to the best of our knowledge, this is correct.

The theory proposed here places the burden of maturation on A-chains, on non-local θ-role assignment. Another logical possibility within the Government Binding grammatical model would be to assume that the binding conditions in their entirety do not mature until a later stage.[9] While we think that the choice between A-chains, as presented here, and the binding conditions in general is an empirical issue which is yet to be determined, it is of some importance to us to point out here that there is no conceptual advantage to assuming that the binding conditions (rather then A-chain formation) mature. If, indeed, the binding conditions mature, it is clear that the maturational stage does not determine only the availability of NP-movement, but also the assignment of grammatical coreference. Thus such a change could be extended to a larger domain. On the other hand, there is no reason to assume that the formation of A-chains, made necessary by the θ-criterion, is conceptually the same as the binding conditions, which regulate the assignment of grammatical reference. While both are subject to similar structural conditions, they derive their logical necessity from rather different grammatical principles. In short, as A-chain formation and the binding conditions do share some structural properties, it would not be surprising to us if, indeed, the maturational stage involves both. On the other hand, we do not think that restricting the maturational stage to the formation of A-chains is problematic, nor do we think that there is an apriori reason to assume that its extention so as to cover the entire binding phenomena is necessarily an improvement.

3.3. The Acquisition of Passive Constructions in Hebrew

Our account of the acquisition of verbal passives in English rests crucially on the theoretical assumption that the derivation of these passive constructions involves NP-movement and hence the formation of an A-chain. We mentioned above that in Hebrew, as well as in English, the acquisition of adjectival passives precedes the acquisition of verbal passives, although there is no reason to assume that the latter are more complex from the morphological point of view. A natural extention of this study is thus to ask whether there is any evidence that the derivation of verbal passives in Hebrew involves the formation of A-chains, while the derivation of adjectival passives does not.

In Borer and Grodzinsky (1986) it is argued that all passive verbs in Hebrew are ergative (or unaccusative, in the senses of Burzio, 1981, and Perlmutter, 1978, respectively). It has been often observed that there are two kinds of intransitive verbs (see Perlmutter, 1978; Burzio, 1981). One type of intransitive verb obeys the pattern in (29a). The sole argument of the verb is generated in the [NP, S] position, the subject. In that position it is assigned a thematic role. The second type of intransitive verb follows the pattern in (29b). In that type of construction, the argument of the verb is generated in the [NP, VP] position, the object position, and it is assigned thematic role in that position. It is this latter type which we will refer to as ergative verbs, following the terminology of Burzio (1981).

(29) a. NP V
    b.   V NP

In various adult grammars (e.g., English, French), independent considerations will rule out the configuration in (29b), unless the post-verbal argument moves to the subject position. Concretely, this fact is accounted for in the Government Binding model by assuming that intransitive verbs cannot assign abstract Case and that in these languages the assignment of nominative Case in a post-verbal position is impossible. This, however, is due to factors which need not concern us here. In other grammars (e.g., Italian, Spanish, Hebrew), such movement is not necessary, as nominative Case assignment in the post-verbal position is possible.

Returning now to the derivation of verbal passives in Hebrew, note that if we assume that all passive verbs are ergative in the sense made clear above, then the rule which derives passive verbs from active verbs performs some morphophonemic changes on the one hand, and absorbs the subject θ-role on the other hand, on par with the absorption of subject θ-role in English.[10] In Hebrew, as is typical of Semitic morphology, different active verbal patterns give rise to different passive verbal patterns. A very sketchy paradigm is given is (30). In each of the patterns, the consonants *K.T.L.* represent the location of the consonants of the tri-consonantal root. The vowels, as well as other consonants, represent the vocalic pattern and additional affixation. The verbs are inflected in the 3rd-masc-sg., past tense, following a traditional practice in the description of Semitic languages. In (31), some examples of the different patterns are given:[11]

(30) | *active pattern* | *passive pattern* | *dominant meaning* |
|---|---|---|
| 1. KaTaL | niKTaL | undetermined |
| 2. KiTeL | KuTaL | intensive |
| 3. hiKTiL | huKTaL | causative |

(31) 1. *patax*; *shamar*; *baxar*   *niftax; nishmar; nivxar*
       opened; kept; chose   was opened/kept/chosen
    2. *piter*; *serek*; *xilek*   *putar; sorak; xulak*
       fired; combed; distributed   was fired/combed/distributed
    3. *hisbir*; *he'evir*; *histir*   *husbar; hu'avar; hustar*
       explained; relocated; hid   was explained/relocated/hid

Given the assumption that all passive verbal patterns in Hebrew are ergative in nature, the rule deriving passive verbs from active verbs would leave the subcategorization and the internal θ-role assignment of the active verb intact, resulting only in the absorption of the external θ-role. Unlike English, the verbal nature of the output is not changed. and thus, when compared with (21) above, (32) is the statement of the rule deriving verbal passives in Hebrew:

(32)   the passive morpheme absorbs the external θ-role (and may optionally transmit it to the object of *by*).

We will assume here that the possibility of feature neutralization is not available in Hebrew, resulting in the absence of under-specified categories in that language.[12] Thus, following the derivation, the derived form remains a verb — an ergative verb, which assigns θ-role internally, and which does not assign an accusative Case. Note, now, that if the derivation of verbal passives gives rise to ergative verbs, the completion of a derivation in which these verbs are involved requires one of two steps. A sentence with an ergative verb may be derived in either of two ways. It may be generated with an absent [NP, S] position (following the analysis of ergative constructions offered in Borer, 1986). As nominative Case in the adult grammar of Hebrew may be assigned to the post-verbal subject, the subject may simply remain in the post-verbal position, giving rise to the S-structure in (33a). On the other hand, if the [NP, S] position is generated, but is left empty, due to its non-thematic nature, the post-verbal subject must move into the [NP, S] position, so as to avoid a violation of the binding conditions. In that position it may be assigned nominative Case in the standard way. This move will lead to the grammatical S-structure illustrated by (33b):

(33) a.   [$_S$ [$_{VP}$ hugsha [$_{NP}$ 'ugat tapuxim]]]
             served-pass. cake apples

       'an apple-cake was served'

b. [s [NP 'ugat tapuxim]i [VP hugsha ei]]
     cake apples   was-served

Considering first the derivation of (33b), note that it must involve the formation of an A-chain. In order to see that this is so, consider the D-structure representation of (33b). Recall that all passive verbs are ergative, and that as such, they have only an internal argument, to which they assign θ-role, but no Case. Thus (33b) is base-generated as (34);

(34)   [s [NP e] [VP hugsha   'ugat tapuxim]]
             served-pass. cake apples

If no movement takes place in (34), the derivation would be ruled out, as the [e] in the [NP, S] position will not be bound. Subsequently, the argument in the post-verbal position must move to the [NP, S] position. However, following the Projection Principle, a trace must be left in the [NP, VP] position in order for the verb to assign θ-role there at S-structure. At S-structure, θ-role is assigned to 'apple-cake' through the A-chain which it forms with its coindexed trace, as in (35). In this sense, the derivation of (33b) parallels exactly the derivation of verbal passives in English:

(35)   'ugat tapuximi hugsha [e]i
        cake apples   served-pass

Some independent evidence for the ergativity of passive verbs in Hebrew comes from the following facts discussed in Borer and Grodzinsky (1986). In Hebrew, a prepositional phrase with the preposition le- (roughly 'to') can function as a possessor of an NP in the clause. Thus consider the following sentences:

(36) a.   ha-yalda 'axla li   'et   ha-tapu'ax
        the-girl   ate to-me acc the-apple

        'the girl ate my apple'

b.   ha-yeled shavar li   'et   ha-xalon
        the-boy   broke to-me acc the-window

        'the-boy broke my window'

c.   ha-kelev shaxav li   'al ha-mita
        the-dog   lay to-me on the-bed

        'the dog lay on my bed'

An important fact to be noticed with respect to (36a—c) is that the 'owned' NP is always in the VP. Thus there is no implication in (36a—c) that the girl, the boy or the dog respectively are 'mine'. There is, on the other hand, a clear meaning that the apple, the window and the bed, respectively, are 'mine' or pertain to me in some important way. Furthermore, an attempt to couple the possessor PP with a subject NP leads to ungrammaticality in the following sentences:

(37) a. *ha-kelev shaxav li
         the dog   lay to-me

b. *ha-yalda yashva li
    the-girl   sat to-me

c. *ha-po'alim 'avdu li
    the-workers worked to-me

The facts in (36)—(37) can be easily explained, if one assumes that the possessor PP is a clitic attached to the verb, and that it must c-command the 'possessed' NP. This configuration is met with respect to the possessed NP's in (36), but not in (37), thus leading to the grammaticality of the former, but the ungrammaticality of the latter.

There is, however, a class of counterexamples to this generalization. This class consists of some verbs of the *KaTaL* form (the heterogenous verbal class), some verbs of the *hitKaTeL* form (the reciprocal-reflexive form) and all of the passive verbs. Thus consider the following examples:

(38) a. ha-maftexot naflu li
        the-keys   fell   to-me

        'my keys fell'

b. ha-xalon   nishbar li
   the-window broke   to-me

   'my window broke'

c. ha-pgisha   hukdema   li
   the-meeting was-advanced to-me

   'my meeting was advanced'

d. ha-'uga ne'exla li
   the-cake was-ate to-me

   'my cake was eaten'

The systematic way in which passive verbs (and others) allow for the possession relation between the *le-* PP and the surface subject need not be viewed as a counterexample to the explanation given above, if we assume that at D-structure, the surface subjects of these verbs occupies a post-verbal position. Thus the correct representation of (38a—d) actually contains a trace in the post-verbal position, and it is the *c*-command relations between the possessor PP and that trace, which allows the explanation above to be maintained. On the other hand, this conclusion lends support to our contention that all passive verbs in Hebrew are ergative in nature.

Consider now the acquisition of verbal passives in Hebrew. Recall that given the assumption that all passive verbs are ergative, the derivation of clauses involving these forms requires either the formation of an A-chain, as in (33b), or post-verbal nominative assignment, as in (33a). Considering (33b) first, recall that we assume that the formation of A-chains does not mature until a later stage. It is this late maturation which prevents the children from deriving verbal passives in English, while allowing them the derivation of adjectival passives. The latter, while equally complex morphologically, are entirely lexical, and as such, they do not require syntactic movement, and subsequently, the formation of an A-chain. It is thus clear that to the extent that the derivation of verbal passives in Hebrew also involves the formation of an A-chain, we do not expect them to emerge until a later age. At the same time, we expect children to master adjectival passives, the derivation of which is exactly parallel to the derivation of adjectival passive in English, and does not require the formation of A-chains.

Now consider (33a). It would seem that Hebrew speaking children, confronted with the impossibility of A-chain formation, would resort to this option: they would leave the internal argument in its original position, post-verbally, and would assign nominative Case to it there, an option available in the adult grammar. There is, however, evidence which points out clearly, that at the stage of development discussed in this paper, Hebrew speaking children do not possess knowledge of the mechanism which enables them to assign nominative Case post-verbally. In spontanous speech, VS word orders are extremely rare, in spite of the fact that such word orders are very common both in adult speech and in children's literature. It should be noted that this word order is not only rare in constructions involving ergative verbs, but also in constructions which involve postposition of the subject and verbal fronting, both processes which require post-verbal nominative Case assignment. Thus consider the following percentages from elicited production (there are 16 children in each of the age groups):[13,14]

(39)	Age	No. of Utterances	VS Orders no. Percent
	3-0—3;11	548	10 1.64%
	4;0—4;11	690	20 2.89%
	5;0—5;11	744	32 4.3%
	7;0—7;11	967	79 8.17%

It is thus plausible to conclude that the device which enables the child to assign nominative Case post-verbally is not available at the stage at which adjectival passives (but not verbal passives) are derived. In this respect, the early grammar of Hebrew speaking children resembles the grammar of speakers of English and French, and differs from the adult grammar of Spanish, Italian and Hebrew itself. It follows that the path illustrated by (33a) is blocked for the child as well. Thus there is no way for the child to derive a well-formed verbal passive, a fact which accounts for their absence in the early grammar.[15]

To summarize, we have shown that verbal passives in Hebrew are similar to verbal passives in English in one crucial respect: their derivation involves the formation of an A-chain. As such, we expect the same delay in their development as exists in English. An additional step of this argument, however, necessitated showing that the derivation of verbal passives without the formation of A-chains, which is possible in the adult grammar of Hebrew, is not available to the child. Data concerning word order and agreement in Hebrew strongly suggests, that this option indeed is not available at the stage discussed in this paper.

4. CAUSATIVE-INTRANSITIVE CONSTRUCTIONS.

4.1. *Overgeneration and Correction: An Analysis*

In this section we would like to show how the assumption that in the early grammar chain formation is impossible can account for the elimination from the grammar of overgeneration of the type illustrated in (15). Again, in order to understand what is going on in the early grammar, it is useful to understand what is happening in the adult grammar. We observed above that there are two kinds of intransitive verbs, corresponding to the pattern in (29), repeated here as (40):

(40) a. NP V
     b.   V NP

We will assume, following suggestions of Burzio (1981) that in the adult grammar of English, all verbs which exhibit causative-intransitive alternation are ergative verbs. Thus a verb such as *move* is listed lexically as taking one argument, which is base-generated in the object position and which is assigned a thematic role (θ-role) by *move* in that position (see (41a)). Given the fact that in English the object of *move* cannot be assigned Case in that position, movement must take place, yielding the representation in (41b):

(41) a. e moved the doll
     b. the doll$_i$ moved [e]$_i$

The considerations which lead us to postulate movement and trace in (41b) should be familiar from the discussion of the derivation of verbal passive in Hebrew above.

Let us now turn to the causative operation. The causative morpheme (which is 0 in English), when attached, accomplishes a very specific task: *in the presence of a θ-role, it adds a θ-role*. The simplicity of the formulation is derived from what we would like to call *The External Argument Principle*, and which we formulate as (42):

(42)   *The External Argument Principle*:

> Unless otherwise specified, all arguments or θ-roles which are added or deleted by a morphological operation are external. All added arguments are of the type *agent*.

Two points are worth noting here. First, note that the passive rule obeys the External Argument Principle, in that the θ-role eliminated/absorbed is the external one. Note further that the Projection Principle implies that the causative rule, adding a θ-role, may not apply in the syntax and must apply in the lexicon. The principle in (42) will ensure the correct application of the causative rule, adding an external argument to *move* which is an agent. This addition would result in the sentence in (43):

(43)   Peter moved the doll

In (43) no movement need take place, as the addition of an external subject role to the verb *move* makes it possible for the verb to assign Case to the post-verbal argument (see Burzio, 1981, for discussion). As one last question, consider why in the adult grammar of English the sentence in (44) is ungrammatical:

(44)   *Peter giggled the doll

The verb *giggle* is not an ergative verb. Rather, it has the pattern in (40a). We would like to utilize now a statement of markedness, in assuming that the causative rule, in its unmarked application, does not involve the *internalization* of an argument (we are using the term *internalization* here in the sense of Williams, 1981). We mean markedness here in a very specific sense: we assume that the unmarked rule is the less costly rule, i.e., the rule that requires the least computation. From this point of view, a rule which adds an external argument without internalization involves less computation, and is thus less marked, than a rule which requires internalization prior to such addition. We do not intend to claim here that internalization rules are not common in natural languages, and in fact, exactly such an internalization rule is required in order to account for the causativization rule in Modern Hebrew.

Interpreting the unmarked rule of causativization in such a way, note that the application of the causative rule to a verb such as *move* does not entail any change in the assignment relationship of the verb and does not require any internalization. The verb still assigns a θ-role to *the doll* in the same position, i.e., the post-verbal position. Thus the application of the causative rule to a verb such as *move* is unmarked in the specific sense defined above. On the other hand, if a θ-role is added to the verb *giggle*, and the External Argument Principle is obeyed, it is clear that the assignment relations between the verb and the previous subject must be changed: the subject must become an object, i.e., it must be internalized. Thus the application of the causative rule to *giggle* is marked.

Now let us consider the language learner. In the early grammar, as we suggested above, the process of A-chain formation is not available. It follows that NPs must appear in the very same position in which they are assigned θ-roles. Now consider the two types of intransitive verbs depicted in (40), coupled with the observed fact that in English, type (40b) must undergo movement. Since A-chain formation is not available to the child, but nevertheless utterances with the D-structure of (40b) are available in the input (e.g., the doll moved), s/he is led to the only hypothesis which is compatible with the data: the hypothesis that all intransitive verbs that s/he was exposed to thus far are of the type (40a), i.e., their argument is base-generated in the subject position.

Now consider the causative rule. Since the child is exposed to pairs such as the ones given in (14) above, s/he must deduce that a causative rule exists in English. On the other hand, since in his/her lexicon all intransitives are of the (40a) type, s/he also deduces that English allows for a marked application of the causative rule, i.e., that the causative rule in English involves the internalization of the intransitive subject. However, after concluding that such is the English rule, we expect exactly the overgeneration which indeed occurs. Since in the child's grammar there is no formal distinction between *giggle* and *move*, it is only natural that the causative rule should apply to both of them, resulting in the sentences in (15).

Note, incidentally, that the process of causative formation suggested here is extremely plausible for the child, given the kind of errors the child does make, when compared with possible errors which the child does not make. Thus we find the child systematically using intransitive verbs transitively, but we find no intransitive use of transitive verbs. Thus mistakes such as (45) do not occur in the early grammar:

(45) a. *the cake eats
     b. *the movie sees
     c. *the doll punished

This state of affairs changes drastically once A-chain formation is available. The child realizes immediately that s/he must re-evaluate the formal representation given to the entries of intransitive verbs, as some of them may, in fact, have the representation in (40b). S/he further realizes that for these latter types, the unmarked application of the causative rule is possible. We may assume, then, that the child embarks upon a search for positive evidence that will determine which of the intransitive verbs in his/her lexicon are ergative verbs. Such positive evidence is available in abundance: first, only subjects of ergative verbs appear in the object position (in causative constructions). Second, only ergative verbs appear as passive participles, either in adjectival or in verbal constructions. Once the child determines which intransitives are ergatives, and given the fact that only ergatives may undergo causativization, the overgeneration ceases instantly.

To summarize, overgeneration in the causative constructions is the result of a wrong lexical representation of ergative verbs. This representation, which is wrong from the adult's grammar viewpoint, is the only grammatical representation which the child may give, while obeying the constraints imposed by the early grammar. Once these constraints are lifted, and chain formation is possible, the wrong representation is corrected and the overgeneration ceases. In other words, the earlier rule involved a marked application, which resulted in a larger range of lexical items which served as input to the application of the rule. A later version of that same rule entailed an unmarked application, restricted to a smaller range of lexical items as input. Note that although we assume a process of correction here, it is not the rule which is corrected. The adult rule still involves the addition of an external argument, and thus the analysis of these constructions conforms to our requirement that no rules be discarded. The correction is in the representation in lexical entries of the relations between the verb and its arguments. The causative rule remains unchanged in principle, and the only modification in it involves a simplification: a choice of the unmarked operation over the marked operation. This fact gives rise to an interesting hypothesis: the possibility that whatever reinterpretation occurs with respect to earlier formulated rules, they will involve the simplifications of earlier formulations, made available by factors introduced by maturation. Rather than assume, then, that the grammar always becomes more complicated, we assume that it is sometimes simplified, along options which are available but which cannot be utilized in the early grammar.[16]

4.2. *The Acquisition of Hebrew Causative Constructions*

In this section we will show how the system developed for English causative-intransitive constructions carries over to Modern Hebrew. It will be shown that Hebrew speaking children, like English speaking children, overgenerate causative verbs. Unlike the case for English speakers, however, such overgeneration does not actually cease, but continues well into puberty, serving as one of the major foundations for neologisms and slang. The latter phenomena will be explained by appearling to the marked nature of the causativization rule in Hebrew. The child data in this section is based on the work of Berman (1981a, 1981b, 1982) and Berman and Sagi (1981).

As mentioned above, the verbal paradigm of Hebrew is composed of
a basic consonantal root and of a number of patterns, each displaying a
typical array of affixes and having a particular vocalic melody. Concretely, the verbal paradigm of *hiKTiL* is the one associated usually
with causative meaning, while the source form (to the extent that such
source form exists) is *KaTaL*. The rule mapping from the *KaTaL* form
to the *hiKTiL* form is quite productive (although there are gaps in the
paradigm), and it applies both to transitive and intransitive forms. On
the other hand, we find *hiKTiL* forms in the adult grammar which are
not derived from a *KaTaL* source, alongside *hiKTiL* forms which have
a semantic meaning that is compositionally deduced from the meaning
of the source *KaTaL* form combined with causation. This situation is
illustrated in the following table:

(46)   *KaTaL form*   *hiKTiL form*

    a. 'axal   'ate'   he'exil   'caused to eat, fed'

	KaTaL form		hiKTiL form	
a.	'axal	'ate'	he'exil	'caused to eat, fed'
	lavash	'put on clothes'	hilbish	'caused to put on clothes'
	ra'a	'saw'	her'a	'caused to see, showed'
	shama	'heard'	hishmi'a	'caused to hear'
	rakad	'danced'	hirkid	'caused to dance'
	yashav	'sat'	hoshiv	'caused to sit'
	'amad	'stood'	he'emid	'caused to stand'
	caxak	'laughed'	hicxik	'caused to laugh, amuse'
	nafal	'fell'	hipil	'caused to fall'
b.	katav	'wrote'	hixtiv	'dictated'
	kara	'read'	hikri	'read aloud'
	batax	'had confidence'	hivti'ax	'promised'
c.	*lavan		hilbin	'caused to become white'
	*kashav		hikshiv	'listened'
	*bara		hivri	'became well'
d.	dakar	'stabbed'	*hidkir	
	kara9	'tore'	*hikri9a	
	xalam	'dreamt'	*hexlim	

While the correlation between semantic function and morphological
paradigms is never complete, as is illustrated above for the causative
paradigm, it is nevertheless relatively regular, and as we will show
below (and see also references above), at least for the causative constructions, children tend to associate the verbal paradigm *hiKTiL* with
regular causative meaning in a systematic way. Thus we find typical

cases of overgeneration, i.e., the formation of causative verbs in the *hiKTiL* pattern from existing *KaTaL* form, with entirely regular compositional causative meaning assigned to these verbs. Consider the following examples (from Berman and Sagi, 1981):[17]

(47)

KaTaL form		*Overgenerated hiKTiL form*		*Correct form*
shata	'drank'	hishta	'caused to drink'	hishka (irreg.)
taka	'stuck'	hitki'a	'caused to get stuck'	—
gar	'resided'	higir	'caused to spent the night'	—
yashan	'slept'	hishin	'caused to go to bed'	hishkiv (from shaxav, 'lied down')
saxa	'swimmed'	hisxa	'caused to swim'	—
calal	'dived'	hiclil	'caused to dive'	—

Alongside the forms in (47) attested in children, we also find cases of over-regularization in children, where roots which appear in patterns other than *hiKTiL* with a causative meaning are mistakenly conjugated as *hiKTiL* forms by the children. This is illustrated by the following table (from Berman and Sagi, 1981). Note that the verbs in (48), while appearing in the *KaTaL* form, nevertheless have a meaning of causation (i.e., cause to be smeared, cause to burn, etc.). On the other hand, there are no cases of overgeneration featuring the *hiKTiL* form without causative meaning (e.g., no *hiKTiL* forms with an argument structure of an intransitive verb):

(48)

Correct form		*Over-regularized form*
marax	'smeared'	himri'ax (himri'ax)
daxaf	'pushed'	hidxif (madxifa)
xalac	'took off shoes'	hexlic (lehaxlic)
saraf	'burned'	hisrif (masrif)
hafax	'turn inside out	hehefix (mahafixa)

(The forms in parenthesis are the forms actually attested in the samples, inflected for gender, number and tense).

We assume that the forms in (48) disappear gradually, as the child realizes that there are other forms in the language (and utilizing the same root) which have the same meaning. However, it is very plausible to conclude that at the ages in which the forms in (47) and (48) are attested in children (roughly 3;0 until 6;0 for (48), and at least 7;0 or perhaps later for (47), see below) the children possess a productive morphological rule of causative formation, which converts the source *KaTaL* form to an *hiKTiL* form, with the strict compositional meaning of *cause* to *KaTaL*. This rule is responsible for the production of utterances which are attested in adult speech, alongside the production of the forms in (47) and (48).

Consider now the nature of the rule in question. On a par with the rule which converts ergative verbs to causative verbs in English, we may say that the causative rule in Hebrew, apart from performing obvious morphophonemic changes, adds an argument, which, given The External Argument Principle must be external and must be an agent. Note, however, that the adult rule in Hebrew differs in an important way from the adult rule of English: the adult rule of Hebrew specifically allows what we have referred to as a marked application, i.e., the internalization process. This is clearly the case, since in Hebrew, transitive verbs, with a clear external argument, can undergo the causativization rule, giving rise to three place predicates. Such are the verbs 'eat', 'see', 'hear', 'put-on cloths' and others (see (46a) above).

Now consider this situation from the viewpoint of the language learner. As the child learning Hebrew is clearly assuming that the causative rule is regular and productive, the overgeneration illustrated in (47) follows. Notice, however, that this overgeneration is not based on a wrong assumption with respect to the nature of the rule involved, as was the case for the learner of English. Recall that the English learner erronously assumed that the rule is marked, and hence would apply to any intransitive verb. However, as the rule in English is unmarked, overgeneration resulted. On the other hand, the rule in Hebrew *is* marked, and the child assuming it to be so is correct. Consequently, the ability of the Hebrew speaking child to form A-chains, which we assume to mature later on, should not influence in the least the overgeneration of causative forms. In fact, we predict that such overgeneration would not cease at all, barring here the influence of social factors on productive processes of word formation.[18] Concretely, what this state of affair amounts to is the claim that the overgenerated forms in (47) are possible but non-occuring words of Hebrew, that is, words which are well-formed, but which are missing from the lexicon of Hebrew due to accidental gaps. It is these gaps which give rise to lexical innovations (such as slang formation). On the other hand, the overgenerations produced by English speaking children are not possible words of English (in using the term possible non-occuring word we are following the distinction drawn in Halle, 1973, and much subsequent morphological literature).

Independent evidence for the status of the forms in (47) as possible non-occuring words comes, indeed, from productive processes of word-formation found in adults. Thus we find among slang items causative forms such as *hilxic* 'caused to be pressured' from *laxac*, 'pressured', *hishpix*, 'ejaculate', related to *shafax*, 'poured', and others.

Concluding, we saw that the rule of causativization in Hebrew and in English performs the same operation: it inserts an argument, in accordance with The External Argument Principle. However, the application of this rule in the adult grammar of English is unmarked, whereas Hebrew utilizes a marked version of this rule. From the viewpoint of the language learner, this leads to a somewhat different array of facts. The English learner, given his/her inability to form A-chains, must assume at first that the English rule, as well, is marked. As a result, the class of lexical items which can serve as input to that rule is increased, and overgeneration results. When the learner realizes that A-chain formation is possible, s/he is driven to re-evaluate the application of the causative rule, resulting in the conclusion that the rule is unmarked, and that the class of possible inputs to it is smaller. Overgeneration ceases. On the other hand, the Hebrew child, at the same time, re-confirms his/her original hypothesis, that the rule is marked, since even after A-chain formation is possible, there is much positive evidence that indicates that the rule applies in a marked fashion. Consequently, overgenerations do not cease, and are not, strictly speaking, over-generations at all, they are simply cases of possible non-occuring words, which serve as a foundation for neologisms and slang formation.

5. CONCLUSION

We have provided arguments in favor of a theory of language acquisition which is at least partailly based on the maturation of specific linguistic abilities. The particular Maturation Hyposthesis that we have entertained is that the ability to form A-chains matures. We have argued, based on child language data, that at an early age both English and Hebrew-speaking children form lexical (adjectival) passives, but not verbal passives. This follows from the Maturational Hypothesis. Furthermore, at this same earlier stage, both English and Hebrew-speaking children overgeneralize causative verbs. The overgeneration follows from assuming a marked application of a morphological rule, which involves internalization as well as the insertion of an external argument. In the case of Hebrew, the child is learning an essentially correct rule. The adult causative rule *is* marked in this specific sense, and overgeneration in this case simply gives rise to well-formed neologisms. In the case of English, the marked application is a result of an erronous representation of ergative verbs, which is forced by the unavailability of A-chains. When maturation occurs, relevant positive evidence allows the reanalysis of these representations, causing a retreat to the unmarked adult rule.

We have advanced our hypothesis quite tentatively. Even if maturation plays a key role in language acquisition, it may turn out, under deeper analysis, and considering a wider array of phenomena, that the particular Maturation Hypothesis has to be reformulated. It would be surprising if this were not the case. In this paper we hope to have opened up a large new array of possible explanations in language acquisition.

NOTES

* The research on which this paper is based was partially supported by NSF grants BNS-78-270YY and BNS-84-19475-01. First versions of these ideas were developed in and presented to the 1984 UC Irvine Seminar on Language Acquisition and Linguistic Theory. Nina Hyams provided a number of useful suggestions, and we also benefitted from discussions by Neil Elliott and Rita Manzini. Mary-Louise Kean provided an extensive critique of an earlier version of this paper and also told us much about biological maturation. We would like to thank Ruth Berman and Dorit Ravid for discussion and for giving us data.

[1] Mary-Louise Kean informs us that the areas of the brain responsible for human linguistic capacity undergo significant development well into the first decade. She suggests that a maturational hypothesis seems quite plausible, given the biological evidence. She has marshalled a good deal of evidence toward this position.

[2] Interestingly, adjectives derived from non-actional verbs such as *see* and *like* may be improved significantly in the adult grammar by further affixation. Thus compare (6a—b) with (ia—b):

(i) a.   the unseen doll; the doll seems unseen.
   b.   the well-liked doll; the doll appears well-liked.

This state of affairs suggests that the constraint against adjectives derived from non-actional verbs is not a derivational constraint, but rather a condition on well-formed outputs (i.e., a contraint on what is a semantically possible adjective). Thus the derivation of adjectives such as *seen* is not ruled out in itself. We return to the nature of this constraint below.

[3] Several counterexamples to this claim are cited by Roeper (1983), who notes the grammaticality of sentences such as (i—ii):

(i)   the code was unbroken by the Russians
(ii)   the island was uninhabited by Mankind

While supplying a complete explanation for the grammaticality of (i—ii) is outside the scope of this paper, we believe it to represent an exception rather than a norm. Specifically, it seems that in sentences such as (i—ii), the adjectives combined with the by-phrase form complex predicative adjectives, and thus restrictions apply to the complement of the *by*-phrase which do not usually apply. Thus compare (i—ii) with (iii—iv):

(iii)   *the code was unbroken by John
(iv)   *the island was uninhabited by the Robinsons

It appears that the ungrammaticality of (iii—iv) when compared with (i—ii) derives from the fact that *unbroken by John* does not make a sufficiently general complex predicate, unlike, say, *uninhabited by Mankind*, a fact which suggests that (i—ii) are not necessarily problematic for our account. Note, as additional support for our claim, that these complex predicates may appear in canonical adjectival positions, as in (v) (and compare with (vi), where a *by*-phrase is excluded in our system):

(v)   uninhabited by mankind though this island was, the Robinsons decided to build their summer home there.
(vi)   *torn by the fierce dogs though this doll was, John decided to keep it.

[4] An interesting question concerns the disappearance from the speech of children of overgenerations of the type cited in these examples. We assume that to the extent that there are well-formed adjectives in the language which convey the meaning expressed by the adjective, the child will eliminate the over-generated adjectives when confronted with positive evidence that another form exists in the language. We have no explanation at this point for the disappearance of forms such as meshu'al, for which the language does not have any other adjectival form. It should be noted that verbal passives are also less common in adult everyday speech than adjectival passives, and that this relative rarity might account for their late emergence in the child's speech. On the other hand, they are amply present in other forms of input, which are presumably available to the child at that age (ages 4—7). Thus they are quite common in the speech of radio and TV announcers. Furthermore, their relative rarity in speech still does not account for the precise time at which they actually emerge, as it is implausible that around age 7 children are more exposed to these forms than they are at earlier stages.

[5] No attempt is made in this paper to explain the conjunction of properties associated with the participial morpheme, either in adjectival constructions or in verbal constructions. It is clear that a complete account of the passive rule must address itself to the question of whether these properties are derived from one another or not. Thus, for instance, in the work of Stowell (1981) it is assumed that subcategorization is appended to θ-role assignment. On the other hand, we are aware of no adequate account which

derives the elimination of Case from the elimination of subject θ-role, or vice versa. For some discussion, see Chomsky (1981) and Marantz (1984).

[6] In Borer (1984) and in Borer and Wexler (1984) it is assumed that the Projection Principle should be interpreted as a condition on features, and not as a condition on assignment. This is, in some respects, similar to Marantz (1984). Following this assumption, processes which alter the assignment relations between an assigner and an assignee do not violate the PrPr, as long as all features which the assigner possesses are actually assigned. Thus, for instance, the absorption of a θ-role does not constitute a violation of the Projection Principle. Note, however, that the specifications in (19) violate the Projection Principle regardless of the way in which it is interpreted.

[7] The way that we have stated the Projection Principle in (17), the lexical features have to be preserved at all syntactic levels. The lexical features are taken to be the output of the lexion. Thus rules can eliminate or add features within the lexicon, but not at the syntactic levels. This view differs from the one expressed in Roeper (1983), who assumes that the Projection Principle (in a weakened version) restricts the application of lexical operations as well.

[8] Note that the specifications in (21) as stated do not violate the Projection Principle only if it is interpreted as a condition on features and not as a condition on assignment, as the θ-role which is assigned to the [NP, S] position in the active is not assigned there in the passive derivation (see N. 6 for discussion). Alternatively, it might be argued that a verb is specified to assign an external role (rather than specifying that it must be assigned in the [NP, S] position), and that this role is either absorbed or assigned externally — to the object of the *by*-phrase, thus maintaining the Projection Principle as a condition on assignment. This last possibility was proposed to us by L. Rizzi (p.c.). Note that this solution still leaves problematic the absorption of accusative Case. One more important point needs to be made with respect to the distinction between verbal passive and adjectival passive. Note that while the former allows underspecification and absorption, no underdeterminacy is allowed in the latter. Forms derived lexically, it seems, must be fully specified. In Borer and Wexler (1984) it is proposed that this is due to the Lexical Determinacy Principle, which, in effect, does not allow lexical entries to be underdetermined. As adjectival passives are lexical entries, but verbal passives are not, the Lexical Determinacy Principle applies to the former only. For detailed discussion and motivation see the reference.

[9] For example, one might assume that for a young child, no item can receive reference from another linguistic item. Thus an anaphor could not receive reference from its antecedent. On this view, young children could not correctly understand, say, reflexives. There is no reason to think that this is true. For research suggesting that the assignment of reference is available at an early stage, see, among others, Otsu (1981) and Wexler and Chien (1985).

[10] Note that in order for our morphological system to go through, it in necessary for the passive verbs to be derived in the syntax, and not in the lexicon. An argument to this effect is, in fact, easy to make, but it will take us outside the scope of this paper.

[11] The actual form of verbs in Hebrew is further affected by morphophonemic alternations and phonological rules which need not concern us here. At any rate, the picture in (30) is a somewhat idealized one, which suffices for the purposes of this paper.

[12] We do not offer here any explanation for this difference between English and Hebrew. The possibility of offering such an explanation rests heavily on a more

elaborate theory of feature neutralization than is available at present, and thus depends greatly on future research.

[13] The data on word order and agreement in Hebrew comes from a study in progress which is currently being conducted in Tel-Aviv University by Ruth Berman. We are extremely grateful to Ruth Berman for making this material available to us, and to Ruth Berman and Dorit Ravid for discussing with H. Borer different aspects of their project. In the enclosed sample we are systematically excluding existential constructions in Hebrew, formed with the particle *yesh* (and its negative counterpart *'eyn*). The reason for this exclusion is twofold. First, it is not clear that *yesh* and *'eyn* are in fact verbal in nature. Thus, for instance, they do not exhibit verbal agreement and may not be inflected according to tense. Second, there is strong evidence that in colloquial adult speech the post-particle NP is accusative and not nominative.

[14] Unfortunately, there is no data available on 6-year olds in this survey. Interestingly, however, of the 5-year olds checked, one patterns systematically with the 7-year olds. Thus the figure cited for 5-year olds, which falls between the younger group and the 7-year olds, is somewhat misleading. 15 of the 5-year olds checked performed precisely on a par with the 3 and 4-year olds, and VS orders were 2.77% of their total utterances. The other child on the other hand, patterned with the 7-year olds, producing an extremely high rate of VS orders: 20.6 of the utterances. While we have not conducted detailed measurements, the 'advanced' 5-year old seems to be further along than the other 5-year olds in other respects as well (cliticization, construct-state, complex embedding and other constructions appear in the former's speech but not in the latter's). Note, by the way, that the figures in (39) are not trivially necessary, in the sense that children must do better with advancing age. SV orders, although perfectly grammatical, nevertheless decrease with age.

[15] Note that we are claiming here that post-verbal nominative Case assignment is a late development, and that in the early grammar it is not attested. In much recent literature (notably, Rizzi, 1982, and subsequent studies) it is assumed that post-verbal nominative Case assignment and the availability of null pronominal subjects follows from the same factor. If this is correct, then we also predict that there will be no pronominal subject drop in early grammar either. This prediction runs contrary to the studies of Hyams (1983), who argues convincingly that children initially have a null-subject grammar, and that only later on do speakers of non-null subject langauges realize that their grammar needs to be corrected. If, indeed, Hyams is correct, then it would seem that the two phenomena cannot be given a unified grammatical explanation. This line is independently argued for in the work of Safir (1982), who claims that two parameters are involved in explaining these phenomena, and not one.

[16] Note that sentences such as "John giggled the doll" and "Mary vanished the mouse" are accessible to adults (that is, adults know precisely what they mean), while sentences such as "the cake eats" and "the mouse banished" are not. This might indicate that a residue of the marked application is, in fact, present in the adult's grammar, not entirely discarded, rendering these 'comprehensible' atterances highly marked, rather then strictly ungrammatical.

[17] Berman (1982) reports that alongside the forms in (47)–(48) Hebrew speaking children also use the *KaTaL* forms to indicate causative meaning, as in the following examples:

(i) a.   *ra'iti* 'et ha-ciyurim   le-aba   cf. her'eyti
         saw-I acc the-drawings to-Daddy   showed-I

   b.   lidya, 'ima   'oxelet 'oti hayom, lo 'at   cf. ma'axila
         Lydia, Mommy is-eating me today, not you   is-feeding

It seems to us, however, that this production pattern (all examples of which are from
the same child, age 2;6—2;11) does not reflect a productive process of causative
formation rule, and does not correspond to the stage of overgeneration in the formation
of English causatives reported by Bowerman. Rather, the productive stage described by
the data in (47)—(48) corresponds to the stage described by Bowerman, both in terms
of the approximate age and in terms of productivity. The stage illustrated by the data in
(i) appears, on the other hand, to reflect an earlier stage in the acquisition of derivational morphology, where the derivational relationship between '*axal* and *he'exil*, 'ate'
and 'fed' is perceived, but the morphological rule mapping from one to the other has
not been mastered yet. The description of the characteristics of that particular stage and
the questions raised by its existence are outside the scope of this paper.

[18] It is plausible to assume that a pressure for conservative use of language would bar
growing children in a school set-up from using self-produced neologisms, even if these
are well-formed morphologically. We thus assume that to the extent that children no
longer use some of the forms given in (47) it is because these vocabulary items are
typically associated with 'baby-talk', and are thus socially unfavored by the growing
child. In other words, neologisms of the type discussed here probably receive negative
feed-back, comparable, say, to that received by *ain't* and similar tokens.

REFERENCES

Aoun, J.: 1979, 'A short note on cliticization', ms. MIT, Cambridge.
Berman, R.: 1981a, 'Regularity vs. anomaly: The acquisition of Hebrew inflectional
    morphology', *Journal of Child Language* **8**, 256—82.
Berman, R.: 1981b, 'Language development and language knowledge: Evidence from
    the acquisition of Hebrew morphology', *Journal of Child Language* **8**, 609—26.
Berman, R.: 1982, 'verb-pattern alternation: The interface of syntax, morphology and
    semantics in Hebrew child language', *Journal of Child Language* **9**, 169—92.
Berman, R. and I. Sagi: 1981, 'On word-formation and word-innovation in early age',
    Balshanut Ivrit Xofshit, 1981:18 (in Hebrew).
Berwick, R.: 1982, *Locality Principles and the Acquisition of Syntactic Knowledge*,
    Ph.D. dissertation, MIT Dept. of Electrical Engineering and Computer Science.
Berwick, R. and A. Weinberg: 1984, *The Grammatical Basis of Linguistic Performance:
    Language Use and Acquisition*, MIT Press, Cambridge.
Borer, H.: 1983, 'The projection principle and rules of morphology', in *Proceedings
    from the 14th meeting of the North Eastern Linguistic Society*, University of
    Massachusetts, Amherst.
Borer, H.: 1984, *Parametric Syntax*, Foris Publications, Dordrecht.
Borer, H.: 1986, 'I-subjects', *Linguistic Inquiry* **17**, 375—416.

Borer, H. and Y. Grodzinsky: 1986, 'Lexical cliticization vs. syntactic cliticization: The case of Hebrew dative clitics', in H. Borer (ed.), *Syntax and Semantics* **19**, Academic Press, New York.

Borer, H. and K. Wexler: 1984, 'The maturation of syntax', paper presented at the Amherst Symposium on Language Acquisition, May 1984.

Bowerman, M.: 1982, 'Evaluating competing linguistic models with language acquisition data: Implications of developmental errors with causative verbs', *Semantica* **3**, 1—73.

Burzio, L.: 1981, *Intransitive Verbs and Italian Auxiliaries*, Ph.D. dissertation, MIT. To be published by D. Reidel, Dordrecht.

Chomsky, N.: 1965, *Aspects of the Theory of Grammar*, MIT Press, Cambridge.

Chomsky, N.: 1981, *Lectures on Government and Binding*, Foris Publications, Dordrecht.

de Villiers, J., M. Phinney, and A. Avery: 1982, 'Understanding passives with non-action verbs', paper presented at the 7th Annual Boston University Conference on Language Development, Boston.

Gleitman, L.: 1981, 'Maturational determinants of language growth', *Cognition* **10**, 103—114.

Gleitman, L. and E. Wanner: 1982, 'Introduction', in E. Wanner and L. Gleitman (eds.), *Language Acquisition, the State of the Art*, Cambridge University Press.

Halle, M.: 1973, 'Prolegomena to word formation', *Linguistic Inquiry* **4**.

Hyams, N.: 1983, *The Acquisition of Parameterized Grammars*, Ph.D. dissertation, City University of New York, New York. To be published by D. Reidel, Dordrecht.

Horgan, D. M.: 1975, *Language Development: A Cross-Methodological Study*, Ph.D. dissertation, University of Michigan.

Jaeggli, O.: 1981, 'A modular approach to Romance agentive causatives', ms., USC.

Jaeggli, O.: 1982, *Topics in Romance Syntax*, Foris Publications, Dordrecht.

MacNamara, J.: 1972, 'Cognitive basis for language learning in infants', *Psychological Review* **79**, 1—13.

Marantz, A.: 1984, *On the Nature of Grammatical Relations*, MIT Press, Cambridge.

Maratsos, M. P.: 1983, 'some current issues in the study of the acquisition of grammar', in J. Flavell and E. Markman (eds.), *Child Psychology*.

Maratsos, M. P., D. E. C. Fox, J. Becher, and M. A. Chalkley: 1983, 'Semantic restrictions on children's early passive', ms. University of Minnesota.

Marcus, M.: 1979, *A Theory of Syntactic Recognition for Natural Language*, MIT Press, Cambridge.

Marr, D.: 1982, *Vision*, W. H. Freeman, San Francisco.

Otsu, Y.: 1981, *Universal Grammar and Syntactic Development in Children: Toward a Theory of Syntactic Development*, Ph.D. Dissertation, MIT.

Perlmutter, D.: 1978, 'Impersonal passives and the unaccusative hypothesis', in *Proceedings from the 4th Meeting of the Berkeley Linguistic Society*, Los Angeles.

Pinker, S.: 1979, 'Formal models of language learning', *Cognition* **1**, 217—283.

Pinker, S.: 1983, 'Productivity and conservativism in language acquisition', paper presented in the Symposium on Leaning, University of Western Ontario, London.

Pinker, S.: 1984, *Language Learnability and Language Learning*, Harvard University Press, Cambridge.

Rizzi, L.: 1982, *Issues in Italian Syntax*, Foris Publications, Dordrecht.

Roeper, T.: 1983, 'Implicit arguments and the projection principle', ms.. University of
    Massachusetts, Amherst.
Safir, K.: 1982, *Syntactic Chains and the Definiteness Effect*, Ph.D. dissertation, MIT.
    To be published by Cambridge Press.
Siegel, D.: 1970, 'Non-sources for un-passives', in J. Kimball (ed.). *Syntax and
    Semantics II*, Seminar Press, New York.
Stowell, T.: 1981, *Origins of Phrase Structure*, Ph.D. dissertation, MIT, To be published
    by MIT Press, Cambridge.
Wasow, T.: 1977, 'Transformations and the lexicon, in P. Culicover, A. Akmajian and
    T. Wasow (eds.), *Formal Syntax*, Academic Press, New York.
Wexler, K.: 1982, 'A principle theory for language acquisition', in E. Wanner and L.
    Gleitman (eds.), *Language Acquisition, the State of the Art*, Cambridge University
    Press.
Wexler, K. and Y. C. Chien: 1985, 'The development of lexical anaphors and
    pronouns', *Papers and Reports on Child Language Development*, No. 24.
Wexler, K. and P. Culicover: 1980, *Formal Principles of Language Acquisition*, MIT
    Press, Cambridge.
Williams, E.: 1980, 'Predication', in *Linguistic Inquiry* **11**(1).
Williams, E.: 1981, 'Argument structure and morphology', *The Linguistic Review* **1**(1).

AMY WEINBERG

COMMENTS ON BORER AND WEXLER[1]

1. THE THEORETICAL STATUS OF THE 'MATURATION HYPOTHESIS'

Borer and Wexler present two types of arguments in favor of their 'maturational account' of language acquisition. One type is conceptual; claiming that, contrary to popular belief, there is no reason *not* to adopt a maturational theory. In addition, they claim that this framework is more compatible with the research goals and principles of linguistic theory. In addition, the account is also supposed to avoid the pitfall of unjustified reliance on evidence from the linguistic environment. The second set of arguments is designed to show that the maturational theory is more empirically justified in that it can use a uniform set of principles to handle certain cases better than non-maturational accounts.

I believe that Borer and Wexler (hence B & W) have done an excellent job of establishing this approach as a *bona fide* alternative at the conceptual level. In particular, the arguments from simplicity that are supposed to make maturational theories suspect are shown to be spurious. Moreover, the style of empirical argument that they present is quite interesting. They try to give a uniform account of the developmental patterns observed in two distinct constructions (the passive and causative-ergative constructions). This kind of approach is particularly congenial from the standpoint of current linguistic theory (particularly the government-binding approach) because in this theory the notion of a construction is derivative.[2] Principles apply across construction types and we would expect a lag in the development of some principle to have effects throughout the grammar. In this comment I will try to show that while B & W's work is quite conceptually sound there are important empirical problems. The problems show that a unified approach is in fact not possible at least in terms of the maturational principles that B & W provide. The interest of B & W's paper, I think, goes beyond whether the particular analyses proposed succeed. As will be seen in the body of the paper, a plausible non-maturational account of B & W's

173

Thomas Roeper and Edwin Williams (eds.), Parameter Setting, 173—187.

data involves considerably sharpening the notion of "possible triggering stimulus" and "data available to the child". Thus even if a maturational account is ultimately to be rejected the environmental factors that are crucial to making a non-maturational account run will be better understood to the extent that we consider the 'maturational' alternative.

The paper will proceed as follows. I will start by trying to independently justify the markedness assumptions needed by Hyams (1983), thereby eliminating the argument for a maturational treatment for this case and undermining the conceptual arguments based on goodness of fit between maturational accounts and parameterized grammars. Next, I will suggest that B & W's treatment of the passive construction must be substantially revised for empirical reasons. Then, I will show that the Hebrew passive data are not explained by the maturational account. Finally, I will show that there are conceptual problems with their treatment of the causative construction and that when these are taken care of, the causative data also cannot choose between maturational and non-maturational theories.

2. BRIEF SUMMARY OF THE MATURATIONAL THEORY

The essence of the maturational theory is the claim that parts of a child's grammatical competence may be unavailable at early stages of language development. This is coupled with the claim that the availability of these principles does not arise from any development of other general cognitive or perceptual capacities.[3] There is a qualitative change in the mental makeup of the language learner. Reaching a certain age 'triggers' the availability of a set of principles of adult competence that were hitherto unavailable to the child. *Triggering* is to be strictly contrasted with *learning*. For the cases under discussion, the child learns nothing. Rather, aspects of her innate endowment simply become available for grammar construction at different points in her development.

This approach heavily restricts the reliance we must place on ordering of environmental input. As B & W mention, non-maturational accounts often attribute a language learner's late control of a construction to the late or infrequent occurrence of that construction in the linguistic sample.[4] By contrast, because the maturational approach attributes staggered development to the staggered availability of linguistic constraints, principles, or operations, we can explain language development even under conditions of an unchanging linguistic environment.[5]

3. THE MATURATION HYPOTHESIS AND
MARKEDNESS THEORY

One of the arguments for this approach comes from consideration of cases where linguistic theory gives the same markedness value to two grammatical options and nonetheless one of these options seems to be available earlier in the course of language development. The 'maturation hypothesis' can explain this by claiming that the option corresponding to the earlier stage is simply maturationally prior to the other choice. B & W discuss the important study of Hyams (1983) in this light. Hyams elegantly explains a series of simultaneous developmental changes by claiming that the child's first hypothesis is that her language allows 'Null Subjects'. This hypothesis correctly characterises languages like Spanish or Italian but must be modified to correctly describe English. Even though this theory explains the facts in an interesting way, B & W point out that one would like to know *why* the [+Null Subject] option is chosen first and why the data that disconfirm it (the presence of expletive subjects in a language) are not acted on by the child until rather late in acquisition (what they call "the triggering problem"). They propose their maturational theory as an answer. The [+Null Subject] option is simply maturationally prior and since the other option is not available to the child until a certain point, no evidence provided by the linguistic environment can lead her to this conclusion.

It seems to me though that there is another, non-maturational account of these facts. Goldin-Meadow (1979) has noticed that there is a statistical correlation at the two word stage between intransitive verbs and the presence of overt subjects in children's speech. Children will tend to delete the subject of a sentence if the verb is transitive. We can explain these data on the natural assumption that children use their innate endowment to constrain the grammars governing their own linguistic output. Under this assumption, the Extended Projection Principle (Chomsky, 1981) should apply to the two word stage as well. This entails that the subcategorised objects of transitive verbs must be linguistically expressed. However, at the two word stage there seems to be an extralinguistic constraint that limits output to two words.[6] In order to conform to the Extended Projection Principle within the limitations of the memory constraint the child must express the object and drop the subject. However, if a child assumed the [−NULL SUBJECT] value of the PRO DROP parameter, her early utterances would be ungrammatical for these transitive cases.[7] Assuming that grammar governs early outputs as well thus forces the child to adopt the [+NULL SUBJECT] option as a first hypothesis. Hyams argues that the presence of expletive subjects in a language triggers the switch from [+] to [−] NULL SUBJECT. True expletive subjects only occur in multi clausal structures so it is not surprising that it takes some time for the child to become aware of their presence because as Otsu (1981) observes, multi clausal structures are misanalysed by children at early stages of acquisition. Independently needed principles explain the observed developmental sequence in this case and so we don't need to invoke maturation to make the account in terms of parameters run.

4. ON THE DEVELOPMENT OF THE PASSIVE CONSTRUCTION

B & W offer the following account of the development of the passive:

(1) There is a stage where children cannot form A-chains and therefore can only form "lexical or adjectival passives".

(2) Adjectival passives (at least in English) are restricted by a [+SR] condition on adjective formation that rules out adjectives that are [−direct action], except when these [−SR] adjectives inherit this feature from a [+SR] affix.[8] In addition, since the argument structure change associated with the adjective forming rule *deletes* the subject argument, adjectival passives never occur with *by* phrases.

(3) Putting (1) and (2) together, we predict a stage where passives, formed only from direct action verbs are correctly comprehended. At the same stage, we also predict that short passives, but not long passives are correctly comprehended.

The fact that we can use the same principles to unify *both* facts about passive development might be taken as an argument for this approach because maturational accounts of these facts used different principles to explain each of these facts (see Berwick and Weinberg, 1984; Maratsos, 1978). A closer inspection shows that unifying treating these phenomena as one leads to incorrect empirical predictions. Maratsos and Abramovitch (1975) showed that long and short passives are acquired *at the same time* in the course of development.[9]

Thus a developmental theory should not separate these two types of passives into different maturational components. More importantly, these data show that internalisation (as opposed to deletion) should be an option for the *lexical* passive.[10]

Maratsos and Abramovitch's data are to be expected because we can show independently that the adjective forming rule involved in passive *internalises* rather that *deletes* the θ-role associated with the subject position at DS.[11] B & W argue for deletion over internalization by noting the inability of the 'by' phrase to cooccur with prenominal passive participles. However this can be attributed to the fact that if the '*by*-phrase' were to occur before the modified noun the structure would violate Williams' "*Head Final Filter*", a filter that bars non-head final material from occuring in prenominal position.[12] The only other possibility is to place the '*by*-phrase' after the noun. However the phrase remains an *ex*ternal argument and so the lexical specifications of the adjective are still not satisfied. Thus we correctly predict the ungrammaticality of (3) and (4).

(*3)   the uninhabited by the British island

(*4)   the uninhabited island by the British

Passive adjectival participles in other positions that cooccur with '*by*-phrases' sound fine to my ear:[13]
  a. The island was uninhabited by civilized people, but linguists like to live there.
  b. The problem was unsolved by any linguist until Sue came along and licked it.[14]

Since full passives can be constructed using either a lexical or syntactic passive rule, we cannot (and given the data, should not) try to reduce their acquisition to the presence of the verbal passive rule.

More importantly, it is crucial to B & W's story that the class of lexical (adjectival) passives exclude non actional predicates. However, this claim is also quite dubious. B & W test whether a participle is verbal or adjectival by seeing whether it can appear in prenominal position or as the complement of a verb like 'seems'. The [+SR] verbs that can't occur in these positions are taken to be accidental gaps in the paradigm because in these positions,

the context can improve those (actional adjectives -ASW) but does little to improve non-actional adjectives. (B & W, 1984: 18.)

It seem to me however that context helps in both kinds of cases. So for example, (5a) and (5b) seem considerably improved by context (5c) and (5d):

(5) a.   ?a loved child
    b.   ?The child seems loved
    c.   After seeing so many orphans, a loved child is a pleasure to see.
    d.   The child seems loved, but then she shows up with all those bruises.

There is also a rather long list of [−SR] adjectives that seem to be perfect even without context:[15]

(6)   a respected woman
           an admired man
           an appreciated complement
           a despised dictator
           a loathed criminal
           an expected retort

This means that adjective formation should not be restricted to action verbs. If this is true for English, then even if it is not true in all languages, children have to learn whether adjective formation is constrained by the [+SR] restriction in their language. Therefore, even if we assume such a restriction, we must explain why the presence of non-actional passives in adult English doesn't lead the child to remove this restriction from her adjective forming rule even at early stages. It seems both maturational and non-maturational theories are in the same boat and everyone must rely on something like the fact that non-actional passives are rare in the child's early linguistic input.[16]

This fact was used by Berwick and Weinberg (1984) to give a non-maturational account of passive development. We claimed that the child assumed that affixes were associated with a unique set of properties. In addition we assumed that the '-ed' ending involved in passive participle formation was not distinguished from the earlier comprehended past tense forming '-ed'. This entails that both passives and past tense verbs are case assigners. Passives at an early stage would be analysed as in (7).

(7)   The boy was hit   e.
        [+NOM]   [+OBJ]

As Chomsky (1981) argues however, movement to an A-position from a case marked position violates Principle C of the Binding Theory (the case marked trace is a variable and is not A-Free). Such movement also creates a case conflict because an element is associated with two cases. To create the correct structures for licit passive interpretation, we claim that the child has to give up the idea that a morpheme is associated with a unique set of properties.[17] We assumed that she would do this conservatively. If a verb appeared enough times in a non-interpretable environment, the child would mark the verb as taking an exceptional 'ed' affix that absorbed case. Since actional verbs occur more widely in the child's early linguistic environment, we claimed that they would be correctly comprehended first. We assume that at some point in development the child notices cases where the past-tense and participial forms of a verb are distinct and thus realises that passives are formed by 0 affixation and are distinct from '-ed' past tense endings. This allows the formation of passive participles that do not violate the Principle of Unique Association. It is important to see the special use that environmental factors are put to here. Conservative learning (the need for highly salient examples to push a language learner to a certain grammatical option) is derived from the fact that option is not highly valued by the learning mechanism. This use of environmental evidence is quite different from the kind criticized in Wexler and Culicover (1980).

5. THE HEBREW PASSIVE

B & W claim that the absence of A-chain formation can explain why Hebrew children do not seem to produce verbal passives until school age. It is difficult though, to see how their account actually explains the data they cite. They state the adjectival passive rule as

(19) a. $[+V -N] \rightarrow [+V +N]$ resulting in the elimination of accusative case features.
     b.   The elimination of the subject θ-role.
     c.   The externalization of the internal argument.
          (B & W p. 25)

In the case of the verbal passive, the morphological part of the rule adds passive morphology to the basic verbal pattern and

> absorbs the external θ-role (and may optionally transmit it to the object of by)
> (B & W p. 41.)

This morphological change combines with A-chain formation to form verbal passives in adult Hebrew. Even assuming that A-chaim formation is not available at early stages of development, we are at a loss to explain why the child couldn't form an analogue of verbal passives using the following entirely lexical rule that does not involve A-chain formation.[18] The rule would

a.   add the morphological pattern associated with verbal passives
b.   Internalize the external θ-role.
c.   Externalize the internal θ-role.

We have no explanation for why the Hebrew child does not produce verbal passives (albeit by misanalysis) because nothing in linguistic theory bars the adoption of the incorrect alternative above in the early stage. Banning A-chain formation is simply not sufficient.[19]

6. CAUSATIVES

B & W want to use the inability to form A-chains to explain the overgeneralisation of the causative construction to cases like (8).

(*8)   John giggled the doll

They attribute the overgeneralisation to the fact that both these cases (true intransitives like "Mary giggled") and ergatives ("The doll broke") are treated as intransitives at the early stages. They claim that this is due to the fact that the ergative analysis is not available at this stage because it involves the formation of A-chains, Since both cases are analysed in the same way as intransitives, the appearance of a case like (9) in adult speech can only signal to the child that (8) must be grammatical as well. B & W claim that both cases are formed by a marked form of a causativization rule that adds an external argument and internalizes the previously external argument, yielding (9)

(9)   Mary broke the doll.

In addition, B & W argue that the account in terms of the maturation of A-chains can explain why the overgeneralisation disappears. In their words:

> This state of affairs changes drastically once A-chain formation is available. The child realizes immediately that s/he must re-evaluate the formal representation given to the entries of intransitive verbs . . . S/he further realizes that for these latter types the unmarked application of the causative rule *is* possible . . . Once the child determines which intransitives are ergatives, and given the fact that only ergatives may undergo causativisation, the overgeneration ceases instantly.

It seems to me that there are conceptual problems with this second assertion. Notice that this case differs from the two preceding ones in that the pressure for grammar change comes solely from the *possibility* of an alternative analysis. In the previous two cases there was positive evidence in the stimulus that the child's previous analysis was incorrect (the 'non-actional' English passives cannot be interpreted given the early passive rule and a class of Hebrew passives cannot be analyzed as adjectival.) According to B & W, the early analysis is sufficient to handle all the positive evidence and since overgeneralizations can only be coupled with *negative* evidence to induce correction, their presence cannot trigger reanalysis. Moreover, we do not want the mere *possibility* of reanalysis in terms of A-chains to force reanalysis in these terms. To see why, consider the case of 'able' affixation. This is a lexical rule that changes verbs into adjective and externalizes the THEME argument.[20]

(10) a. NP_1^{-able} [____]$_V$ NP$_2$ → NP$_2$[____] +able (by NP$_1$)
  b. Mary beat John   John is beatable
      America (can) win the war The war is winnable by America

Given that this construction does not involve the use of A-chains. It should occur at the early stages of development. Once A-chain formation becomes available, however, the rule would be reanalyzed in terms of A-chain formation. Since A-chain formation processes do not distinguish thematic classes of predicates, we would predict overgeneralizations of the following types:

(*11) John is promissable
    *John is giveable candy [On the model of "John was given some candy".]

The only way to recover from these overgeneralisations is again, by correction and thus we want to avoid placing the child in this position by forcing reanalysis only when there is some overt positive evidence in the stimulus that a previous analysis cannot handle. B & W's notion of 'marked rule' provides us with a way of doing this for the causative case. 'Markedness' in the relevant sense means deriving a structure using a rule with more computation than another available derivation.[21] On the assumption that ergatives are treated as intransitives at the early stage, they can be linked to their causative counterparts only by using the *marked* version of the causativisation rule. Once the 'A-Chain' formation option is available though, if we change the analysis of ergative verbs, from intransitives to true ergatives, we can relate them to their causative counterparts using the unmarked version of the causative rule. Again there is a problem though because we seem to be exchanging markedness for markedness. In order to use the unmarked causative rule, we must assume a 'marked' derivation for the basic ergative structures. In the 'early' analysis the D-structure is equivalent to the S-structure but now we must add the cost of NP-Movement to the derivation of these structures. Again, it seems that there is no motivation for reanalysis in terms of A-chains. In addition notice that these facts make the maturational account superfluous. Given B & W's markedness assumptions, the ˜ child would choose the intransitive analysis for ergative constructions even if an analysis in terms of A-chain formation was available. Therefore, in terms of the ability to explain the early stages of overgeneralisation, the two analyses are on a par as both would give a unique analysis to true intransitives and ergatives at the early stage.

Let me now take a stab at explaining what causes the overgeneralisation to cease in English. As B & W note, English passives can only be formed from transitive verbs. In contrast to Germanic languages, passives like (12) are ungrammatical.

(12) a. It was danced.
     b. It was slept.

If we can show that some passives can only be derived from the ergative version of verbs like 'break', we can provide the child with the necessary positive evidence to reach the conclusion that ergatives cannot be analysed as intransitives. Furthermore, if we can show that this data, though part of the Primary Linguistic data is sufficiently exotic, we can motivate a time lag between the time the child mis-analyses ergatives as intransitives and the time when the data allows her to correct her mistake. Manzini (1983) and Chomsky (class lectures and forthcoming) argue that so called implicit arguments (arguments that are part of the interpretation, but not phonetically realized) may control a PRO as shown in (13):

(13)   The boat was sunk PRO to collect the insurance.

This sentence is interpreted as meaning that the boat was sunk by the same person who wanted to collect the insurance.

They also show that implicit arguments correspond to internalized subjects and thus if a sentence has no thematic subject, then the sentence will only be grammatical if an overt argument can act as the appropriate controller. This is shown in (14).

(*14)   The boat sank PRO to collect the insurance.

Since this is an ergative structure it has no thematic subject. The overt subject is actually the preposed object, so no argument has been internalized and there is no appropriate argument to control the PRO.[22]

A final fact is that there are two types of passives from ergative verbs. One has the causative interpretation (15)

(15)   The vase was broken by Mary

This can have the interpretation that Mary caused the vase to be broken. We can see that this must be derived from the transitive (causative) form of 'broken' because there must be a thematic subject to internalize and serve as the implicit controller of the PRO in (16).

(16)   The vase was broken in order to collect the insurance.

In addition though, there is a passive form with no implied agent and a stative meaning. This seems to be the preferred reading with the present tense of these constructions as shown in (17)

(17)   The glass is broken.

The fact that there is no implicit argument can be verified by noticing that such constructions are semantically deviant for the same reason as cases like (14). Since there is no implicit argument the subject, which is an inappropriate controller of the PRO is the only argument around to control.

(18)   The vase is broken to collect the insurance

As was shown above neither the adjectival nor verbal passive eliminates the subject. Therefore, we can only derive a passive like (17) (with no implicit argument), from a structure that had no thematic subject to begin with. This means that (17) must be derived from a the ergative form of these verbs. However, as we mentioned, passives can only be formed from *transitive* verbs. Therefore, given a structure like (17) in an appropriate context to force the 'stative' reading, the child would be forced to give up his previous analysis of ergatives as transitive verbs. Such sentences are plausibly part of the PLD, however contexts that would bias language learners to the stative reading in the passive case would presumably not occur with great frequency and so it might take the child some time to revise his previous analysis.

7. CONCLUSION

The logic of and conceptual arguments for the maturational approach look sound. In addition, we noted the elegance of the kind of explanations attempted. We discovered however that the cases discussed did not motivate the type of theory as a *necessary* part of the theory of language development. Non maturational theories could explain the developmental patterns in all cases cited. Along the way we noted the empirical inadequacies of the principles needed by Borer and Wexler to account for the passive case and proposed an alternative maturational account of the development of this construction. The maturational account was also found to be lacking as an explanation for the loss of overgeneralisation of the causative construction in English and a non maturational argument was proposed.

NOTES

[1] I would like to thank Norbert Hornstein, David Lightfoot, and Tom Roeper for helpful comments.
[2] See Chomsky (1981), Ch. 1, for details.
[3] This does not mean that there is *no* general cognitive development occuring. It merely means that general cognitive development is not sufficient to explain all the facts about language development and thus the theory requires additional internal maturational principles.
[4] The cases that they discuss are particularly interesting in this regard because 'late' occurence of a construction can't be attributed to some unfolding extra-linguistic

capacity (developing memory, ability to handle complicated input, etc. since the triggering data consists of very short, simple sentences.

[5] It is important to emphasize that Wexler and Borer's account duplicates the reliance on a uniform set of principles to govern grammar construction at *all* stages of development that is characteristic of non-maturational accounts formulated by generative grammarians. This uniformity constrains the hypotheses available to the child in a way that a theory using both grammatical and extragrammatical linguistic principles could not.

[6] Note that Goldin-Meadow's observation suggests that the notion "two word stage" can't be subsumed under the notion "+Null Subject Parameter". If there weren't some kind of extra-linguistic restriction on number of words, then we would predict that Subjects would be dropped equally frequently in both the transitive and intransitive case.

[7] A case like "hit Daddy", with the obligatory presence of the object needed to satisfy the Extended Projection Principle would still be ungrammatical because the absence of a subject in a (−Null Subject) language is prohibited.

[8] They cite the prefix '*un*' and we might add the suffix '-*able*'.

[9] Borer and Wexler cite the production data taken from Horgan (1975) to show that short passives appear before long ones. As has been noted many times however, production data cannot act as a very subtle probe, particularly when length factors occur as independent variables in the structures being compared. One cannot rule out the possibility that Horgan's subjects understood both types of passives, but only produced short passives because of independent constaints on length of utterance.

[10] "The average number of sentences acted out accurately was 5.00 out of eight possible for full passives and 5.00 for short truncates." Maratsos and Abramovitch (1975) p. 147.

[11] Both options are quite compatible with the framework proposed in Borer (1984).

[12] See Williams (1982) for discussion.

[13] See also Roeper (1983) for additional examples.

[14] The passive participles that do occur with '*by*-phrases' are argued to be adjectival because they occur as left dislocated elements in 'though preposing' sentences. This test cannot be a diagnostic for adjectival status because *any* post copular structure including clearly verbal passives like (d) can be preposed in these cases:

   a. S': [PRO exercising] though John was, Mary still said he was getting fat.
   b. NP: [military victory] though it was, the attack on Grenada was a political disaster.
   c. VP: [given a toy] though the baby was, the brat still cried anyway.
   d. [expected to win though he was], McEnroe was beaten in the early rounds.

Even if this were not the case B & W's examples do not undermine the claim that adjectival passives occur with internalized rather than deleted arguments.

[15] In any case, the (+SR) restriction is peculiar in that actional verbs, the '*un-*' prefix, and the 'able' suffix (at least) must be marked (+SR) and it is difficult to see how these form a natural class.

[16] Pinker (1982) cites De Villiers who claims that non-actional passives very rarely occur in the adult speech that children hear at early stages.

[17] The unique association of affixes to properties at least as a first hypothesis seems quite necessary to guarantee efficient learning. As Berwick and Weinberg point out, if

we don't assume such a principle, then the fact that the child figures out that an affix is associated with some properties when attached to a verb 'A' would not allow him to induce its function with respect to a verb 'B'. We would expect affix formation to proceed verb by verb. Bowerman (1981) has shown though that once morphemes are decomposed into "root + affix" components, affixation is completely regular; in fact, over-regularised.

Tom Roeper (personal communication) suggests some needed clarification of the way in which this principle functions in this case. The affixation of the past tense '-ed' ending onto intransitive verbs does not cause the same developmental difficulties for the child as does passive '-ed' affixation. Assuming that intransitive verbs were not case assigners, one might think that this is unexpected given our Principle of Unique Association. In this case, the past tense '-ed' ending would have different case assigning properties in the transitive and intransitive cases. We can deal with this potential counterexample in one of two ways. We might want to claim that the past tense '-ed' ending rather than being inherently case assigning, inherited the case properties of the root that it attached to. In that case, passive '-ed' in transitive or intransitive verbs would be distinguished from the passive '-ed' suffix in that the former was a case inheriting while the latter was a case absorbing suffix, thus cutting the data in the appropriate way. Another way to handle this case would be to deny the premise of the argument; namely we might claim that intransitive verbs retain their case assigning property but do not assign a *theta*-role to the object position. The independence of case and *theta*-role assignment is demonstrated in the case of passives where case is not assigned, but *theta*-role is assigned to the object position. Intransitives would be seen as cases where the case assigning property of a verb was (vacuously) retained without corresponding *theta*-role assignment. See Koopman (1984) and Travis (1984) who argue extensively for the independence of case and *theta*-role assignment.

[18] This rule is modeled after the rule forming adjectives from verbs by adding the suffix 'able' (See below for discussion of this rule.)

[19] One might consider the inapplicability of the morphological analysis proposed to handle undergeneralizations in the English case to the present construction to count against such an analysis for either case. This is an incorrect analogy though because the morphological solution was designed to explain the existence of the early stage in the development of the English passive without having to characterise this stage as a possible parameter of UG. Since B & W (mistakenly as we argued above) characterised this early stage as a possible parameter (incorrectly excluding non direct-action verbs as inputs to the adjective forming rule) they are lead to expect their account of the English case to generalise to the Hebrew construction. We showed that their account is unsuccessful here and after correctly redescribing the English case we do not expect the morphological solution to generalise either.

[20] See Williams (1982) for details.

[21] "We mean markedness here in a very specific sense. We assume that the unmarked rule is the less costly rule, i.e. the rule that requires the least computation." (B & W, p. 49.)

[22] The sentence is deviant because the overt subject is an inappropriate controller because it is inanimate and can't collect insurance.

REFERENCES

Berwick, R. and A. Weinberg: 1984, *The Grammatical Basis of Linguistic Performance*, MIT Press.

Borer, H.: 1984, 'The projection principle and rules of morphology', *NELS* **14**, University of Massachusetts publication.

Bowerman, M.: 1981, 'Evaluating competing linguistic models with language acquisition data: Implications of developmental errors with causative verbs', *Semantica* **3**, 1—73.

Chomsky, N.: 1975, *Reflections on Language*, Pantheon.

Chomsky, N.: 1981, *Lectures on Government and Binding*, Foris Publications, Dordrecht.

Goldin-Meadow. S.: 1949, 'Language without a helping hand', in H. Whitaker and H. A. Whitaker (eds.), *Studies in Neurolinguistics*, vol. 4, Academic Press.

Horgan, M.: 1975, *Language Development: Across Methodological Study*, unpublished Ph.D. dissertation, University of Michigan.

Hyams, N.: 1983, *The Acquisition of Parameterized Grammars*, unpublished Ph.D. dissertation, CUNY.

Koopman, Hilda: 1984, *The Syntax of Verbs*, Foris Publications, Dordrecht.

Koster, J.: 1978, *Locality Principles in Syntax*, Foris Publications, Dordrecht.

Maratsos, M.: 1978, 'New models in linguistics and language acquisition', in M. Halle, J. Bresnan, and G. Miller (eds.) *Linguistic Theory and Psychological Reality*, MIT Press.

Maratsos, M. and R, Abramovitch: 1975, 'How children understand full, truncated, and anomalous passives', in *Journal of Verbal Learning and Verbal Behaviour* **14**, 145—157.

Manzini, Maria-Rita: 1983, *Restructuring and Reanalysis*, unpublished MIT Ph.D. dissertation.

Otsu, Yukio: 1981, *Universal Grammar and Syntactic Development in Children*, unpublished MIT Ph.D. dissertation.

Pinker, S.: 1982, 'A theory of the acquisition of lexical-interpretive grammars', in J. Bresnan (ed), *The Mental Representation of Grammatical Relations*, MIT Press.

Roeper, T.: 1983, unpublished University of Massachusetts ms.

Travis, L.: 1984, *Parameters and Effects of Word Order Variation*, unpublished MIT diss.

Wexler, K. and P. Culicover: 1980, *Formal Principles of Language Acquisition*, MIT Press.

Williams, E.: 1982, 'Another Argument that Passive is Transformational', *Linguistic Inquiry* **13**(1), 160—163.

LAWRENCE SOLAN

PARAMETER SETTING AND THE DEVELOPMENT OF PRONOUNS AND REFLEXIVES

1. INTRODUCTION

In recent writings and lectures, Chomsky has emphasized a shift in focus occurring in linguistic theory during the 1970s and '80s. While earlier models, such as that set forth in Chomsky (1965), directed their attention at positing and characterizing rule systems, in recent years, linguistic theory has focused more on conditions on representation.

This shift has had serious implications for research on language acquisition. Comparing, for example, Chomsky (1965) and Chomsky (1981), it is evident that the ultimate goal of linguistic theory has remained relatively constant: a description of the language faculty that is capable of explaining how the human child is capable of learning rapidly and based on degenerate evidence any actual or potential human language. Such a description must show the child to be capable of considering only a highly constrained set of possible hypotheses about the structure of his native language to account for the ease and rapidity of acquisition. At the same time, it must be broad enough to explain the child's capability of learning, with more or less equal facility, any of the highly diverse languages to which he may be exposed.

Because of the shift in focus described above, it has become possible to relate, with some degree of precision, hypotheses about the conditions on representation that now characterize so much of linguistic research within the framework of the revised extended standard theory and government-binding theory in particular, and the ultimate goals of the theory — an explanation for aspects of the language acquisition process. For if the child is constrained in his consideration of hypotheses to exactly those left available by the theory (the number available may exceed one within a parameterized view of linguistic universals), then the theory offers an explanation for the fact that the child has not wandered farther afield in his attempts to learn his language. To the extent that the theory predicts with precision the hypotheses that a child will actually consider, it is at least descriptively adequate with respect to the acquisition data.

Thomas Roeper and Edwin Williams (eds.), Parameter Setting, 189—210.
© 1987 *by D. Reidel Publishing Company.*

It should be noted that before this shift in focus, it was very difficult to relate the articulated goals of linguistic theory with any particular set of events in the language acquisition process.[1] While attempts were made to describe children's utterances in the notation of the then-current theory, see, for example, Menyuk (1969), Bloom (1970), McNeill (1970), it was not at all obvious how such descriptions furthered our knowledge about linguistic theory and its goals in any interesting way. Thus, it should not be at all surprising that Newmeyer (1981), a reasonably thorough description of the history of generative grammar through the mid-1970s, barely mentions language acquisition research at all.

During the past decade, however, considerable experimental language acquisition research has made its way into the literature, whose goal has been to investigate the child's use or non-use of various constraints in his understanding (and less often, production) of a variety of linguistic structures. The argument underlying much of this research is as follows. Linguistic theory predicts that the child will be limited in the ways he can understand certain structures. If the child's interpretation of these structures is indeed consistent with the theory's predictions of how his hypothesis formation is constrained, then the acquisition data lend support to the theory, which had been developed on independent grounds. If, on the other hand, the child shows himself not to be constrained in his hypothesis formation, at least not as predicted by the theory, then either the theory is incorrect with respect to its explanatory goals or some other explanation must be posited consistent with the existence of linguistic universals, such as the child's being insufficiently mature to apply the innate constraint. The more interesting case is the child whose interpretations are constrained, but not exactly as predicted, because it is more difficult to explain his performance apart from his application of a theory different from the one posited by linguists at the time. For this reason, language acquisition research of this kind can be a source of data that argues for reevaluation of current theoretical claims.

The research to be discussed in this paper fits into the research paradigm just described. Children were asked to act out with toy animals sentences containing reflexives and pronouns in order to determine whether their interpretations of the test sentences reflect their application of constraints that linguistic theory claims should limit their ability to construe sentences in certain ways. The results indicate that the children are constrained in their responses — but not precisely as the theory predicts they should be. Consequently, certain suggestions are proposed for revisions in some aspects of the theory that are consistent both with the introspective data that motivated the theory in the first place, and with the evidence from child language presented in this paper and in other recent work.

2. A BRIEF LOOK AT BINDING THEORY

It has long been observed that both of the sentences in
(1) are ungrammatical:

(1) a. *Della remembered that Perry had helped *herself.*
    b. *Della remembered that *Perry* had helped *him.*

To explain this fact, a number of locality priniciples have been proposed in the literature, restricting the interpretation of the reflexive in (1a) to an antecedent in its own clause, and restricting the interpretation of the pronoun in (1b) to an antecedent outside its clause. This complementarity is captured by the principles of the binding theory presented in (2), where D is the domain in which these principles apply (see Chomsky, 1980, 1981).

(2) a.   An anaphor must be bound in D.
    b.   A pronoun must be free in D.

In English, the overt anaphors are reflexives and reciprocals. 'Bound' means bearing the same referential index as an element that c-commands it, and 'free' means not bound. If we assume that D includes at least the tensed clause, then *herself* has no possible antecedent to which it can be bound in (1a) except *Della*, and *Della* is not within D, causing a violation of principle (2a). The problem with (1b) can be similarly described with reference to principle (2b).

In English, the same principles governing (1) also govern (3), where the embedded clauses are infinitival.

(3) a. *Paul asked Della to ignore *himself.*
    b. *Paul asked *Della* to ignore *her.*

In addition, these principles account for a wide range of data involving binding across noun phrase boundaries, with the binding restrictions operating when the noun phrase has a subject, as in sentences like (4).

(4) a. *Tragg* found Della's picture of *himself.*
   b. *Tragg found *Della's* picture of *her.*

From sentences like (1), (3) and (4), it appears that the principles stated in (2) apply in the domains of subjects. Just in case a pronoun or reflexive is in a subject domain, its interpretation is controlled in part by (2). Chomsky's *specified subject condition* captures this generalization.

Several additional observations must be made. First, not all languages work in such a coherent manner. As Harbert (1982) points out, citing a plethora of other work, in many languages, such as Icelandic, there exists an asymmetry between (1) and (3). Only in (1) do the binding principles rule out the relevant interpretations. That is, sentences corresponding to (3a), but not (1a), are grammatical in many languages. Second, many languages do not have picture noun phrase constructions such as (4). That is, in many languages, noun phrases simply do not have subjects. It is not at all clear that the binding principles need to be stated as generally for those languages. Finally, consider sentences like (5).

(5) a. Paul believes himself to be a good detective.
   b. *Paul believes that himself is a good detective.

Chomsky (1981) accounts for these sentences by extending the notion 'subject' to include both overt subjects and the agreement element of tensed clauses, calling this enlarged concept 'SUBJECT'. The reflexive in (5a) can be bound to *Paul* since there is no intervening SUBJECT. In (5b), on the other hand, the reflexive is in the domain of the SUBJECT in the embedded clause, and thus binding is not possible under (2a). It should be noted, however, that for languages such as Icelandic, collapsing the various conditions under which the binding principles apply will produce results not entirely consistent with the data, as Harbert points out. Earlier theories, such as Chomsky (1981), which lacked the notion SUBJECT, avoided this problem in that it is possible for languages to differ with respect to which of a number of possible domains may be included in D for any particular language. That is, it is possible to claim that Icelandic has a nominative island condition, but not a specified subject condition.[2]

Returning to the discussion in the introductory section of this paper, it is possible to relate the outline of the binding principles discussed in this section with particular claims about the language acquisition process. The theory of binding, stated as principles of universal grammar, involves a set of claims about what the child must learn, and what the child already knows, in the sense that he or she will not consider more than a limited set of the possible hypotheses that can account for the phenomena discussed above. As for what must be acquired on the basis of experience, the set of anaphors and pronouns for any language is not predictable from linguistic universals. In the sentences presented above, the child must learn that the reflexive forms are anaphors, and the pronominal forms are not. This task is by no means trivial, a fact to which we shall return below. Secondly, the child must learn the definition of D for the language being learned. As we saw above, languages exhibit variation with respect to the environments in which the binding principles operate. For some languages, such as English, they operate quite broadly, across tensed and infinitival clause boundaries, and across noun phrase boundaries when the noun phrase has a subject. However, many languages do not have noun phrases with subjects, and some languages have binding principles that apply only across tensed clause boundaries. Given this parametric variation, children must learn which type of language he or she is learning in order to properly define D for his or her own language. Whether children initially have a particular, unmarked hypothesis about this is a question of fact, which has thus far not been answered by theory-internal considerations. Third, the child must have the two principles in (2). Finally, the child must be able to recognize the array of embedded structures that define the domain of the binding theory in order to be able to apply the principles of that theory.

The experiments to be described below address themselves to the four preconditions described above. Children were tested, in three experiments, on a variety of English sentences containing pronouns and reflexives. The results indicate that children have considerable difficulty defining D, and may have some difficulty distinguishing between pronouns and anaphors. Whether they have both (2a) and (2b) under their control is also questionable. Explanations for these results will be offered in terms of the general principles discussed above, and in terms of proposed revisions in the binding theory suggested recently by Freidin (to appear).

3. THE EXPERIMENTS

The subjects were thirty-seven children, ages four to seven. For purposes of data analysis, they were divided into two groups, a younger group of nineteen children with mean age, 4, 10, and an older group of eighteen children, with mean age, 6, 0. The children all attended day care centers and nursery schools in the Boston area.

The procedure was as follows: the experimenter and the child sat across from each other at a table containing four toy animals representing the four noun phrases used in the experimental sentences, and photographs of each of the toys. Practice sentences were then presented, giving the child the opportunity to familiarize himself both with the identity of the animals and with the task of acting out the sentences using the animals and the pictures. The experimental sentences, thirty in all (two are not discussed at all in this paper), were then presented to the child, one by one. After the sentence was presented to him, the child acted it out with the toys and pictures, and the experimenter noted on the score sheet what the child did.

All of the children received exactly the same number of tokens of the various sentence types described in the next three subsections. However, eight different versions of the questionnaire were used, each version containing different combinations of lexical items. This was to preclude the results reflecting only the child's conceptualization of what certain animals are likely to do. A substantial number of verbs and predicates were used and selected at random.

The various questionnaires presented the sentences in complete cycles (no syntactic structure was heard twice until every other structure was heard once), and the order in which the various structures was presented varied from questionnaire to questionnaire.

3.1. *Experiment 1*

Test Sentences. In this study, children were presented with sentences such as the following:
1.   The dog said that the horse hit himself.
2.   The dog said that the horse hit him.
3.   The dog told the horse to hit himself.
4.   The dog told the horse to hit him.
These sentences differ along two parameters. First, while 1 and 3

contain reflexives, 2 and 4 contain pronouns. Second, while the embedded clause in 1 and 2 is tensed, the embedded clause in 3 and 4 is infinitival. Thus, this experiment is designed to test whether children's binding principles are complementary, that is, whether D is the same for principles (2a) and (2b), and whether the presence or absence of tense makes a difference in their performance.

The children received four tokens of each of the four sentences listed above. The experiment, however, contained eight conditions. Half of the presentations of each sentence type occurred following a misleading pragmatic cue, designed to trick the child into choosing a discourse topic as the antecedent of the proform. For the sentences with reflexives, the pragmatic lead mentioned the nonlocal animal. Thus, the pragmatic lead for sentences 1 and 3 would be PL1.

PL1.   This is a story about the dog.

For those sentences containing pronouns, the pragmatic lead mentioned the local noun phrase. The lead for 2 and 4, then, would be PL2.

PL2.   This is a story about the horse.

Following earlier work of Barbara Lust, the pragmatic cues were directed at learning whether the children's principles are impervious to pragmatic considerations.

Results. The results for Experiment 1 are presented in Table I.

TABLE I
Percentage of correct responses experiment 1

Condition	without misleading cue	with misleading cue	total
1	95	88	92
2	49	46	48
3	82	70	76
4	36	39	38

First, the age of the child made no difference in the number of correct responses, $F < 1$. Nor did age interact significantly with any of the effects otherwise tested. Therefore, as is clear from the presentation of Table I, the results for the two age groups were collapsed for all statistical analysis.

The presence of the misleading cue made the sentences slightly more difficult for three of the four conditions, and slightly easier for one of them. The effect of the cue, however, was not significant, $F(1,35) =$ 2.80, $p = .103$. Consequently, for further analysis of the data, the sentences with and without the cues were combined. However, later analyses that compare the results of the various experiments with each other use only those sentences without the pragmatic cues since no such cues existed in the other experiments. There were no significant interactions between the presence or absence of the cue and any of the other factors.

The two factors of primary interest, the effects of tense and of type of proform, were both significant. Children correctly responded to sentences with pronouns only 43% of the time, while responding correctly to sentences with reflexives 84% of the time. This difference is highly significant. $F(1,35) = 33.25$, $p < .001$. Similarly, those sentences with tensed embedded clauses were significantly easier (70% correct) than sentences with infinitival complements (57% correct), $F(1,35) = 13.82$, $p = .001$. It is important to note that there was no significant interaction between the type of proform and the type of complement. That is, each of these factors independently affects the ease of interpretation, and requires separate explanation. Throughout, virtually all of the incorrect responses consisted of a reflexive-like pronominal interpretation, or a pronoun-like reflexive interpretation.

Thus far, the results leave for explanation these conclusions: that pragmatics are irrelevant, that tensed embedded clauses are easier than infinitival ones, and that reflexives are easier than pronouns.

3.2. *Experiment 2*

This experiment contained only two sentence types:
  5.   The dog found the horse's picture of himself.
  6.   The dog found the horse's picture of him.
The key to answering these correctly was to choose the picture of the toy horse for 5 and the picture of the toy dog for 6. These sentences were placed randomly through the questionnaires as described above, and the children heard two tokens of each sentence.

Results. The results are startling. The children got 85% of the tokens of 5 correct, but answered correctly only 1% of the tokens of 6. An additional analysis of variance was performed comparing the results of

Experiments 1 and 2 according to type of proform (reflexive or pronoun) and place in which the proform is embedded (tensed clause, infinitival clause or noun phrase). Because of the low correct response rate for sentence 6 of Experiment 2, there was a significant interaction between these two factors. $F(2,35) = 10.88$, $p < .001$. That is, the child's ability to interpret correctly sentences containing pronouns depends crucially on the type of structure in which the pronoun is embedded. This fact also must be explained.

3.3. *Experiment 3*

The sentences in Experiment 2 actually differ from those in Experiment 1 in two ways, only one of which is theoretically interesting. The sentences in Experiment 2 are 'picture' noun phrase sentences, which may have a number of peculiar properties. To determine whether the types of constituent in which the proform is embedded makes the sentences harder to understand independent of the binding principles, Experiment 3 was devised, whose sentences are as follows:

7.   The dog said that the horse found the picture of himself.   86%
8.   The dog said that the horse found the picture of him.   38%
9.   The dog told the horse to find the picture of himself.   68%
10.   The dog told the horse to find the picture of him.   23%

The percentage next to each sentence indicates the percentage correct. Here, again, the children were presented with two tokens of each sentence type.

Both the type of proform (pronoun or reflexive) and the type of clause into which it was embedded (tensed or infinitival) were varied systematically. Unlike Experiment 1, however, the proforms were all contained in picture noun phrases that were themselves embedded in the embedded clauses. Because the picture noun phrases contained no subjects, as the theory predicts, it is the subject of the embedded clauses that defines the binding domains. For the sentences with reflexives, the horse is the antecedent, and the dog is the only possible antedent in the sentences containing pronouns.[3]

As the results indicate, the sentences with reflexives were again easier than those with pronouns, and the sentences with embedded tensed clauses were easier than those with embedded infinitival clauses. An analysis of variance was performed on the sentences in Experiments 1 (without the misleading cues) and 3 combined. Interestingly, the type of constituent in which the proform was embedded, clause or noun phrase, was significant. $F(1,35) = 4.14$, $p = .002$. That is, it is harder for children to interpret sentences with proforms embedded in noun phrases that are themselves embedded in complement clauses, than it is for them to interpret sentences with proforms embedded directly in the complement clauses themselves. Crucially, there was no interaction between either the type of constituent and the type of proform, or between the type of constituent and the type of embedded clause (tensed or infinitival), $F < 1$ in both instances. This last set of facts is important because it indicates that the presence of the picture noun phrase makes the sentences more difficult by a constant. But recall in our comparison of Experiments 1 and 2 that the presence of the picture noun phrase interacted significantly with the type of proform. Subtracting about 10% from the scores on Experiment 1 roughly yields the results in Experiment 3. But no such analysis can be made with respect to a comparison of Experiments 1 and 2. This means that it is not merely the presence of the picture noun phrase that makes the children answer incorrectly on sentence 6 of Experiment 2 almost 100% of the time. Rather, it is something related to the syntactic structure. In particular, it is something that characterizes the sentences in Experiment 2, but not those in either Experiment 1 or Experiment 3. The only such characteristic is the fact that the noun phrase in which the proform occurs in Experiment 2 contains a subject, and that subject noun phrase plays a crucial role in the proper application of the binding principles. Therefore, also ripe for explanation is the fact that children have so much difficulty with sentence 6 of Experiment 2 in light of all of the other results. This question is a part of the larger question of how children define the domain D in which the binding theory applies.

4. ISSUES IN THE DEVELOPMENT OF LOCALITY PRINCIPLES

In this section, I will address some of the issues discussed in Section 2 in light of the results of the experiments described in Section 3. In particular, the four prerequisites for control over the theory — distinguishing between pronouns and anaphors, defining D, applying principles (2a) and (2b), and recognizing the relevant syntactic structures — will be seen to play a role in the children's interpretations.

4.1. *Why Sentences with Pronouns are More Difficult than Those with Reflexives*

Over all, children responded correctly on 81% of the sentences containing reflexives, but on only 34% of those containing pronouns. In all three experiments, every sentence with a reflexive was easier than its counterpart with a pronoun. One possible conclusion is that children, at some early stage of development, have principle (2a), but not principle (2b). Jacubowicz (1983) presents results consistent with this account. Over a wide range of sentence types, Jacubowicz found children correctly interpreting sentences with reflexives more frequently than similar sentences containing pronouns. Deutsch and Koster (1982), looking at the development of Dutch as a first language, also found children having an easier time with reflexives than with pronouns. They appear to explain their results in terms of the generally pragmatic nature of nonreflexive pronoun interpretation. And Otsu (1981) also found children making more errors on sentences with pronouns than on corresponding sentences with reflexives, although Otsu does not draw any conclusions from this fact.

In the experiments described in the previous study, ten of the thirty-seven subjects were consistently able to interpret correctly sentences with reflexives, while consistently interpreting sentences with pronouns as though they contained reflexives. Children were placed in this group if the difference in performance on the two sentence types was at least 80%. For example, a child who correctly interpreted 95% of the sentences with reflexives, but only 15% of the sentences with pronouns is said to interpret both proforms as reflexives. Although this criterion is somewhat arbitrary, this characterization of the children's performance would appear to be justified.

The question remains, however, whether the relative ease of sentences with reflexives in which principle (2a) applies means that children, at some early stage, lack principle (2b) altogether. For several reasons, I believe that this conclusion is incorrect. Rather, as I will argue, the source of the problem lies with children's confusion about which principle applies to particular forms in English. This explanation makes sense since there is no necessary relationship between particular words, such as *him*, and particular principles of the binding theory, such as (2b).

First, in Solan and Ortiz (1982), we presented bilingual children with the Spanish translations of the sentences in Experiment 1.

(6) a.   Juan dijo que Pedro se golpeó.
         Juan said that Pedro hit himself.
   b.   Juan dijo que Pedro lo golpeó.
         Juan said that Pedro hit him.
   c.   Juan ordenó a Pedro golpearse.
         Juan told Pedro to hit himself.
   d.   Juan ordenó a Pedro golpearlo.
         Juan told Pedro to hit him.

The results showed children interpreting correctly sentences with pronominal clitics more frequently (57%) than those with reflexive clitics (41%). The difference is significant. See Solan (to appear) for a more detailed discussion. It would make little sense to claim that the relative ease of reflexives in English is caused by children's 'not having' principle (2b) in lilght of these results. Rather, it would appear that something distinct in the nature of the proforms in the individual languages is at work.

In Spanish, the reflexive clitic 'se' plays other roles as well. It is the spurious dative clitic in sentences like (7),

(7)   Juan se lo dio.
         Juan to him it gave.

and acts as an impersonal marker in sentences like (8).

(8)   Aquí se habla español.
         Spanish is spoken here.

Thus, it should not be surprising for children to suffer some confusion in trying to determine which principle, (2a) or (2b), applies to the clitic se. With regard to lo(and la), the accusative clitics, on the other hand, children should have relatively little difficulty since these proforms are unambiguously pronominals.

A somewhat different story obtains with respect to the relevant English proforms. While himself is unambiguously reflexive, him is arguably a reflexive in sentences like (9).

(9) a.   John saw a snake near him.
   b.   John has passion in him.

Kuno (forthcoming) argues that at some level of representation, say S-structure, the pronouns in (9) are abstract reflexive markers, REFL. A later spelling rule (likely occurring between S-structure and phonetic form) determines whether REFL will be realized as *himself* or *him*, for example. The spelling rule, according to Kuno, makes crucial use of REFL's semantic role in its clause.

Assuming something like Kuno's analysis to be correct, it is at least conceivable that children learning English will initially conclude that certain pronouns, such as *him* and *her*, are subject to principle (2a), the principle that governs anaphors. Additional support for this proposition comes from the fact that children initially are reluctant to rule out forward pronominal reference under any circumstances. See Solan (1983) and references cited therein.

Second, as far as I know, no language has anaphors but lacks pronominals. It would be an unusual state of affairs with respect to the theory of markedness for children's initial hypothesis to be completely at odds with this observation. It is generally assumed that there is some relationship between the acquisition process and the theory of markedness. This assumption would be undermined if children did not have principle (2b) at all.

For the reasons discussed above, I will tentatively conclude that, at some initial stage in the development of English, children erroneously conclude that principle (2a) applies to both reflexives and pronouns, despite their knowledge of both principles of the binding theory.[4]

4.2. *The Domain of the Binding Principles*

Two other facts require explanation: the relative ease of tensed sentences in contrast to infinitival sentences, and the extraordinary difficulty that children have with sentences like 6 from Experiment 2, repeated below:

  6.   The dog found the horse's picture of him.

Children correctly interpreted this sentence type only 1% of the time, a result that is unusual. Both of these results implicate issues concerning the domain, D, in which the principles apply. Although they will be discussed in turn, I will conclude that the relative ease of tensed sentences is unrelated to aspects of the binding theory and parameter setting, but follows rather from certain differences in the processability of the relevant sentence types. As for sentences like 6, on the other hand, these have serious implications for the proper statement of the binding theory and the setting of parameters.

4.2.1. *Why tensed sentences are easier than infinitives.* Recall from Section 2 that in some languages, such as Icelandic, principle (2a) does not rule out the binding of a reflexive across an infinitival clause boundary. From this, it is possible to conclude that some languages lack the specified subject condition but do have the tensed S condition, the latter ruling out binding across any tensed S. Harbert (to appear) argues that the notion SUBJECT is itself parameterized, with some languages, like English, choosing both manifestations of SUBJECThood, and others, like Icelandic, choosing only that part of the definition that includes the AGR element of tensed clauses, that is, the part corresponding to the propositional island constraint.

As noted in Section 3, children performed significantly better, in both Experiments 1 and 3, when the sentence contained a tensed embedded clause than when it contained an infinitival one. From this fact it is inviting to conclude that children initially hypothesize that English, like Icelandic, defines the domain of principle (2a) narrowly. This conclusion makes additional sense in light of Picallo (1984), showing the relevance of tense domains in other areas of the grammar. Nonetheless, several reasons exist for rejecting this explanation for these results. First, returning to Harbert (to appear), there is apparently a correlation between whether a language allows binding across an infinitival clause boundary and whether principle (2b) applies to rule out the possibility of coreference in sentences like (10).

(10)   Della loves her job.

Languages like English in which (10) is grammatical do not allow sentences like (11).

(11)   *Della told Tragg to stay away from herself.

Languages like Icelandic, on the other hand, allow (11) while (10) is ungrammatical unless it is uttered with a genitive reflexive instead of a genitive pronoun.

To the extent that children allow coreference in sentences like (10), it indicates that they are not applying the Icelandic version of the binding principles, in which coreference would be impossible. Although

I have not examined children's comprehension of this types of sentence, I have looked at children's understanding of sentences like (12).

(12)   After his run, the dog hit the horse.

Presumably, (10) and (12) operate equivalently with respect to principles (2a) and (2b). The results, as reported in Solan (1983), show children allowing coreference 57% of the time, more than for any other sentence type in an experiment containing a wide variety of syntactic structures. This is *prima facie* evidence that children are not applying the Icelandic version of the binding principles. Since, as Harbert (to appear) argues, it is the English version that is the unmarked one, it should not be surprising if the evidence from child language indicates that children are not initially choosing the marked alternative.

Second, experimentation in Spanish, discussed in Solan (to appear), indicates that one must be careful about drawing broad conclusions from the fact that tensed clauses are generally easier. In a set of experiments, children were presented in Spanish with sentences like (13) and (14).

(13) a. Juan trató de golpearse. Juan tried to hit himself.
     b. Juan trató de golpearlo. Juan tried to hit him.

(14) a. Juan dijo que se golpeó. Juan said that (pro) hit himself.
     b. Juan dijo que lo golpeó. Juan said that (pro) hit him.

In Spanish, a pro-drop language, the subject of a tensed clause need not be articulated. Here, children performed significantly better on the sentences in (13) than on those in (14) (89% vs. 80% correct). That is, the sentences with infinitival clauses were easier.

Because English requires the presence of a subject, it would be impossible to conduct this study in English. While these data may be subject to various interpretations, they lend additional support to the tentative conclusion that children do not initially incorrectly set the parameter governing the value of D. That is, children do not appear to assume that the domain of the binding principles in English is equivalent to that of Icelandic. It is conceivable that the difficulty that children have interpreting sentences with infinitival complements is the result the fact that for these sentences, not only must they determine the antecedent for the proform, but they must also determine the antecedent for the empty complement subject, PRO. That PRO has only one possible antecedent in (13) can explain its relative ease. This explanation, however, should be regarded as tentative, and subject to further investigation.

4.2.2. *The domain of the disjoint reference principle.* In this section, I will address the issue of why sentence 6 from Experiment 2 was so difficult. Before doing so, however, it is necessary to elaborate on some aspects of the binding principles stated in (2).

First, the statement of the principles in (2) implies that the domains in which principles (2a) and (2b) apply are identical. But as sentences like (10) illustrate (repeated below), this is not the case.

    (10)   Della loves her job.

As pointed out by a number of scholars, for example Freidin (to appear), Huang (1982) and Harbert (to appear), *her* is not in the domain of a SUBJECT within its NP in (10), in that, by definition, the SUBJECT must be distinct from the proform.[5] Thus, the binding domain for *her* is the entire sentence, and principle (2b) should rule out coreference between *Della* and *her*. It does not. Huang and Freidin propose somewhat different alternatives for dealing with this fact and related facts. Both involve defining D differently for the two binding principles. I will adopt Freidin's alternative throughout the remainder of this discussion.[6]

According to Freidin's analysis, the domains for principles (2a) and (2b) are (loosely) as follows:

    (D_a)   An anaphor must be bound in the domain of an accessible SUBJECT.

    (D_b)   A pronoun must be free in its governing θ-domain (where NP and S are the θ-domains).

In essence, D_a is equivalent to the domain proposed in Chomsky (1981). D_b, however, differs from that proposed by Chomsky in that the notion SUBJECT is not relevant at all. Thus, a pronoun must be free in the NP or S containing it and a governor of it. This accounts for (10) in that *her* is free in its NP, *her job*, and is therefore available to be bound to *Della*.

One consequence of Freidin's alternative is that coreference should be possible in sentences like (15).

(15)   John found a picture of him.

Chomsky's earlier work predicts that disjoint reference is required in (15). Although coreference is not preferred, it does seem possible, especially when (15) is compared to sentences like (16).

(16)   *Perry cross-examined *him*.

It is possible, consistent with Freidin's statement of the domain of (2b), to explain whatever difficulty exists with (15) in terms of the Avoid Pronoun principle, discussed in Chomsky (1981). That principle, which is merely a strategy in English, suggests that a pronoun not be used when the grammar will mandate the desired interpretation without one. Thus, the fact that coreference is not preferred in (17), although it is permitted by the grammar.

(17)   John likes his writing books.

Coreference is obligatory, because of control theory, when the pronoun is absent. Since, for sentences like (15), coreference is obligatory when a reflexive is present instead of a pronoun, coreference will not be preferred when a pronoun appears, even though disjoint reference is not mandated by the grammar.

Returning to the domain of principles (2a) and (2b), the differences between the domains can be elaborated upon further. Principle (2a) is a true locality principle. It dictates that a SUBJECT is an absolute barrier to the interpretation of a reflexive. That subjecthood is the defining concept should not be surprising since for many languages, such as the Romance languages and possibly Japanese as well, reflexives can only be bound to subjects. Let us assume that binding of reflexives to a subject is the unmarked case, and that a child must learn from positive evidence that his language allows additional binding if indeed it does. That is to say, principle (2a) is parameterized, with one value of the parameter being unmarked.

With respect to principle (2b), Freidin's version of D_b disallows local interpretation of a pronoun within its governing NP or S. Is this the unmarked case? Williams (1981) points out that constructions like (15) are relatively rare across languages, and are therefore likely to be marked structures. Moreover, the fact that NP is a θ-domain in English may also make English marked, in that languages generally do not permit structures like (18), in which the passivization rule has applied within an NP.

(18)   the enemy's destruction of the city

Keeping these facts about markedness in mind, it is at least conceivable that children, beginning with the unmarked hypothesis, initially assume that D_b is the domain for (2b), but that S is the only possible governing θ-domain.

The next issue is which S domains are governing S domains. It would seem to be necessary to use the definition of governing category taken from Chomsky (1981):

(19) α is the governing category for β if and only if α is the minimal category containing β and a governor of β, where $\alpha =$ NP or S.

That is, a pronoun must be free in an S containing it and a governor of it, provided that there is no other NP or S in which the pronoun is more deeply embedded.

Note that even under the child's narrower interpretation of D_b, sentences like (10) can be accounted for:

(10)   Della loves her job.

Since the NP, *her job*, is still the governing category for *her*, D_b does nothing to rule out coreference between the pronoun and the subject of the sentence. The pronoun has no governing S domain. However, once children come to terms with the fact that in English θ-roles are assigned in NP as well as in S, they should abandon this initial hypothesis. Thus, they do not need positive evidence from sentences containing pronouns and reflexives to move from the initial, unmarked value of the parameter (only S defines θ-domains) to the marked, correct value for English (both NP and S define θ-domains). This is significant because positive evidence that coreference is impossible in sentences like (4b) will not be forthcoming:

(4b)   Tragg found Della's picture of her.

Looking now at the data from Experiment 2, the sentence that children were entirely unable to interpret was the one that has exactly the same structure as (4b):

6.   The dog found the horse's picture of him.

That children choose the horse as the antecedent of the pronoun almost 100% of the time follows from the fact that they are incorrectly employing D_b, at least in part. For D_b, while predicting that the binding principle should not apply to this sentence, does not in and of itself explain why children should not simply assign arbitrary reference to pronouns in these sentences. Given that the binding theory does not apply here, some independent principle must be adduced.

Two factors seem to mandate local interpretation for sentence 6 of Experiment 2. First, the expression, "the horse's picture", is ambiguous. It can mean either a photograph with an image of the horse, or it can mean a photograph belonging to the horse. If children initially interpret the expression as meaning the former, then the fact that the binding theory does not apply would automatically free them to interpret the sentence according to its most sensible contextual meaning. The fact that the sentences with pragmatic miscues made the sentences no more difficult leads to the conclusion that children would not have interpreted the sentences in this way universally if their binding restrictions had prohibited such an interpretation. Secondly, it is possible that children employ some sort of minimal distance principle in interpreting semantically degenerate items when the grammar does not dictate otherwise. Here, where the binding principles are not restricting interpretation, such principle may take effect.

Finally, although from their high percentage of correct responses I have assumed that children know both (2a) and D_a, the results of these experiments are actually not finely enough tuned to lead to that conclusion. In all instances, the nearest NP to the reflexive is also the nearest subject. It is impossible to conclude from these results exactly what children consider to be the domain of reflexives: the nearest NP or the nearest subject. Because I have also had to introduce the concept 'governing category' into the child's version of principle (2b), a better understanding of the child's version of (2a) may prove to be especially illuminating in painting a clear picture of the binding principles during the early stages of acquisition. More research designed to answer this question must be conducted.

5. CONCLUSION

In this paper, I discussed a series of experiments designed to reveal some properties of children's initial hypotheses about the binding principles' application to English. The results are not easily explainiable in terms of Chomsky's (1981) statement of the domain of the binding principles, but are much more easily accounted for in terms of the revisions proposed by Freidin (to appear). A number of differences among the various sentence types, while inviting explanation based on deep principles of universal grammar, appear to be better explained with reference to ease of processing and language particular phenomena. Given the complexity of the language faculty in humans, this complicated mixture should not be surprising.

ACKNOWLEDGEMENT

This work was supported in part by a grant to Catherine Snow by the Milton Fund of Harvard University. I wish to express my gratitude both to that fund and to Catherine Snow. I would further like to thank Chip Morrison for his participation in this project. Comments from many workshop participants have been very valuable.

NOTES

[1] See also Brown (1971) for some discussion of how predictions for child language development derived from notions of complexity inherent in the then-current theory fail to be borne out by the developmental facts.

[2] This entire discussion will be refined in Section 4 below. In particular, it is possible to account for both the English and Icelandic facts within a parameterized view of the notion SUBJECT, in which a language may choose either both prongs of the definition, or only that prong corresponding to the propositional island condition, the latter being a marked varient. See Harbert (to appear).

[3] This may not be true for some speakers. Moreover, the revisions of the theory proposed by Freidin (to appear) discussed below predict that for sentences with pronouns, the binding theory does not restrict interpretation here. That the nonlocal interpretation is the more likely one must be explained on independent grounds. See Section 4.2.

[4] Aspects of the child's processing strategies may also be relevant. If the child at first assumes that semantically degenerate elements are to be interpreted locally (a correct assumption for empty categories), he may use some sort of distance principle, regardless of the type of proform. This would explain the performance of those children who uniformly interpreted all sentences as if they contained reflexives.

[5] Actually, this follows not from the definition of SUBJECT, but from the definition of 'accessible' SUBJECT. In (10), the noun phrase has a SUBJECT, but it is not an accessible SUBJECT.

[6] Huang argues that principle (2b) applies when the pronoun is in the domain of a SUBJECT, regardless of whether the SUBJECT is accessible. This accounts for

sentences like (10). But, as Freidin (to appear) points out, it does not account for sentences like (i).

(i) *Della* believes *her* to be a genius.

In (i), *her* is a subject, not accessible within its S. Therefore it should be free within the embedded clause, and binding between it and *Della* should be possible. Since it is not, the revisions proposed by Huang are not descriptively adequate with respect to this type of sentence.

REFERENCES

Baker, C. L.: 1979, 'Syntactic theory and the projection problem,' *Linguistic Inquiry* **10**, 533—582.

Bloom, L.: 1970, *Language Development*, MIT Press, Cambridge, Massachusetts.

Brown, R.: 1971, 'Derivational complexity and order of acquisition in child speed', in R. Brown, *Psycholinguistics*, Free Press, New York.

Chomsky, N.: 1965, *Aspects of the Theory of Syntax*, MIT Press, Cambridge, Massachusetts.

Chomsky, N.: 1980, 'On Binding', *Linguistic Inquiry* **11**, 1—46.

Chomsky, N.: 1981, *Lectures on Government and Binding*, Foris Publications, Dordrecht.

Deutsch, W. and J. Koster: 1982, 'Children's interpretation of sentence-internal anaphora', *P.R.C.L.D.* **21**, 39—45.

Freidin, R.: to appear, 'Fundamental issues in the theory of binding', in B. Lust (ed.), *Acquisition Studies in Anaphora: Defining the Constraints*, D. Reidel, Dordrecht.

Harbert, W.: 1981, 'Should binding refer to SUBJECT?', paper presented at the meeting of the North Eastern Linguistic Society, MIT.

Harbert, W.: to appear, 'Markedness and the bindability of subject of NP', in E. Moravcsik, J. Wirth and F. Eckman (eds.), *Proceedings of Conference on Markedness*, Plenum.

Huang, C.-T. J.: 1982, *Logical Relations in Chinese and the Theory of Grammar*, unpublished doctoral dissertation, MIT.

Jacubowicz, C.: 1983, 'On markedness and binding principles', paper presented at Conference on Government and Binding, Cornell University.

Matthei, E.: 1981, 'Children's interepretations of sentences containing reciprocals, in S. Tavakolian (ed.), *Language Acquisition and Linguistic Theory*, MIT Press, Cambridge, Massachusetts.

McNeill, D.: 1970, *The Acquisition of Language*, Harper & Row, New York.

Menyuk, P.: 1969, *Sentences Children Use*, MIT Press, Cambridge, Massachusetts.

Newmeyer, F.: 1980, *Linguistic Theory in America*, Academic Press, New York.

Otsu, Y.: 1981, *Universal Grammar and Syntactic Development in Children: Toward a Theory of Syntactic Development*, unpublished doctoral dissertation, MIT.

Picallo, C.: 1984, 'The Infl node and the null subject parameter', *Linguistic Inquiry* **15**, 75—102.

Solan, L.: 1983, *Pronominal Reference: Child Language and the Theory of Grammar*, D. Reidel, Dordrecht.

Solan, L.: to appear, 'Language acquisition data and the theory of markedness: Evidence from Spanish', in E. Moravcsik, J. Wirth and F. Eckman (eds.), *Markedness*, Plenum.

Solan and Ortiz: 1982, 'The development of pronouns and reflexives: Evidence from Spanish', paper presented at the Boston University Language Development Conference.

Williams, E.: 1981, 'Language acquisition, markedness, and phrase structure, in S. Tavakolian (ed.), *Language Acquisition and Linguistic Theory*, MIT Press. Cambridge, Massachusetts.

DANIEL L. FINER

COMMENTS ON SOLAN*

1. INTRODUCTION

Experimental results are presented in Solan's paper which demonstrate that there is a contrast between children's interpretation of reflexives and pronouns and the interpretations that are assigned to these elements in the adult grammar. In brief summary, Solan found that both reflexives and pronouns are likely to end up bound in their governing categories — a situation what accords with Principle A of the Binding Theory (an anaphor is bound in its governing category), but that runs counter to Principle B (a pronominal is free in its governing category). In addition, Solan's data also show violations of Principle A of the Binding Theory (anaphors were construed with an antecedent external to their governing category); these latter violations occurred more frequently in infinitival than in indicative clauses.

My remarks on Solan's interpretation of his findings fall roughly into two categories, those concerning Principle A, and those concerning Principle B. In Section 2, I suggest that another type of sentence is relevant to the difference in reflexive bindings that was found between indicative and infinitival complements. If Solan's analysis of his data is correct, the differences should not emerge if this type of sentence is also used. A second part of Section 2 discusses Solan's arguments against the claim that his subjects have different values set for a few parameters. Here I conclude that some of the arguments he gives are inconclusive, and I suggest that another argument might be given in favor of his position. The set of comments in the third section address the Principle B violations, and here I attempt to relate these facts to the earlier ones involving reflexives.

2. PRINCIPLE A

Recall that there was a statistical difference between the degree to which the children made mistakes in infinitival versus tensed comple-

211

Thomas Roeper and Edwin Williams (eds.), Parameter Setting, 211—219.
© 1987 *by D. Reidel Publishing Company.*

ments. That is, sentences like (1) in Solan's experiment were an arena
for fewer mistakes than were sentences like (2).

(1)   The dog said that the horse hit himself.

(2)   The dog told the horse to hit himself.

In (1), the children obey the rules of English; *himself* was construed
with *the horse*, but in (2), *the dog* was taken as the antecedent for the
reflexive to a greater degree, even though *the dog* is external to the
domain in which the reflexive should be bound.

Solan first discusses the possibility that the children are, in some
sense, speaking Icelandic, since reflexives can be non-locally bound in
the Icelandic counterparts of (2), but not in (1). One analysis of the
Icelandic-English contrast (which he attributes to Wayne Harbert) is
that the grammar of Icelandic obeys the Tensed-S Condition, but lacks
the Specified Subject Condition.

Assuming this account is basically correct, we could then propose
the initially plausible hypothesis that the children are simply applying
the binding principles of Icelandic (i.e., they have not yet discovered
that the SSC is operative in English). Solan suggests, however, citing
experimental data from Spanish to support the point, that the Icelandic
hypothesis is not at all what is going here. Instead, he proposes a
processing account of the differences between the interpretations of (1)
and (2). He first observes that the relevant form of (2) is in fact *The dog
told the horse [PRO to hit himself]*. He then suggests that not only must
the child find an antecedent for the reflexive, he must also find a
controller for PRO in addition. The computational load is thus greater,
and more mistakes are likely to be made. According to Solan, then, the
confusing PRO factor is what accounts for the difference between the
interpretations of (1) and (2).[1]

Solan's explanation leads one to expect that if sentences like (2) were
replaced by those in (3) (where PRO does not occur) in an experiment
such as that under discussion, the PRO-factor would be filtered out;
children's interpretations of (3) should look more like what is found for
(1).

(3)   The dog $\begin{Bmatrix} \text{a. wants} \\ \text{b. expects} \end{Bmatrix}$ the horse to hit himself

     c.   The dog believes the horse to have hit himself.

To restate the point, there is no PRO in (3), and thus there should be no extra processing load; the interpretations of (3) should agree with the interpretations of (1), not (2), if Solan is correct in his analysis of the children's behavior. If, on the other hand, the interpretations of (3) fall together in the charts with the interpretations of (2), then this hypothesized PRO-factor would appear to have nothing to do with the contrasts in question. If the results were to conform to this second possibility, then the Icelandic hypothesis would still deserve to be entertained (but see below). Another set of experiments is in order.

Another reason why Solan rejects the Icelandic hypothesis concerns sentences like (4) and (5):

(4)   Della$_i$ loves her$_i$ job.

(5)   *Della$_i$ told Tragg to stay away from herself$_i$.

The correlation he notes is that while English has (4), it does not have (5), and while Icelandic has (5), it does not have (4), unless the pronoun is a genitive reflexive. The argument runs as follows: Children cannot be speaking according to Icelandic parameters since they appear to understand sentences like (4) in the manner indicated above, contrary to what the grammar of Icelandic would predict (disjoint reference).

There are two implicit assumptions here, both open to question. The first is that *her* is not an English version of the Icelandic genitive reflexive in this context, i.e., an anaphor. If it were such, then children's English would look more like Icelandic than if it were not. In this regard, it has been suggested in various places that there is suppletion in the genitive pronominal system; although the phonetic form is the same, there are two forms of the possessive pronoun, one anaphoric and one pronominal.[2] If this is true, then this argument of Solan's loses its force; these children may well be speaking Icelandic.

The second assumption appears to be that there is a direct grammatical correlation between the occurrence of SSC violations and the occurrence of genitive reflexives. The natural question here is, why should we expect there to be such a correlation? That is, the question of whether or not the SSC is operative may well be independent of the occurrence of genitive reflexives (and vice versa), and so (4) and (5) may be irrelevant to the present issue. Some language (call it 'Iceglish') might fail to obey the SSC but still lack genitive reflexives. Here the question is simply whether these two features are instantiations of a single abstract parameter, or whether two separate parameters are involved.

In short, the Icelandic hypothesis can be maintained in the face of (4) and (5) under an analysis involving suppletion in English, or, alternatively, it can be argued that (4) and (5) are simply irrelevant to the question of whether of whether or not the children are applying Icelandic binding principles (where a distinction is made between a given language's inventory of nominal expressions and the principles governing the distribution of these nominal expressions).[3]

On the other hand, besides the data from Spanish and Solan's other considerations, there is a further reason to reject the Icelandic hypothesis. If the Language Acquisition Device is equipped with the 'Subset Principle' (cf. Berwick and Weinberg, 1984; Wexler and Manzini, this volume) the child, when presented with a parametric choice, will, ceteris paribus, project the grammar with the parameter setting that produces a subset of the grammar with the other parameter setting. For present purposes, it is enough to note that a grammar with both TSC and SSC yields a subset of the strings allowed by a grammar with only TSC (Jackubowicz, 1984, makes this point as well).[4] Aside from other considerations, there is thus reason to reject the Icelandic hypothesis with respect to the contrast between (1) and (2). That is, under the Subset Principle, the child would assume *ab initio* that both the TSC and SSC are operative, and then, upon exposure to positive evidence (e.g., Icelandic), extend binding domains where necessary. Holding the Subset Principle constant then, we must find some explanation other than that involving a separation of the TSC from the SSC for the childrens' interpretations of (1)–(2), since the Subset Principle would force a binding domain smaller than that allowed by the SSC's absence to be entertained first.

To return briefly to the suggested replacement set of sentences offered earlier in (3), if it turns out that the results of this counterfactual experiment pattern with the indicatives in Solan's experiment, then both his processing explanation and the Subset Principle are supported. If there remains a discrepancy between infinitives and indicatives when PRO is controlled for, however, then there is room to make the argument that the childrens' grammar at this stage lacks the SSC (regardless of whether or not the rest of the grammar of Icelandic comes along as extra baggage; see above), and so much the worse for the Subset Principle (but see below).

3. PRINCIPLE B

One can say at least two things about the the three sorts of NP's found in natural languages. Anaphoric expressions, those items falling under Principle A, *must* have an antecedent. Names, variables, etc. (*R*-expressions), those items falling under Principle C, must *not* have an antecedent. Let us assume that children also believe the second proposition. What, then, do they know about pronouns? At one stage of their linguistic development, according to Solan's work, they are disposed to treat items like *him* in roughly the same fashion as they treat anaphors, i.e., they bind them in their governing categories. But here care is needed. We must not jump immediately to the conclusion that they are violating Principle B.

The question is, are these small speakers in fact violating Principle B (or do they not have it?), or do they simply not know what counts as a pronominal, i.e., they don't know which expressions fall under Principle B (they have Principle B, but they don't have pronominals)? With respect to the former option, I agree with Solan in his comments — at some stage Principle B does operate with generality, and it is difficult to imagine how it might arise if not there from the beginning. The other picture is more plausible: Children have Principle B in some form, but they are not yet aware which expressions fall under it. Presumably, they are on the lookout for such a class of items.

A pronominal, as adults know it, can appear in two contexts that are relevant to the child. It can be free, with no antecedent in sight,

(6)   He left

or it can be bound from outside its clause.

(7) a.   John$_i$ believes [that he$_i$ will get no mail]
    b.   Bill$_i$ wants [Mary to like him$_i$]

For all a child knows, the pronominal in (6) may well be an *R*-expression; it is free. (7), with its intended interpretations, shows bound pronominals. Although the items are bound, they are bound from outside the clauses in which they occur. Given that they are bound, however, there may be pressure on the child, at some stage of linguistic development, to take anything that is bound as an anaphor. If this occurs, the pronominals in (7) will be mistakenly classified as anaphors, and the child then has positive evidence (albeit false) that the binding domain of anaphors must be extended beyond the clause in which they occur. Once this domain is enlarged so that the bindings in (7) are treated as exemplifying Principle A of the Binding Theory, two things will then follow. One, pronominals (read 'anaphors' here) can be locally bound, and two, anaphors (real anaphors) can be non-locally bound (in the same way as the pronominals are bound in (7) under the false assumption that they are anaphors).

Let us assume that the child hears sentences like those in (7) and constructs the intended interpretations. At this point, he might say to himself "Anaphor! Principle A, bound in its governing category." The rest of the unconscious reasoning might run as follows: There is positive evidence that items like *he* can be bound. When they are bound, they are bound outside their immediately containing clauses. If the Subset Principle is active, binding domains will grow as the positive evidence rolls in. That is, start small and expand when necessary. The child has seen it necessary to postulate an extended binding domain, and this domain properly includes the smaller non-extended one. Once the domain is enlarged to cover sentences like (7), it follows that the immediately containing clause of the pronoun is also included in this domain. Apparent violations of Principle B follow immediately, despite the lack of positive evidence to this effect. Also, since the binding domain for anaphors has been extended (albeit mistakenly) non-local anaphor bindings like those discussed in the previous section will emerge.

At this envisioned stage, the child is applying Principle A to both anaphors and what in the adult grammar are pronominals. In addition, there is also, presumably, positive evidence available to the child which shows pronominals occurring with no antecedent (e.g. (6)).[5] At this point, the child might assume that a pronominal may occur with no antecedent, but when there is a possible one, it must be bound. Evidence contradictory to this latter assumption would soon roll in (if it hasn't already), in the form of something like (8):

(8) a.   John$_i$ believes [that he$_j$ will get no mail]
    b.   Bill$_i$ wants [Mary to like him$_j$]

The situation as I've described it would be fairly marked — a blind application of the Subset Principle to Principle B phenomena would force the child to choose the analysis where pronouns pattern with *R*-expressions, since the set of strings where pronouns have no antecedents is a subset of the set of strings in which pronouns sometimes have antecedents. There is, on the other hand, positive evidence to which the child has access that shows that pronouns can have antecedents (e.g., (7)). With this degree of markedness, the situation would be very unstable and it would push the child to hit upon the idea that *he, him*, etc. can be classified as falling under this previously dormant Principle B, with a corresponding readjustment of the definition of the relevant governing category with no worries about binding from outside (which still counts as free in this new domain). At this point, the items whose binding patterns induced the extended Principle A effects would now be classified otherwise, and there would be no need to have such a large governing category. The child's classification of anaphors would approximate the adult's, and the governing category could then collapse in size.

4. CONCLUSION

In the preceding section, I have attempted to construct a likely story in which the children's mistaken interpretations of pronominals and their mistakes in reflexive bindings receive a unified account under the Subset Principle. The classification of pronouns as items falling under Principle A expands the binding domain, and once this occurs, reflexives can be bound where (in the adult grammar) pronouns can be. Even though in Section 2 it was suggested that the Subset Principle would prevent the postulation of an extended binding domain for reflexives, the aberrant interpretation of pronouns can serve as a trigger, and thus they can give rise to mistaken reflexive bindings. In this light, I think that it is still plausible that the children are, to some degree, entertaining the idea that the binding domains of their target language might be determined by, as it turns out, the parameter that shapes part of the grammar of, for example, Icelandic. Solan's interpretations of the facts are different; the mistakes discussed in Section 2 might well have arisen because of PRO. We appear to agree that the mistakes surrounding the interpretation of pronominals probably arose from misclassification, but there is room for disagreement on what the trigger of that misclassification might have been, and what relation this misclassification has to the rest of the data.[6]

NOTES

* These comments are a response to the version of Larry Solan's paper that was circulated prior to the conference. Depending on the form of the published version, my comments may turn out to be irrelevant or inaccurate. Apologies to Larry in advance. Preparation of the manuscript was supported in part by the MIT Center for Cognitive Science through a grant from the A. P. Sloan Foundation's Program in Cognitive Science.

[1] Solan does not suggest that the children are mistakenly taking *tell* to be a subject control verb. If they were in fact doing so, then the explanation for their interpretations of the reflexive would follow straightforwardly. Helen Goodluck informs me (personal communication), however, that children have subject vs. object control straightened out by the time they reach the age of Solan's subjects.

[2] This is suggested in Chomsky (1981) and Goggin (1982), among other places. Baker (1983) proposes a different feature system for nominal expressions, $[\pm \text{pronoun}]$ and $[\pm \text{near}]$, where anaphors and pronominals share the feature $[+\text{pronoun}]$ and are differentiated with respect to $[\pm \text{near}]$. Genitive pronouns are then left unspecified for $[\pm \text{near}]$.

[3] As Solan notes, Harbert (1982) notes a correlation between the occurrence of genitive reflexives and long-distance reflexivization, and then observes that if binding domains were restricted to NP and S and stated in terms of government only, with no reference to SUBJECT, both types of reflexivization could then be viewed as violations of Principle A. This unification would be impossible if SUBJECT were a determining factor in the definition of the binding domain. While such a situation might open up the logical space of anaphora to make room for a genitive reflexive, there is no necessary connection here between such an element and a transclausal reflexive, especially since the correlation here is in terms of *violations* of a binding principle. Harbert also gives some arguments against the proposal that the genitive is a disguised reflexive (see previous note).

[4] A necessary assumption here is that the strings that are relevant for determining subset relations display binding relations, perhaps in the form of suffixal subscripts.

[5] Ken Wexler has pointed out (personal communication) that the 'free' use of pronouns comes in very early in child language. See also Montalbetti and Wexler (1985) for a revision of Principle B which will account for many of the Principle B violations under discussion. Interestingly enough, in a pilot study of the second language acquisition of English reflexive binding patterns by native speakers of Korean, Finer and Broselow (to appear) found behavior very similar to that displayed by Solan's subjects. That is, the Korean speakers showed a tendency to take non-local antecedents for reflexives in infinitival clauses and local antecedents for reflexives in tensed clauses. Also, pronominals were treated similarly.

[6] Space limitations prevent me from discussing other issues that Solan raises, in particular that of whether the governing category of anaphors should be distinguished from that of pronominals. In this regard, see Chomsky, 1984, where identical domains are proposed, but where the effects derived are identical to those derived by Freidin's restatements. There also appears to be an interesting covergence from different areas on the idea that theta-domains (or their equivalents) are relevant to binding (Bach and Partee, 1980, the papers in Bresnan, 1982, Freidin's proposals cited by Solan,

Chomsky, 1984, etc.). As a last point, it should be noted that merely because SUBJECT is a partial determinant of the governing category for an anaphor, this does not guarantee that the anaphor will be bound by a subject. This alone will not capture the 'subject-orientation' of certain anaphoric elements; something else is required, perhaps along the lines of proposals by Borer (this volume) or Finer (1985), where INFL/AGR (coindexed with the subject) plays an active role in determining the antecedent.

REFERENCES

Bach, E. and B. Partee: 1980, 'Anaphora and semantic structure', *Papers from the Parasession on Pronouns and Anaphora*, CLS, University of Chicago.

Baker, C. L.: 1983, 'A revised theory of binding for definite pronouns, reflexives, and reciprocals', ms., University of Texas, Austin

Berwick, R. and A. Weinberg: 1984, *The Grammatical Basis of Linguistic Performance*, MIT Press.

Borer, H. (this volume), 'Comments on Jakubowicz' paper'.

Bresnan, J. (ed.): 1982, *The Mental Representation of Grammatical Relations*, MIT Press.

Chomsky, N.: 1981, *Lectures on Government and Binding*, Foris Publications, Dordrecht.

Chomsky, N.: 1984, *Knowledge of Language: Its Nature, Origins, and Use*, ms. MIT (to be published by Praeger).

Finer, D.: 1985, 'The syntax of switch-reference', *Linguistic Inquiry* **16**(1).

Finer, D. and E. Broselow: to appear, 'Second language acquisition of reflexive binding', in S. Berman *et al.* (eds.), *NELS* **16**, GLSA, University of Massachusetts, Amherst.

Goggin, J.: 1982, 'A non-sentential approach to "Clausal" NP's', *Texas Linguistic Forum #21*, University of Texas, Austin.

Harbert, W.: 1982, 'Should binding refer to SUBJECT?', in P. Sells and J. Pustejovsky (eds.) *NELS* **12**, GLSA, University of Massachusetts, Amherst.

Jakubowicz, C.: 1984, 'Markedness and binding principles', in C. Jones and P. Sells (eds.), *NELS* **14**, GLSA, University of Massachusetts, Amherst.

Wexler K. and R. Manzini (this volume), 'Parameters and learnability in binding theory'.

MARIANNE PHINNEY

THE PRO-DROP PARAMETER IN SECOND LANGUAGE ACQUISITION*

INTRODUCTION

The parameterized model of Core Grammar that has been recently proposed by Chomsky (1981) has a two-fold function. As a part of the framework of linguistic theory, the model accounts for some systematic differences between languages, and accounts for a wide variety of constructions within an individual language. As part of the framework of Acquisition Theory, it can account for developmental stages in the acquisition process of a first language, including both stages of a single language and cross-linguistic comparisons (Otsu, 1981; Phinney, 1983). However, only a few researchers (White, 1983, 1985; Flynn, 1983, among them) have applied this model to the problem of second language acquisition.

The problem of how a second language is acquired by an adult is an interesting one. Ideally, one would like to assume that the acquisition device which operates during first language acquisition continues to operate during the acquisition of the second language, although perhaps less efficiently, since L2 competence rarely approaches that of the native speaker in an adult. If the LAD is still operational at some level past puberty, then the same constraints and conditions which operate in the acquisition of a first language should operate in the second. The setting of parameters (Chomsky, 1981, 1982) should thus be necessary in L2 acquisition as well as in L1 acquisition.

It has been assumed that the possible settings of the Core Grammar parameter can be ranked on a scale of markedness, and that the initial state of the acquisition device entails that all the parameters are set to the unmarked setting. To reset a parameter to a more marked setting requires certain input data which serve to confirm that the parameter in question is indeed marked in that language. If the language utilizes the unmarked setting, then the initial assumptions will be met by the input data, and the parameter will never be changed.

This model leads to predictions about the acquisition process which can be supported by empirical data. These predictions can include

221

Thomas Roeper and Edwin Williams (eds.), Parameter Setting, 221–238.

acquisition order and relative difficulty of certain constructions within a particular language, or relative order of acquisition across languages. A construction which is unmarked, or a parameter setting which is unmarked, should be relatively easy and acquired at an early stage, all things being equal. Constructions and parameters which are marked should cause more difficulty and be acquired later. There is some evidence to support these predictions from data on infinitives (Phinney, 1981) and White (1981) discusses several previously published studies from this point of view.

If we assume that Core Grammar and this model of the Acquisition Device are relevant to second language acquisition as well as to first, then these parameters and markedness considerations should be involved. Although the adult L2 learner is not in quite the same situation as the child, in that one language has already been learned and the parameters set for that language, the same process must hold to a certain extent in acquiring the L2. Parameters may have to be re-set according to the data available from the second language.

This paper will examine the role of the pro-drop parameter (Chomsky, 1981) and markedness in causing errors in the interlanguage, the intermediate stage between L1 monolingualism and the final L2 competence reached by the adult learner. Evidence from the L2 acquisition of English and Spanish will be presented to support the claim that parameter resetting must occur in L2 acquisition, and that a delay in resetting the parameter will induce systematic errors in the L2 learner's production. In addition, it is suggested that markedness considerations can account for directional differences in difficulty. The theory has the advantage over traditional L2 approaches to learner errors, Contrastive Analysis (CA) and Error Analysis (EA), in that it is more powerful and leads to further implications concerning the interaction of Core Grammar and the LAD.

1. PREVIOUS APPROACHES TO L2 ACQUISITION

Applied linguists have been concerned for many years with the problem of predicting and explaining difficulties which occur during the process of learning a second language. Two approaches which have waxed and waned in the past few years are Contrastive Analysis (CA) and Error Analysis (EA). Both approaches are in fact independent of linguistic theory; any framework may be used as the basis of analysis.

CA was formulated primarily to "predict and describe the patterns that will cause difficulty in learning, and those that will not cause difficulty" (Lado, 1957) in learning a foreign language. Based on the hypothesis that a careful description of both the native language and the target language would permit prediction of learning difficulties, CA assumes no particular linguistic framework, although CAs have been done using structuralist descriptions (Lado, 1957), generative phonology (Ritchie, 1967), and generative transformational grammar (Stockwell *et al.*, 1965). In the last decade, however, the use of current linguistic models has become less common in CA. In fact, CA itself seemed to decrease in popularity in the seventies as proponents discovered that there were difficulties with the theory that made predictions inaccurate and directional predictions almost impossible.

For example, Stockwell *et al.* (1965) present a contrastive analysis of Spanish, with a view towards explaining difficulties found by English students learning Spanish. (Note that they do *not* discuss the other direction, an area which has been the focus of considerable EA research.) Concerning the well-known fact that overt pronominal subjects are rarely used in Spanish, they propose a "Simple Sentence Transformation" called Subject Omission. They first describe the pattern in Spanish, then state, in a section called *Learning Problems*, "The English speaker will tend to overuse subjects — and in doing so will sound emphatic and aggressive" (p. 421). There is no discussion of whether certain contexts may be more prone to error than others, or whether this overuse of subjects might be related to any other linguistic factors. In their hierarchy of difficulty (Chapter 11), "Spanish third person subject omission" is considered to be Category 2 on a 16 point scale, while "English first person and second person subjects obligatorily expressed, Spanish optionally so" is Category 14, implying that the former is far more difficult than the latter. Without empirical data, this claim is difficult to evaluate. Their hierarchy is based on a comparison of obligatory vs. optional rules, which is closely dependent on the analyses selected for the two languages, and is not dependent on any more abstract notions of grammar or the LAD. In fact, the data to be presented here suggests that their predictions are incorrect.

In predicting the difficulties to be encountered in the L2 acquisition process, CA assumes that difficulty is correlated with the distance between two languages on some scale of typological difference (not specified). James (1971) notes that it is generally accepted that "some languages are harder to learn than others, given a certain L1 as a starting point" (p. 62). There is a general layman's perception of this point; ask any undergraduate at any college in the United States which language is the easiest (to fulfill a language requirement, for example), and chances are s/he will say "Spanish" or possibly "French" but certainly not "Russian". James went on to state that "since it seems that some languages are not intrinsically more difficult than others . . . we must conclude that the L1 is the crux of the matter" (pp. 96—97). The parameterized model of Core Grammar provides a theoretical model for challenging that statement. Recent discussions of parameters and markedness seems to suggest that some languages may indeed be intrinsically more difficult. If a language has selected the highly marked setting for several parameters, it will require more input data of a particular type to acquire, and thus will be 'more difficult'.

As the use of CA declined and more emphasis was placed on psychological reality in linguistic theory and language acquisition, attention began to focus on the errors learners make. Corder (1967), in a landmark EA paper, proposed that error analysis fit squarely into a model of psycholinguistic processes, assuming that the learner of a second language makes use of the same acquisition device used by the child in acquiring the first language. The L2 learner's errors were thus systematic and evidence of the acquisition system and of the learner's transitional competence.

For psycholinguistics, both CA and EA have weaknesses. CA, in the classical sense, can be predictive but non-directional, and thus fails to satisfy the intuition that some languages *are* easier than others. It is clearly dependent on the linguistic model being used for the analysis; if the theory changes, so do the predictions made by CA. As such, it is more a model and methodology than a theory. EA, on the other hand, is data-driven. It can be predictive only by utilizing observations of what has happened previously. While there are theories of how inter-language develops (Selinker, 1972), error analysis itself is only a methodology. From a psycholinguistic point of view, it seems reasonable that CA and EA are actually two sides of the same coin; one provides a means of approaching part of the L2 acquisition problem theoretically, although it is incomplete without a specified theoretical model. The other provides a method of analyzing the data from the acquisition process.

2. THE PLACE OF UNIVERSAL GRAMMAR

The role of Universal Grammar in L2 acquisition and the effect such considerations have on the data analysis have been a recurrent theme in applied and theoretical linguistics since the mid-1970s. Following claims then being made about UG (Chomsky, 1972), Celce-Murcia (1972) proposed that the universalist hypothesis was necessary if "meaningful work is to be done in the area of contrastive syntax" (p. 12). Although her work on comparatives utilized a concept of markedness (Chomsky and Halle, 1968), no implications for the learning process were made beyond stating that the unmarked member of an opposition pair like *hot-cold* is usually the first learned by a child.

Since then, consideration of markedness has recurred in different forms, although the references are sparser than one might expect (Rutherford, 1982). Eckman's (1977) Markedness Differential Hypothesis utilized markedness relations stated in universal grammar, although he referred to implicational universals rather than the more intrinsic markedness assumed in a parameterized grammar. In reviewing several L2 acquisition studies, Rutherford concludes that the results "are not inconsistent with the principles of core grammar" (1982:98), although he feels that at this point it is mostly useful with low-level syntax (undefined).

Zobl's (1983) projection model of markedness comes closer to that used in the terms of Chomsky (1981). In his model, a construction is unmarked if the acquisition device requires no data to arrive at it. The more data that is needed, and the more revisions required in the grammar, the more marked the construction will be. The initial state of the learner is assumed to be his/her competence in L1; thus Zobl's view of markedness is determined by the relationship between L1 and L2.

With regard to the L2 acquisition process, Zobl's model may be more correct than that which has been proposed for the L1 process. The unmarked state has been assumed to be the initial state of the LAD. However, once a language has been learned and the grammar modified, it is not necessary to assume that the learner of a second language would return to the initial state. A discussion of markedness in L2 acquisition would thus have two levels; the intrinsic Core Grammar markedness settings of the initial state, and a secondary level which would refer to the resetting process.

Despite the current interest in markedness as a factor in L2 acquisition (Eckman, 1977; Rutherford, 1982; Zobl, 1983), few researchers have considered it within a parameterized model of Core Grammar. In fact, the model itself has hardly been utilized in studies of L2 acquisition (Flynn, 1983; White, 1983a, 1985, are notable exceptions). Clearly, if the model has relevance for L1 acquisition, as has been suggested (Hyams, 1983; Phinney, 1983), it should be relevant for L2 acquisition as well. Within this model, markedness refers to settings of particular parameters (Chomsky, 1981). In L2 acquisition, the target language may require different settings of a parameter than the native language. Since some settings are determined to be marked in Core Grammar, in that they require a certain amount of supportive data in the input to be instantiated, markedness has an intrinsic quality which Zobl (1983) does not attribute to it.

This view of markedness has been assumed to have certain implications for first language acquisition, namely that the unmarked setting is the default setting, and requires little or no substantiating input data to be acquired, while more marked settings require positive evidence to be 'reset' and incorporated into the developing grammar. In second language acquisition, the implications are somewhat more complicated.

There are two possibilities for the initial period of L2 learning. One is to assume that the L2 learner will begin from scratch, so to speak, that the parameters of Core Grammar will be initialized at the unmarked settings for the L2, and that acquisition will then progress in much the same way as a child's would. This would imply that there would be no interference effects, and that the settings of the parameters in the L1 would have no effect on the learning of the second language. The vast amount of available data on the reality of L1 interference suggests that this approach is untenable. The second possibility assumes that the learner begins with the settings of L1, and generalizes them to L2, until the input data force him/her to reset.

White (1983a) outlines eight possibilities for the markedness interactions of a given parameter. Here, I shall discuss only two possibilities: when the two languages differ on the setting for the parameter, one utilizing the unmarked setting, the other the marked.

Assume that in language X, parameter P is unmarked. A speaker of X then begins to learn language Y, in which the same parameter is marked. The learner, in going from a system in which the setting is unmarked to one in which it is marked, will require a great deal of substantiating input, just as a child would in learning Y as a first language. In other words, acquiring native-like competence in the constructions that depend on the parameter will be difficult for the speaker of X. On the other hand, a native speaker of Y, in trying to learn X, may start by assuming that the parameter is marked, as it is in Y. If the parameter is such that the consequences of the unmarked setting violate the implications of the marked setting, then the evidence needed to reset the parameter will be readily available in the input data. Acquiring native-like competence in the relevant constructions in X may thus be less difficult for the speaker of Y.

This scenario is somewhat different than that proposed by White (1983a). In her model, the learner going from a marked L1 to an unmarked L2 would continue to use the marked setting of the parameter even at the later stages. In fact, both accounts may be possible, depending on the nature of the construction involved.

2. THE PRO-DROP PARAMETER IN L2 ACQUISITION

One parameter which has received considerable attention in the literature is the pro-drop parameter, which involves a cluster of properties, including absence of pronominal subjects, free inversion of subjects, and possibly occurrences of [that e]; it may also be related to the use of verbal agreement (Chomsky, 1981, 1982; Hyams, 1983; Picallo, 1984; Rizzi, 1982; Suñer, 1982; Torrego, 1984). Languages like Italian and Spanish are assumed to use the parameter; languages like English and French do not.

It has been argued that the unmarked setting of the parameter is the setting used by Italian and Spanish (Chomsky, 1982; Hyams, 1983). White (1985) assumes it is marked, in that the presence of empty subjects in the input data would be necessary to instantiate it.[1] If it is assumed that the parameter is correlated with agreement, as suggested by Rizzi (1982) and followed by Hyams (1983), then the evidence for the marked setting (lack of agreement and use of semantically null subjects) would be readily available as well.

2.1. *The Pro-Drop Parameter in Spanish*

Suñer (1982) proposed an interesting analysis for the parameter in Spanish. She argued that Spanish has three types of 'empty' subjects which could be governed by the parameter: *pro*, which can be governed by AGR ([+tense] in her analysis), [e], in the case of postposed subjects; and [Ø], in the case of existential and impersonal sentences like (1) and (2).

(1)   Había mucha gente.
       "There were many people."

(2)   Parece que está enfermo.
       "(It) seems that (he) is sick."

She notes that these sentences never have a pronominal subject, that the subject is semantically as well as phonologically empty, and argues that the subject cannot be PRO or [e], using evidence from gerundive and infinitive constructions.

Suñer claims that the use of [Ø] subjects in these constructions is a variation along the [+obligatory subject] parameter she proposes. While it is generally assumed that empty subjects are one of the main manifestations of the parameter, in most cases it is assumed that sentences like (1) and (2) are parallel to the more common case of (3), where the empty subject is referential.

(3)   Leemos muchos libros.
       Read (1st pl.) many books.
       "We read many books."

Suñer's analysis thus presents a more complex view of the parameter; not only are there empty referential subjects, but there are also truly empty subjects which would then not come under the Binding Conditions. In the more standard analysis, both (1) and (3) are accounted for by the same process. If Suñer's analysis is correct, there may be a difference in the L2 acquisition of the two types of constructions.

2.2. *Evidence for the Pro-Drop Parameter in Acquisition*

There is strong evidence indicating that the pro-drop parameter is involved in first language acquisition. Hyams (1983) discusses the parameter in detail with respect to Italian and English. Her evidence suggests that something like the parameter is operating in the early stages of English, showing a shift from subjectless sentences to the use of subjects just before the acquisition of the verbal morphology. Phinney (1983) provided preliminary evidence that the parameter was in use for younger Spanish speaking subjects, and showed distinct differences between Spanish-speaking and English-speaking children at later stages. If it is assumed that the unmarked setting of the parameter will be used in the initial stages, the available data supports the hypothesis that the unmarked setting of the parameter is as in Spanish and Italian, to allow empty subjects freely, and the children learning English, which uses the marked setting, must reset the parameter during the acquisition process.

If the parameterized model of grammar implies a partially para-meterized acquisition system, then it is reasonable to assume that the parameters will be involved in the acquisition of a second language as well, even if the process may be less efficient in adulthood for whether reason. However, in L2 acquisition, the learner must reset the para-meters, either from unmarked to marked again, or from the setting in L1 to the setting in L2.

If relative markedness does indeed play a role in the L2 usage of the constructions affected by the pro-drop parameter, then assuming the parameter is unmarked for Spanish and marked for English, the follow-ing patterns might be expected. Spanish speakers learning English, in going from a unmarked system to a marked system, should have considerable difficulty. In particular, they should omit pronominal subjects frequently, particularly when the subject can be predicted from the context or in the third person, where there is an agreement marker in the present tense.[2] They should also have difficulty with the im-personal subjects *it* and *there*. If Suñer's (1982) analysis of the para-meter in Spanish is correct, then the fact that those constructions have a [Ø] subject in Spanish should increase the difficulty of learning them in English.

The parameter has been assumed to be correlated in some way with the agreement system, and so the acquisition of the 'agreement' system in English may also be affected. A Spanish speaker learning English will assume that there will be agreement as well as null subjects until the input data proves otherwise. English, having defective agreement morphology, will provide contradictory evidence, delaying resetting of the parameter.[3]

English subjects learning Spanish are going from a marked setting to an unmarked setting in a language with extensive morphological agree-ment. If the initial assumption is that the L2 will have the same settings as the L1, one would expect to find a greater percentage of errors which can be attributed directly to interference, particularly at the initial stages. This would imply overuse of subject pronouns (Stockwell *et al.*, 1965), collapsing of verbal endings to the third person singular, and use of some form of pronoun for *it* and *there*, which might be translations (*él* or a clitic pronoun for *it*, *allá* or *allí* for *there*).

On the other hand, if the LAD returns to its initial assumptions for the parameter settings, English speakers learning Spanish should show patterns which would be similar to Spanish children. They should allow omission of subject pronouns,and include verbal endings, even if not always the correct one. Once they realize that Spanish requires [Ø] subjects in impersonal constructions, those constructions should cause considerably less trouble than for the Spanish ESL students.

These two hypotheses are, of course, opposite ends of a continuum. In reality, English speakers learning Spanish will propably fall somewhere between, with considerable variation depending on the subject. This model cannot be assumed to eliminate the possibility of interference effors; some learners will persist in being dependent on translation, and 'translation' interference is always a real factor, particularly at the beginning levels. Assuming the amount of direct interference to be roughly the same in both ESL and SSL learners, the model can provide a linguistically principled account of some facets of interlanguage.

2.3. *Previous L2 Studies*

Due to the intensive study that has been given to ESL studies, there are considerable published data available on the errors of ESL students of all language backgrounds, including Spanish. This is not the case with English students learning Spanish. There is very little published research detailing the errors which are made by learners of Spanish, and that which is available is not always specific on the points crucial to the evaluation of the hypothesis.

The error patterns common to ESL students are well-known and well-attested for various L1 backgrounds. Moore and Marzano (1979) cite sixty-five error categories found in Spanish speaking children in grades K-6. The twenty most common errors included use of present for past tense (5.1%), improper subject/verb number (2.1%), and third person subject not stated (1.9%). The percentages were very low, which may have been because the subjects were children, exposed to the language in their environment, and not grouped according to ability in English. In a study of adults, Bailey *et al.* (1973), noted that the third person singular -*s* was inaccurate 70% of the time among Spanish speakers.

All ESL teachers will agree that the third person -*s* is extremely difficult for their students, although many will not know why; after all, it is such a simple system, only one ending to remember. But it is precisely this 'simplicity' which causes the difficulty. For all practical purposes, English has no agreement; having determined that, to have one ending on one person in one tense is extremely marked. If a learner has assumed that English is an agreement language (the unmarked case), an impression which may be fostered by paradigmatic teaching methods, then s/he will tend to overgeneralize the -*s* to other persons. This is in fact what many students do. Other seem to cluster the ending on certain verbs (Abraham, 1984), indicating uneven, perhaps lexicalized, acquisition. If the use of agreement or lack thereof is a possible trigger for the setting of the pro-drop parameter, then English provides mixed evidence.

White (1985) presents data from Spanish speakers learning English which reflect grammatical judgements of sentences with empty subjects, designed specifically to test acquisition of the pro-drop parameter. Although she assumes that the parameter is marked and present in Spanish, and thus Spanish speakers are going from a marked system to an unmarked system (English), her data show that Spanish speakers accept subjectless sentences more frequently than French speakers. Her data is not sufficient to settle the markedness setting of the parameter itself, although the data from the French speakers does suggest that the learner assumes that the setting of the parameter in L2 is the same as in L1.

The published data from English speakers learning Spanish is considerably sparser and less conclusive. Guntermann (1978) reported frequency of errors in beginning Peace Corps volunteers. learning Spanish in E1 Salvador. She noted that verb misagreement occured in 8.4% of the corpus, and that native speakers considered errors in person agreement to be more difficult than errors in tense. She does not cite overuse of subject pronouns as an error, although some examples given of students' utterances were corrected by native speakers who deleted the subject pronoun, as in (4).

(4)   Cuando yo fui a casa yo hablaba con Joe.
        corrected to:
        Cuando fuí a casa hablé con Joe.

The only example she gives of an impersonal construction is correct, as in (5).

(5)   En tres años es posible que me casé [corrected to *case*]

Although the verb tense was incorrect, the speaker did not insert a pronoun for *it* in *es posible*. Van Naerssen (1980) also notes that tense was more difficult than person agreement.[4]

Chastain (1981) asked native speakers to evaluate the compositions of students in second year Spanish classes. He notes that the students inserted extra pronouns 37% of the time; however, he states that most of those errors were overuse of clitic pronouns, and there are no instances of overuse of subject pronouns in the published examples. Although Smith (1982) notes a high percentage of "noun phrase omission errors", the omissions she refers to are the omission of the personal *a*, relative pronouns and clitics. She does not cite any noun overuse errors.

From the published data, it appears that English speakers learning Spanish have a great deal of trouble with verbal endings. Van Naerssen (1980) suggests that there is a stage during which the third person singular is used as the default tensed verb, but other research seems to imply that although they may get the endings wrong, they do use them. Tense seems to be more difficult than person, which indicates that the English speakers have determined that Spanish is a [+agreement] language.

With regard to the overuse of subjects hypothesized by Stockwell *et al.* (1965), there appears to be a conspiracy of silence. None of the studies cited mentioned overuse of pronominal subjects as an error, even when native speakers were used to correct utterances of the learners (Guntermann, 1978; Chastain, 1981). In the absence of overt commentary, one can only conclude that it does not pose a sufficiently serious problem for the English speaker learning Spanish to warrant comment. This would seem to provide very indirect support for the hypothesis that learning to omit the subjects is easier than learning to put them in obligatorily.

3. A COMPARISON OF ESL AND SSL LEARNERS

In order to examine the hypotheses discussed here, production data in the form of free compositions were analyzed. Four groups of students were used. Two groups were students in Basic English I and Basic English II at the University of Puerto Rico in Mayaguez. These students have already had twelve years of English instruction in the public schools; however, by normal ESL standards they are at the high beginner to low intermediate level. The other two groups were students in Spanish 110 and 120 at the University of Massachusetts in Amherst. Some students had had Spanish in high school; however, most of the students could be classed as beginners (110) and low intermediates (120). The compositions were written in class as part of the regular class work, in the case of the English students, and as part of an exam in the case of the Spanish students.

The compositions were examined specifically for omission of subject pronouns in obligatory contexts (ESL) and overuse of subject pronouns (SSL) as well as verbal agreement. Because there were unequal numbers of verb forms in the composition, the results within the types are given as percentages, shown in Table I.

In some respects, the data in Table I seem to contradict the published data. In both groups, verbal agreement is more often correct

TABLE I
Subject Pronoun Usage by ESL and SSL learners

	ESL1	ESL2	SSL1	SSL2
Total forms	175	250	304	111
I. Agree. correct	139	183	248	119
(Percent)	(79)	(73)	(82)	(67)
Pro Subjects	.48	.64	.14	.23
Lex. Subjects	.34	.31	.04	.11
Null Subjects	.07	.06	.81	.66
II. Agree. incorrect	35	29	52	49
(Percent)	(20)	(12)	(17)	(28)
Pro Subjects	.29	.38	.08	.27
Lex. Subjects	.43	.59	.10	.10
Null Subjects	.29	.03	.83	.63
III. Impersonals Total	25	38	8	9
(Percent)	(07)	(07)	(03)	(05)
It/el overt	.24	.21	.00	.00
Null it/es	.24	.66	.38	.78
There/alli overt	.20	.03	.00	.00
Null there/hay	.32	.11	.63	.22

than incorrect. This may be partly due to the nature of the assignments; much of the composition was written in first person, which may not be as susceptible to error. Tense errors, where they could be distinguished from verbal agreement errors, were not counted. Spanish speakers learning English did not omit pronominal subjects as much as might have been expected. The total percentage of referential subject omissions was 13% for Group 1 and 6% for Group 2. However, the omissions followed a definite pattern. Sentence initially, referential subject pronouns were never omitted. Most of the omissions occurred in subordinate or conjoined clauses, where the discourse was already focused on the subject. This in fact follows discourse rules in Spanish, where subject pronouns may be used for emphasis, but not where the referent is obvious.[5]

The data from the impersonal constructions is quite different. Although the impersonal constructions made up a small portion of the data base, 56% of the forms in ESL1 were subjectless, and 76% of the forms in ESL2 had null subjects.

The English speakers learning Spanish show that they have learned to omit pronominal subjects, even in the lowest group (SSL1). The total percentage of empty subjects was 83% in SSL1, 65% in SSL2.[6] In the impersonals, there were no instances in which lexical items were used as subjects under interference from English.

4. DISCUSSION

The data from Spanish speakers learning English, both that presented here and that previously published, seem to indicate that the cost of resetting the parameter from Spanish to English is high. The data in Table I also provide indirect support for Suñer's (1982) analysis, in that there is a clear distinction between the impersonal constructions and the use of referential pronouns. The latter seem to be easier to learn.

The data from the English speakers learning Spanish clearly show that the pro-drop parameter is easy to acquire, even when the L1 utilizes the non-pro-drop setting. The impersonal constructions seem to be easier than omitting the referential pronouns, although the data base is too small to test for significance.

The data in Table I also suggest a solution to the problem of the marked setting of the parameter itself. Although most linguists have assumed that the unmarked setting is that exemplified by Spanish and

Italian, White (1983a, 1985) argues that Spanish uses the the marked setting. Following her Table II (White, 1983a), one would expect the following. Spanish to English would be marked to unmarked. Her prediction is that the marked setting, in this case the use of pro-drop, would persist even into the later stages. This prediction is consistent with the assumptions made here, that going from unmarked to marked will result in lingering interference. On the other hand, by her analysis, English to Spanish is unmarked to marked, and the table indicates that at the early stages, the unmarked system would persist. The data presented here clearly do not support that prediction. They do, however, support the claim made here, that going from a marked system (English) to an unmarked system (Spanish) will be less difficult, and most of the students in the SSL1 group showed no reluctance to omit subjects.[7] The data thus support the hypothesis that the unmarked version of the parameter is that used by Spanish.

These data are not sufficient, however, to determine whether the acquisition device resets to the initial unmarked stage when a second language is learned. As Otsu pointed out in his comment to this paper, it is necessary to examine a learner with a marked L1 learning a marked L2. White (1985) has examined such a situation, that of French speakers learning English. Her data indicate that French speakers do not reset to the pro-drop setting before acquiring English, as they show no indication of treating English as a pro-drop language.

5. CONCLUSION

It has been proposed here that the parameterized model of Core Grammar proposed by Chomsky (1981) has relevance for second language acquisition as well as for first language acquisition. The available evidence shows that Spanish students have long-lasting difficulties with subject pronoun usage in English, supporting the hypothesis that going from an unmarked version of a parameter such as the Pro-Drop parameter to a marked version is difficult for the L2 learner. In particular, they have significantly more difficulty with the impersonal pronouns *there* and *it*, which Suñer (1982) analyzed as being distinct from the referential empty subject case. Since those cases are [+pronominal] and using a lexically filled subject is possible, it is not as difficult for Spanish speakers to use the lexical pronouns in English. Omissions still occur at the later stages, and these omissions may be partially dependent on discourse rules. However, if the impersonal constructions are [−pronominal], using a [+pronominal] in English is more difficult.

English students learning Spanish seem to reset the parameter relatively quickly. Even in the lower group, omission of subject pronouns was consistent. No subjects were used in the impersonal constructions, indicating that the students had considerably less difficulty than the Spanish speakers did.

The data presented here suggest that markedness and parameters do play a role in L2 acquisition, although not in precisely the same way as in L1 acquisition. When the L1 utilizes an unmarked setting of a particular parameter, acquiring native-like competence on an L2 which utilizes a marked setting will be difficult and take considerable time. Some learners may never acquire the system fully. When the L1 is marked and the L2 is unmarked, the process of acquisition will be easier. When both L1 and L2 are marked, it was suggested that the parameter will not be reset to the unmarked value first, but will be assumed to continue at the marked value. This implies that the initial state in L2 acquisition is that of the L1; however, if L2 is unmarked, resetting of the parameter takes place rapidly.

This model does not rule out the effects of language transfer; however, it does provide a principled account of certain facets of interlanguage, and provides an explanation for the intuitive sense that some languages are "easier" than others. By utilizing a parameterized model of grammar, areas of difficulty and directionality of difficulty can be predicted with greater accuracy than in traditional analyses, and a theoretically grounded approach to L2 acquisition can be provided.

NOTES

* I would like to thank several colleagues who provided helpful discussion and comments: Francisco Betancourt, Suzanne Flynn, Yukio Otsu, and Lydia White. All errors and lapses in logic are my own responsibility.

I would also like to thank Harlan Sturm and Marie Sheppard of the Spanish department at the University of Massachusetts for allowing me access to their student materials.

[1] This argument, based on learnability and availability of input data, was also made by Phinney (1981) in reference to the Nominative Island Constraint.

[2] This assumes that the parameter is correlated with the use of agreement. Given the defective agreement system in English, this relationship may be weak at best.

[3] If the English input comes primarily from the classroom, where verbs are still often taught in paradigms in Puerto Rico, the impression that English is an agreement language may be fostered.

[4] Van Naerssen also suggested that "there may be a stage in both L1 and L2 in which a basic verb form is used before inflections are added" (1980:153). Although the unmarked verb form may be the third person singular (Phinney, 1983), it is not clear that it is a 'basic' form without inflections.

[5] This may be subject to considerable dialectal and stylistic variation, particularly in Puerto Rican Spanish. To my knowledge, the actual discourse conditions of subject pronoun usage have not been studied in detail.

[6] The decrease in the higher group may be due to the ability to handle more sophisticated topics, so the use of lexical subjects increased.

[7] There were three students out of the 22 in SSL1 who used pronoun subjects with all verbs. They clearly had *not* reset the parameter.

REFERENCES

Abraham, R. G.: 1984, 'Patterns in use of the present tense third person singular -*s* by university level ESL speakers', *TESOL QUARTERLY* **18**(1), 55—70.

Bailey, N., C. Madden, and S. D. Krashen: 1973, 'Is there a "Natural Sequence" in adult second language learning?', *Language Learning* **24**(2), 235—43.

Celce-Murcia, M.: 1972, 'The universalist hypothesis: Some implications for contrastive syntax and language teaching', *Workpapers in TESL*, UCLA 6 (June), 11—16.

Chastain, K.: 1981, 'Native speaker evaluation of student composition errors', *Modern Language Journal* **65**(3), 288—94.

Chomsky, N.: 1972, *Language and Mind*, Harcourt Brace, New York.

Chomsky, N.: 1981, *Lectures on Government and Binding*, Foris Publications, Dordrecht.

Chomsky, N. and M. Halle: 1968, *The Sound Pattern of English*, Harper and Row, New York.

Corder, S. P.: 1967, 'The significance of learner's errors', *IRAL* **5**(4), 161—170.

Eckman, F. R.: 1977, 'Markedness and the contrastive analysis hypothesis', *Language Learning* **27**(2), 315—330.

Flynn, S.: 1983, 'Similarities and differences between first and second language acquisition: Setting the parameters of universal grammar', in D. R. Rogers and J. A. Sloboda (eds.), *Acquisition of Symbolic Skills*, Plenum, New York.

Guntermann, G.: 1978, 'A study of the frequency and communicative effects of errors in Spanish', *Modern Language Journal* **62**(5—6), 249—53.

Hyams, N. S.: 1983, *The Acquisition of Parameterized Grammars*, unpublished Ph.D. dissertation, CUNY.

James, C.: 1971, 'The exculpation of contrastive linguistics', in G. Nickel (ed.), *Papers in Contrastive Analysis*, Cambridge University Press. Cambridge.

Lado, R.: 1957, *Linguistics Across Cultures*, University of Michigan Press, Ann Arbor.

Moore, F. B. and R. J. Marzano: 1979, 'Common errors of Spanish speakers learning English', *Research in the Teaching of English* **13**(2), 161—67.

Otsu, Y.: 1981, *Universal Grammar and Syntactic Development in Children: Toward a Theory of Syntactic Development*, unpublished Ph.D. dissertation, MIT.

Phinney, M.: 1981, *Syntactic Constraints and the Acquisition of Embedded Sentential Complements*. Unpublished Ph.D. dissertation, University of Massachusetts, Amherst.

Phinney, M.: 1983, 'Subjectless sentences in the acquisition of English and Spanish', Presented at *NELS 14*, University of Massachusetts, Amherst.

Picallo, M. Carne: 1984, 'The Infl node and null subject parameter', *Linguistic Inquiry* **15**(1), 75—102.

Ritchie, W. C.: 1967, 'Some implications of generative grammar for the construction of courses in English as a second language', *Language Learning* **17**, 45—69.

Rizzi, L.: 1982, 'WH movement, negation, and the pro-drop parameter', in *Issues in Italian Syntax*, Foris Publications, Dordrecht.

Rutherford, W. E.: 1982, 'Markedness is second language acquisition', *Language Learning* **32**(1), 85—108.

Selinker, L.: 1972, 'Interlanguage', IRAL **10**(2), 209—31.

Smith, K. L.: 1982, 'Avoidance, overuse, and misuse: Three trial and error learning strategies of second language learners', *Hispania* **65**(4), 605—09.

Stockwell, R. P., J. D. Bowen, and J. W. Martin: 1965, *The Grammatical Structures of English and Spanish*, University of Chicago Press, Chicago.

Suñer, M.: 1982, 'On null subjects', *Linguistic Analysis* **9**(1), 55—78.

Torrego, E.: 1984, 'On inversion in Spanish and some of its effects', *Linguistic Inquiry* **15**(1), 103—29.

Van Naerssen, M.: 1980, 'How similar are Spanish as a first language and Spanish as a second language?', in S. D. Krashen and R. C. Scarcella (eds.), *Research in Second Language Acquisition*, Newbury House, Rowley, MA.

White, L.: 1981, 'The responsibility of grammatical theory to acquisition data', in N. Hornstein and D. Lightfoot (eds.), *Explanation in Linguistics*, Longman, London.

White, L.: 1983a, 'Markedness and parameter setting: Some implications for a theory of adult second language acquisition', *McGill Working Papers in Linguistics* **1**(1), 1—21.

White, L.: 1985, 'The "Pro-Drop" parameter in adult second language acquisition', *Language Learning* **35**(1), 47—62.

Zobl, H.: 1983, 'Markedness and the projection problem', *Language Learning* **33**(3), 293—313.

LYDIA WHITE

A NOTE ON PHINNEY

In the context of the current interest in the explanatory role of parameters for language acquisition, it is interesting to speculate whether parameters are relevant only to first language (L1) acquisition or whether they can also explain aspects of non-primary language learning, particularly second language (L2) acquisition. I shall argue that the parametric approach to UG raises potentially interesting research questions for the L2 acquisition field, which I shall outline here.

Before discussing what these questions are, it is necessary briefly to consider why one should even contemplate that UG is of relevance to L2 acquisition. A number of recent papers have pointed out that L1 and L2 learners are both faced with the projection problem (Zobl, 1983; Kean, 1984; Cook, 1985; White, 1985a). That is, second language learners, like first language learners, must acquire a grammar on the basis of impoverished data. Any L2 learner who attains reasonable success in the L2 will end up with very complex and subtle knowledge which was underdetermined by the input. This does not mean that the solution to the projection problem is necessarily identical in both situations but it suggests that one should investigate the possibility that L2 learners have at their disposal the kinds of universal principle which are assumed to the available in L1 acquisition.

Whilst it is relatively uncontroversial that child L2 learning may be mediated by the same principles as govern L1 acquisition, since children are in many cases known to be totally successful at acquiring other languages, the question is more problematic as far as adults are concerned. Adults appear to find L2 acquisition harder than children (though this impression may be based on an overemphasis on phonological difficulties) and many claim that adults cannot successfuly learn an L2 because they are past the 'critical period' for language acquisition. Even granted that there may be a critical period, and the evidence is somewhat controversial, this does not necessarily mean that the effect of the end of the critical period is to wipe out access to UG.[1] There are many other factors that might explain adult difficulties. It thus seems legitimate to investigate whether UG still mediates adult L2 acquisition, as a number of people have recently begun to do.

239

Thomas Roeper and Edwin Williams (eds.), Parameter Setting, 239–246.
© 1987 *by D. Reidel Publishing Company.*

Historically, it was assumed that the major influence on the L2 learner is the mother tongue. This was first formalised in the *contrastive analysis* hypothesis (Lado, 1957) which states that differences between L1 and L2 will lead to difficulties, whereas similarities will enhance L2 acquisition, and that errors in L2 acquisition will be attributable to interference from the L1. In recent years, however, there has been a growing body of research which shows that L2 learners of many different L1s make errors which cannot be traced to the mother tongue, and that these errors are often similar to forms produced by children in L1 acquisition. In addition, for a number of structures, L2 learners go through developmental sequences which parallel those found for L1 development.

Such findings have led to a growing emphasis on universals in L2 acquisition, though these tend to be somewhat loosely defined and are rarely closely identified with principles of UG. One unfortunate effect of this emphasis has been a playing down of the existence of transfer errors, that is, forms attributable to the mother tongue, due to a feeling that they are somehow incompatible with a universals-oriented approach to L2 acquisition (e.g. Dulay *et al.*, 1982). In contrast to this view, there has been a growing revival of interest in language transfer, and attempts to predict and account for when it will occur (e.g. papers in Gass and Selinker, 1983). Even where transfer and universals are considered together, the assumption seems to be that where the former ends, the latter begins. That is, no one as yet has been able to account for transfer as an integral part of a theory of L2 acquisition which assumes that universal principles are crucially involved. I would like to suggest that the concept of parameters may help to do this.

L2 learners are often in the situation of learning a language where the value for some parameter differs from the value instantiated in the L1. Such situations allow one to investigate the question of whether L2 learners are able to reset parameters to the null hypothesis for any new language or whether they transfer the L1 parameter setting, changing to the relevant parameter for L2 only when they encounter evidence that suggests that the L1 parameter is inappropriate. The former hypothesis assumes that the L2 learner can focus on the L2 data sufficiently well to trigger the relevant parameter for L2, regardless of the situation in L1. This view is implicit in the work of Mazurkewich (1984). The hypothesis that the L1 parameter will have some effects is represented in the work of Flynn (1983, 1984), White (1984a, 1985a, 1985b) and

Phinney (this volume), though they differ as to the extent of the effects that they assume.

A hypothesis that I have been investigating recently is that differences in parameter values in L1 and L2 will cause problems, leading to transfer errors. Specifically, the learner will initially fail to notice the difference and will carry the L1 value over, treating the L2 data in terms of the L1 parameter. Taking the 'pro-drop' parameter as a case in point, native speakers of Spanish learning English were found to assume that English does have a number of pro-drop characteristics, including the possibility of null subjects, whereas French speakers did not (White, 1984a, 1985b). In other words, parametric variation offers a potential explanation of transfer errors, with the native speakers of pro-drop languages transferring that parameter to the L2, so that L1 influence falls within a universals-oriented approach to L2 acquisition.

A further line of inquiry is whether there is a difference between principles that have an initial unmarked value, a hypothesis adopted by the learner in advance of any evidence, and those that are truly open. In the former case, one may get the situation outlined by Hyams for pro-drop (this volume) where the L1 learner actually adopts the wrong setting for the mother tongue, by starting off with the unmarked hypothesis for a language that in fact requires the marked. An example of truly open parameters would be head position, where presumably there is no hypothesis in advance of the data, other than the hypothesis that there will be a head position. In L2 acquisition, both these situations are potentially problematic but the case where two languages differ in markedness value for some parameter offers particularly interesting possibilities. If L2 learners can reset UG to the null hypothesis, then they may start off with the unmarked value for a parameter in L2, regardless of its value in L1, as assumed by Mazurkewich (1984). However, if the learner cannot immediately reset parameters to the null hypothesis, then certain problems may arise in the situation where L1 has the marked value and L2 the unmarked, which will not arise where L1 has the unmarked and L2 the marked. Given that *marked* is often defined as requiring positive evidence to trigger it, if L1 has the unmarked value and L2 requires the marked, then presumably the L2 data will eventually trigger the marked value, since the necessary evidence is available. This may or may not take time, depending on whether one considers that the acquisition of marked structures necessarily involves real-time difficulties. However, in the reverse situation, where L1 has already triggered the marked value, and where the learner incorrectly assumes that this is also relevant for L2, negative data may be necessary to tell the learner that marked is the wrong assumption for L2 (c.f. White, 1986). Whilst the precise influence of the markedness value of a parameter in the two languages is debatable, it seems clear that different markedness values in the two languages can lead to predictions concerning directionality of difficulty, as proposed by Phinney (this volume) and by other in the L2 acquisition field.

In the L2 literature, there have for many years been proposals that learners go through a series of 'interlanguage' grammars (Selinker, 1972), and it is often argued that these have the properties of natural languages. If parameters are relevant to L2 acquisition, then one would expect that interlanguage grammars (ILGs) should vary in restricted ways within the limitations prescribed by UG. Whilst an ILG might at some stage be identical neither with the L1 grammar nor the target language grammar, it should nevertheless be a 'possible' grammar, as defined by linguistic theory, and hence pick from the possible parameter values specified by UG. Where a parameter has a range of consequences, these should be found in any ILG that adopts the parameter in question, and when the learner changes from one parameter value to another, one should find related changes in all structures subsumed by that parameter.

A related question concerns how grammar change is brought about in the ILG, how the learner 'retreats' from an incorrect grammar, bringing it closer to the target grammar. Much recent work in L1 acquistion has concentrated on the lack of reliable negative evidence and has focussed on the question of how to ensure learning by means of positive data only. Many L2 learners, however, do get negative evidence in the language classroom, evidence which may trigger grammar change, if they take note of it. In addition, given their prior knowledge of another language, their greater maturity, already complete cognitive development, etc, they may be able to make use of different positive evidence from that used by the L1 learner.

For example, consider Hyams' proposal (this volume) that the presence of expletive elements like *it* and *there* acts as a trigger for the English child to drop the assumption the English is a pro-drop language. If Spanish learners initially treat English as a pro-drop language, as suggested by White (1984a, 1985b), Phinney (this volume), the question arises as to how they subsequently learn that it is not, on the assumption that they will eventually find this out. That is, what triggers reanalysis of the ILG in this case? What data will force grammar change? It seems unlikely that L2 learners will simply notice by themselves that English does not have null subjects; once a particular grammar has been adopted, the data is analysed in terms of that grammar. Given that the presence of pronouns is consistent with pro-drop languages, there seems to be no way for the learner to discover that English is not pro-drop on the basis of positive data from pronouns alone.

Instead, one must consider data which would be sufficient to force grammar change, i.e. data that are inconsistent with pro-drop. Hyams' proposal that the presence of lexical expletives, in conjunction with the avoid pronoun principle, forces change in child grammars, might also work for L2 learners. If this is a trigger for change, one would expect L2 learners to recognize the ungrammaticality of missing expletives at the same time, or before, they recognize the ungrammaticality of missing referential pronouns, and to use lexical expletives at the same time, or before, they use lexical referential pronouns. Experimental evidence seems to be against this. Null expletives are more persistent than null referential pronouns in the grammars of L2 learners (Zobl, 1983; Register, 1984; Hilles, 1986), suggesting that the presence of expletives is not the trigger for change. It appears that in L2 acquisition, at least, the presence of lexical expletives, far from being a source of grammar change, is actually a late aspect of the parameter to undergo revision.

It is also possible that the presence of lexical material in AUX could provide a suitable trigger, since this would govern PRO and, hence, should rule out pro-drop. Apparently for L1 acquisition, the timing of the emergence of subject-auxiliary inversion or negative placement (both of which indicate the presence of lexical material in AUX) is such that it could not trigger loss of pro-drop. However, it is a potential trigger for L2 acquisition, so that positive evidence of a different sort may be available to L2 learners.

There is really no reason to assume that there can be only one line of retreat in L2 acquisition. That is, one might conceive of some learners using negative evidence, while others use positive evidence of various kinds. Where a parameter has a number of consequences, it is conceivable that grammar change could come through any one of them,

and hence a detailed study of parameters may help to determine the
routes available to the L2 acquirer to achieve the target grammar.

A final question that I should like to raise concerns the potential
relevance of L2 data for linguistic theory, and particularly for the
concept of parameters. If we can show that UG is relevant to L2
acquisition, then L2 data constitute a body of data relevant to the
theory, just like data from other areas. For example, in my pro-drop
experiments, I assumed versions of the parameter that incorporate the
possibility of null subjects, of subject-verb inversion, and *that trace*
effects (Chomsky, 1981; Jaeggli, 1982; Rizzi, 1982). It turned out that
null subjects were judged to be acceptable in English but VS was not
judged to be a possible order; this is consistent with views of pro-drop
which consider that VS order is not integral to the parameter (Chao,
1981; Safir, 1982).

Felix (1985) and Wexler and Borer (this volume) propose that
certain aspects of UG might be maturationally triggered, as opposed to
being triggered by other aspects of the data. This is the kind of proposal
where L2 data could be extremely useful. Most second language
learners, whether child or adult, will have gone through the relevant
maturational development before learning their second language.
Therefore, if the L2 learner goes through the same stages as the L1
learner does for some parameter, this suggests that maturation cannot
be involved. By comparing L1 and L2 developmental sequences, one
may be in a position to disentangle maturational aspects of UG from
data-driven ones.

In conclusion, I should like to suggest that the parametric approach
to acquisition opens up an interesting and potentially fruitful interaction
between linguistic theory and the field of second language acquisition.
The formalization of language variation by means of parameters allows
one to attempt to answer the question of how second languages are
acquired and to what extent the mother tongue will have an influence.

NOTE

[1] The question of whether UG is available to adult learners depends in part on one's
view of what happens to UG in adults in general. Is UG nothing but a language acquisition device or does it continue to mediate our first language use throughout our lives?
For example, is it UG that prevents us from making subjacency violations as adults?

This kind of question is rarely discussed and yet it seems particularly important here. If UG mediates all language use, not just language acquisition, then there is no reason to assume that it is not in principle available to adult learners.

REFERENCES

Chomsky, N.: 1981, *Lectures on Government and Binding*, Foris Publications, Dordrecht.

Chao, W.: 1981, 'PRO drop languages and non obligatory control', *University of Massachusetts Occasional Papers in Linguistics* **7**, 46—74.

Cook, V.: 1985, 'Universal grammar and second language learning', *Applied Linguistics* **6**, 2-18.

Dulay, H., M. Burt and S. Krashen: 1982, *Language Two*, Oxford University Press, Oxford.

Felix, S.: 1985, 'Maturational aspects of universal grammar', in A. Davies, C. Criper and A. Howatt (eds.), *Interlanguage*, Edinburgh University Press, Edinburgh.

Flynn, S.: 1983, 'Differences between first and second language acquisition', in D. Rogers and J. Sloboda (eds.), *Acquisition of Symbolic Skills*, Plenum Press, New York.

Flynn, S.: 1984, 'A universal in L2 acquisition based on a PBD typology', in F. Eckman, L. Bell and D. Nelson (eds.), *Universals of Second Language Acquisition*, Newbury House, Rowley, Massachusetts.

Gass, S. and L. Selinker (eds.): 1983, *Language Transfer in Language Learning*, Newbury House, Rowley, Massachusetts.

Hilles, S.: 1986, 'Interlanguage and the pro-drop parameter', *Second Language Research* **2**, 33–52.

Jaeggli, O.: 1982, *Topics in Romance Syntax*, Foris Publications, Dordrecht.

Kean, M.-L.: 1984, 'Seond language acquisition and grammatical theory: A matter of projection and marking', unpublished paper, Max-Planck-Institut.

Lado, R.: 1957, *Linguistics Across Cultures*, University of Michigan Press, Ann Arbor.

Mazurkewich, I.: 1984, 'The acquisition of the dative alternation by second language learners and linguistic theory', *Language Learning* **34**, 91—109.

Register, N.: 1984, 'The pro-drop parameter and its implications for learners of second languages', unpublished paper, University of Wisconsin-Madison.

Rizzi, L.: 1982, *Issues in Italian Syntax*, Foris Publications, Dordrecht.

Safir, K.: 1982, *Syntactic Chains and the Definiteness Effect*, unpublished Ph.D. dissertation, MIT.

Selinker, L.: 1972, 'Interlanguage', *IRAL* **10**, 209—231.

White, L.: 1984a, 'Implications of parametric variation for adult second language learners: An investigation of the pro-drop parameter', to appear in V. Cook (ed.), *Experimental Approaches to Second Language Acquisition*, Pergamon Press, Oxford.

White, L.: 1985a, 'Universal grammar as a source of explanation in second language acquisition', in B. Wheatley *et al.* (eds.), *Current Approaches to Second Language Acquisition*, Indiana University Linguistics Club, Bloomington.

White, L.: 1985b, 'The "pro-drop" parameter in adult second language acquisition',
    Language Learning **35**, 47–62.
White, L.: 1986, 'Markedness and parameter setting: Some implications for a theory of
    adult second language acquisition', in F. Eckman, E. Moravcsik and J. Wirth (eds.),
    Markedness, Plenum Press, New York.
Zobl, H.: 1983, 'Markedness and the projection problem', *Language Learning* **33**,
    293–313.

LIST OF CONTRIBUTORS

Hagit Borer
University of California
Irvine, CA

Daniel Finer
SUNY Stony Brook
Stony Brook, NY

Nina Hyams
University of California
Los Angeles, CA

David Lebeaux
University of Massachusetts
Amherst, MA

Rita Manzini
University College London
London, U.K.

Taisuke Nishigauchi
Shoin College
Kobe, Japan

Marianne Phinney
University of Texas
El Paso, TX

Thomas Roeper
University of Massachusetts
Amherst, MA

Kenneth Safir
43 Mine St.
New Brunswick, New Jersey

Lawrence Solan
208 8th Street
Hoboken, New Jersey

Amy Weinberg
University of Maryland
College Park, MD

Kenneth Wexler
University of California
Irvine, CA

Lydia White
McGill University
Montreal, Canada

Edwin Williams
University of Massachusetts
Amherst, MA

INDEX

249

Printed in the United Kingdom
by Lightning Source UK Ltd.
116578UKS00001B/40-42